2004

THE BERLIN REPUBLIC:
GERMAN UNIFICATION AND A DECADE OF CHANGES

BOOKS OF RELATED INTEREST

The Berlin Republic: German Unification and A Decade of Changes

Editors

WINAND GELLNER
JOHN D. ROBERTSON

FRANK CASS
LONDON • PORTLAND, OR

First published in 2003 in Great Britain by
FRANK CASS AND COMPANY LIMITED
Crown House, 47 Chase Side, Southgate, London N14 BP, England

and in the United States of America by
FRANK CASS
c/o International Specialized Book Services, Inc.
920 NE 58th Avenue, #300, Portland, OR 97213-3786

British Library Cataloguing in Publication Data

The Berlin Republic : German unification and a decade of
    changes
    1. Germany – Politics and government – 1990– 2. Germany –
    History – Unification, 1990 3. Germany – History – 1990–
    4. Germany – Foreign relations – 1990– 5. Germany – Economic
    conditions – 1990–
    I.Gellner, Winand II. Robertson, John D.
    320.9′43′09049

ISBN 0 7146 5393 4 HB
ISBN 0 7146 8328 0 PB

Library of Congress Cataloging-in-Publication Data

The Berlin Republic : German unification and a decade of changes/
editors, Winand Gellner, John D. Robertson.
    p. cm
    Includes bibliographical references and index
    ISBN 0-7146-5393-4 – ISBN 0-7146-8328-0 (pbk.)
    1. Germany – History – Unification, 1990. 2. Germany – Politics
and government – 1990– 3. Political parties – Germany – History – 20th
century. 4. Germany – History – 20th century. I. Gellner, Winand. II
Robertson, John Douglas, 1952–
    DD290.29 .B478 2003
    943.087′9–dc21   2002153038

This group of studies first appeared in a Special Issue of German Politics
(ISSN 0964-4008), Vol.11, No.3 (December 2002),
[The Berlin Republic: German Unification and a Decade of Changes].

Printed in Great Britain by Antony Rowe Ltd., Chippenham, Wilts.

Contents

The Berlin Republic:
German Unification and a Decade of Changes

WINAND GELLNER and JOHN D. ROBERTSON

At the beginning of German unification in October 1990 there were high expectations for where the integration of the formerly East Germany into the German Federal Republic would be within a decade. This collection offers an assessment, now 12 years after unification, of how the most important political event in Western Europe since the end of the Second World War has fared.

Within the academic and journalistic literature, some argue that the expectations have not been met, with new questions arising as to 'if not then when?' Others, of course, say the process has been, under the circumstances, quite successful. Therefore, students of European affairs and comparative political analysis are still left with a series of important questions that require closer scrutiny. For example, what, if anything, went as expected and hoped, and what are the prospects for the future? What, if anything, did not develop as expected, and what lessons can we take from the process and apply to our understanding of German society and politics and the broader process of unification? What, if any, are the political and institutional conditions in Germany that would not have been the same today without unification? And why? What political and institutional issues in Germany have not been seriously affected by unification? And why not?

The 11 contributions in this volume offer comprehensive and in-depth perspectives on these questions and assess the challenges to German democracy that have come with unification. Three articles consider German civic society and political culture since unification: Mi-Kyung Kim and John Robertson draw on the literature of nation-state development to assess the degree of congruence between nation formation and state formation in Germany following unification; Felix Philipp Lutz examines how and why German historical consciousness continues to shape the two political cultures of Eastern and Western Germany, respectively; and Robert Rohrschneider and Rüdiger Schmitt-Beck offer an empirical assessment of the differing levels of trust in political institutions across the two parts of Germany which have grown since unification.

Five articles examine German unification within the context of institutions and the political agenda emerging since 1990: Winand Gellner and Gerd Strohmeier show how the differing traditions of journalism have shaped conflicting media messages across the two parts of Germany since unification, thereby reinforcing many of the cultural differences between Eastern and Western Germany that were present at the time of unification; Karl-Rudolf Korte considers how unification has impacted on decision-making styles and processes within Germany's chancellery system; Thomas Saalfeld offers an in-depth assessment of the many changes to the German party system that have followed unification; Arthur Gunlicks details the complex nature of changes affecting the German federal process as a whole since the two German states united in 1990; and Hellmut Wollmann explores the effects of unification on Germany's local governmental process and structure, and compares Germany's local government responses to post-communist politics with those of Hungary and Poland.

Finally, three articles focus on the economic (domestic and global) consequences and security policy implications of German unification: Michael Münter and Roland Sturm consider the domestic fiscal and monetary consequences of German unification, with an eye to the structural economic implications these changes suggest; Franz-Josef Meiers assesses the foreign and security implications of German unification for the German polity, as well as the broader emerging European defence identity, and the more fundamental Trans-Atlantic security structure; and, finally, Stefan Schirm shows how the global economy and markets have both affected, and in part been affected by, German unification.

The general conclusion to be drawn from the analysis and findings of these papers, taken as a whole, is that while German unification must be rightfully viewed as one of the most successful examples of political and economic transformation (and thus state building) in the modern era, the real costs of such a dramatic social, political and economic change, as well as the long-term prospects for easing some of the pain still felt as a result of this sudden and often traumatic transformation, are challenges the German Federal Republic will face for years to come, with likely real consequences for continued European integration.

The articles included here were (with the exception of the Kim and Robertson contribution) presented originally in earlier draft form at a symposium entitled, 'German Unification: A Decade Hence', held at Texas A&M University, 10–12 February 2002. We wish to thank The Assistant Provost for International Programs of Texas A&M University, Dr Emily Ashworth, The European Union Center of Texas A&M University, and its Director, Dr Michael Laubscher, The German Trans-Atlantic Program, The Political Science Department of Texas A&M University and its Interim Head, Dr Patricia Hurley, and The Program in the Cross-National Study of Politics of the Department of Political Science at Texas A&M University and its Director, Dr Robert Harmel for their support of the symposium.

Analysing German Unification: State, Nation and the Quest for Political Community

MI-KYUNG KIM and JOHN D. ROBERTSON

Unification has confronted Germans with a challenge of historical proportions. Namely, consolidating two former independent nation-states into one. The intention, of course, is to forge a new national identity and clearly define a commonly accepted historical and political purpose for the new nation-state which affords it a legitimate political community. Political community implies a clear sense of common identity among citizens with the new German state. Yet, as all too many observers have noted, consensus and solidarity have been hampered in Germany since its re-unification in 1990 by the persistence of divergent political attitudes and perceptions of a just and legitimate democratic community prevailing within each of the two parts of the unified nation-state.[1] After more than ten years of German unification, Eastern Germans regularly express feelings of 'relative deprivation' and 'the loss of self-respect', despite the fact that wages, pensions and per capita income are almost double their previous levels, following nearly a trillion dollars of German investment into Eastern Germany between 1991 and 2001. The significance of this growing gap in perceptions is underscored when we are reminded that Eastern Germans were relatively more likely to engage in frequent political and economic protest activities than other East and Central European countries, the populations of which had experienced much higher economic dislocation and deprivation during the period 1989–93.[2]

A variety of survey data indicate that the two parts of Germany are distinctly apart on a number of crucial issues that reflect a general difficulty in achieving a common political community. For instance, based on Eurobarometer data from spring 2002, when asked if they 'tended to trust' or whether they 'tended not to trust' eight specified institutions within the German polity, 56 per cent of Western German respondents, on average, tended to support these institutions, while only 46 per cent of Eastern Germans tended to trust the same institutions. The gap was considerably wider for the institution reflecting the broader political culture of a society

Mi-Kyung Kim and John D. Robertson, Texas A&M University

and its commitment to rights, freedoms and privileges – the justice system. Here, 68 per cent of Western German respondents said they tended to trust the German justice system, while less than half, or 48 per cent, of Eastern Germans expressed a similar degree of trust. Additionally, 86 per cent of Western Germans expressed satisfaction with their personal life, compared to 71 per cent for Eastern Germans. Asked if they thought their personal situation had got worse, compared to their personal situation of five years earlier, 24 per cent of Eastern Germans indicated yes, compared to 16 per cent of Western Germans. And, asked if they thought their personal situation was likely to get worse during the next five years, 19 per cent of Eastern Germans indicated yes, compared to 13 per cent of Western Germans. Finally, one indicator of the extent to which the two parts of Germany differ with respect to how they value their national identity may be gleaned from a simple question within the spring 2001 Eurobarometer survey. Asked if they thought the enlargement of the Union would make Germany less important in Europe, 56 per cent of Eastern German respondents agreed, compared to only 49 per cent of Western German respondents.[3]

However, it would be grossly inaccurate to conclude from these observations that Eastern Germans have not supported unification, nor would it be appropriate to suggest that Eastern Germans do not hold unification to be legitimate. Rather, the evidence to date clearly implies that Eastern Germans have yet to achieve a genuine 'nation unification', despite a very successful and evident 'state unification'. Furthermore, this conclusion suggests that the unfinished German unification also has implications and lessons for Europe's on-going unification process.

United Germany is a nation-state which has fused two very different political traditions and cultures into a single federal state structure guided by a common set of institutional mechanisms. It has embedded within its political community competing and often conflicting traditions of stable democracy, as well as developing democracy; traditions of market capitalism, as well as traditions of socialism and command economy. This condition has similarities to those afflicting the European Union as it confronts expansion and extends club membership eastward. Competing cultural, economic and political traditions which extend well beyond the original core of Western Europe present the Union itself with the future possibility of the same *Angst* and *Politikverdrossenheit* which has coloured the political debates of Germany during the period since the fall of the Berlin Wall in 1989.

Beyond the obvious differences in political culture and historical identifications, what are the forces working to slow what had originally been hoped would be a smooth and rapid transition to democracy and full economic integration of the former East Germany following unification?

The answer seems to lie in the nature of collective identity that has emerged in Germany since 1991. If so, then what kind of collective identity should we expect given the nature of unification and the choices surrounding this historic enterprise?

We suggest that the problem of German unification and the lack of total congruence in vision and definition of nation, purpose and identity that characterise the two parts of Germany today are to be understood more clearly as outcomes of the mode and timing of the process of German unification itself. This historical moment immediately became attached to and very much part of the broader processes and pressures associated with European integration, adding the compounding complication of German identity and European identity at virtually the same time to a culture where identity has always carried heavy political costs for Germans and Europeans alike. We begin our analysis by considering how political institutions are interwoven into the process of national identity itself, and the implications of this relationship for the emerging unified Germany since 1991.

INSTITUTIONS AND IDENTITY: STATE AND NATION

The concept of institutions has been defined in a variety of fashions according to the different theoretical perspectives of the schools of thought. For instance, historical institutionalists understand institutions as formal organisations (for example, parties, executive, legislatures), the structures of state (for example, military) as well as informal rules, practices and procedures that guide power and authority transactions in within a political system.[4] Alternatively, one school of sociological institutionalists understand the concept of institutions as 'a web of interrelated norms–formal and informal–governing social relationships', while yet suggesting that institutions are 'the cognitive scripts, categories and models that are indispensable for action'.[5]

In general, for sociological institutionalists, it is difficult to separate the concept of institutions from the concept of identities. These scholars inform us that human actions are socially, culturally and subjectively meaningful. Such social relationships and structures construct institutional patterns of behaviour over time. In this context, institutions imply institutionalised identities, in other words, 'shared' cognitive scripts, categories and models of human actions. In contrast, historical institutionalists are more attuned to the interactions between structure and agency.[6] This school of thought does not believe that human actions can be reduced to social structures. More importantly, as Thelen argues, 'the definition of institutions as shared cultural scripts obscures political struggles among competing scripts and/or conceives of change as the displacement of one script by another'.[7] Thus, following this logic, the concept of institutions cannot be reduced to that of simple identities. Rather, institutions and identity are best understood to be interdependent.

Hans Kohn, in his analysis of nationalism, argues that the nation-state demands a political identity provided through nationalism. Once achieved, nationalism strengthens the legitimacy and viability of political institutions designed to sustain the nation-state.[8] This symbiotic relationship between nationalism, institutions and identity is also an important theme of Stein Rokkan in his conceptual map of state formation and nation-building. His work directs attention to why some countries have succeeded in consolidating their nation-states, while others have failed. Drawing the distinction between state-building and nation-building, Rokkan argues that the consolidation of nation-states has been developed through different historical stages, ranging from the territorial and functional consolidation of states to social assimilation and political integration by cultural standardisation and the extension of political citizenship.[9] These different historical stages establish in their turn the key cultural and political boundaries within society, and between peoples of different nation-states. Therefore, from Rokkan's comparative-historical analysis of modern nation-states, we can draw a more general implication of the relationship between political institutions and political identity: 'legitimate political institutions ultimately require political identities'.

Political institutions obviously do not automatically lead to political identities. Rather, political identities are imagined and invented through the process of cultural integration and cultural politics.[10] If identities are conceived, as we suggest, as 'the idea of boundaries', then national identity can be considered as a symbolic boundary that is 'made by social actors to categorize objects, people, practices, and even time and space' and are 'tools by which individuals and groups struggle over and come to agree upon definitions of reality'.[11] According to the modernist perspectives on nationalism, national identity has been mobilised by the use of mass education systems and mass communication, print capitalism, the inventions of common vocabularies, symbols and cultural traditions, and the reinterpretation and rewriting of history. Anderson and Hobsbawm reflect the view of a number of students of nationalism when they suggest that the role of administrative organisations and disaffected administrators is as important mobilisers of national consciousness. Therefore, as Breuilly points out, the formation of national identity itself becomes a form of politics.[12]

However, when we conceive states as territorial boundaries and national identities as symbolic boundaries, we must not assume that states can easily impose such national identity on their citizens or local communities. In his analysis of state and nation consolidation, Rokkan observes that throughout

European history the identity of periphery localities and subcultures often resists the pressure of cultural-boundary extension emanating from a cultural centre within the broader state. Thus, he claims, 'if you have grown up in a particular community, your chances of acceptance within another are significantly reduced'.[13] There is therefore a reasonable likelihood of an incongruence between the territorial boundaries of state and the symbolic boundaries of nation. It would follow that the one source of difficulty complicating German unification is an incongruence between political institutions of the united Germany, as sources of state boundaries, and national identities, or symbolic boundaries, of the Eastern and Western Germans. More simply, political institutions of the united German state require political identities of the united German nation, a need that has been much more difficult to meet than perhaps originally anticipated during the heady days between November 1989 and October 1990.

To bring clarity and focus to this point, we may turn to Ringmar's concept of 'formative moments' in history.[14] These moments occur when new identities are 'requested' as new institutions are established to confront challenges to the state and nation. All old identities are questioned, disintegrate, or are redefined in order to accommodate the new circumstances. The 1990 unification was such a formative moment in German history. For East Germans, the political institutions of the GDR, which served as symbolic markers for state territorial boundaries, disappeared. At the same time, their old symbolic boundaries became illegitimate in the context of the collapse of communism and the fall of the Berlin Wall. The challenge was to establish new symbolic boundaries in the united Germany. West Germans, on the other hand, had no question of the legitimacy of the political institutions of the Federal Republic. However, the symbolic boundaries associated with the political institutions of the pre-unification FRG did not suffice to justify new state territorial boundaries throughout the newly united Germany. Indeed, they were, and remain to a degree, challenged within the eastern regions of the unified Germany.

Two generations of distinctly different socialisation patterns with distinct political cultures could not be so easily overcome as in the transplanting of democratic institutions into a territory built on a totally alien set of symbols and national identity markers.[15] Andreas Glaeser has documented the persistence of differences in the respective interpretations of self and nation among Western and Eastern Germans.[16] As Glaeser notes, at the beginning of the unification in 1990, both West Germans and East Germans had a presumption of 'the essential unity of the German people' in terms of the history and culture they shared before unification. But unification based primarily on state institutions has transformed the presumption of national identity into a persistent doubt and nagging pessimism over the present and near future course of the newly unified German state.

THE CONTINUITY OF GERMAN POLITICAL INSTITUTIONS AFTER UNIFICATION

Why have the foundations of an identity based on common and shared symbols of nation been so hard to achieve in Germany despite impressive political and economic unification? Why has state unification not led more directly to a sense of common citizenry in Germany? What might account for the disparity between stable and legitimate political institutions across the parts of Germany on the one hand, and the distinctly apparent lack of shared symbolic identities necessary for a political community on the other?[17] While no simple answer may suffice, it seems clear that the key lies in the nature of institutions and their relationship to national identity.

Students of historical institutionalism view institutions as 'enduring legacies of political struggle'.[18] In the previous section, we suggested that German unification is best understood as a formative moment defined by the request for and supply of new political institutions and national identities. Furthermore, from the perspective of historical institutionalists, the formative moment may be considered as a 'critical juncture' wherein institutional changes have been caused by exogenous pressures, essentially external to the political institutions themselves. At that moment of the critical juncture, the resulting new political institutions cannot serve to effectively achieve the consequent development of a common set of shared national symbols necessary for a common definition of national identity unless these new institutions are seen by all principal parties as reflecting a design specifically intended to address the external pressures themselves.

The concept of critical juncture is common in the field of political sociology and comparative political development and is based on the idea that there is a historical moment which propels countries toward different developmental paths. Therefore, the concepts of critical juncture and path-dependence are closely related. And both are powerful tools of conceptual mapping when exploring comparative political development. However, in order to properly apply those concepts to the context of German unification, we must be clear about the circumstances which shaped the unification of the two Germanies. German unification can be properly considered as a critical juncture, thus projecting Germany along a different political development path from the present one, *only if* such unification was realised through the formation and creation of new political institutions. In other words, if the 'critical juncture' actually leads to the building of a new German nation-state based on the *constitutional agreement* between the two Germanies.

This, however, was not the case with German unification in 1990. One of the most important implications which can be drawn from the literature of historical institutionalism for our purposes holds that the institutional changes are path-dependent in that 'the trajectory of change up to a certain point itself constrains the trajectory after the point'.[19] Within the context of German politics following unification, we suggest that the nature of unification is best understood as the lack of 'constitutional agreements' which serve as the foundations for political institutions of the new unified German democracy. The failure to achieve effective constitutional agreements between Eastern and Western perceptions of the proper German nation-state resulting from unification can be traced from the very mode and timing of the democratic adaptation within the GDR during the opening phase of unification, especially between March and October 1990. This path-dependent interpretation suggests that strategies chosen and decisions taken on how to proceed with unification at the moment of the critical juncture itself laid the basis for subsequent difficulties over full acquisition of a shared sense of political community across the two parts of Germany during the decade between 1991 and 2001. While one physical wall collapsed in 1989, others were intentionally or unintentionally constructed in the form of political institutions growing logically from the constitutional design adopted by the unified Germany at the moment of its inception in 1990. National identity and political community have been objectives from the outset, giving secondary importance to political institutional unification and nation-state consolidation.

Indeed, the problem of achieving a common national identity as a basis for a political community with shared symbols of citizenship can be made clear by considering the nature of the democratic transition in Eastern Germany. In *The Third Wave*, Huntington distinguishes four general types of democratic transition: transformation, replacement, transplacement and intervention.[20] According to Huntington, the democratic transition in the GDR is classified as a 'replacement' transition.[21] This was achieved through the organised actions of political opposition groups during the period 1988–89. The problem with assuming that German unification was a replacement transition is that it hides the collective goal of the opposition groups. While a classic replacement transition seeks a revolutionary replacement in scope and scale, it is clear to many students of German politics that during the six months between October 1989 and April 1990 the objective was not revolution, but rather transformation and broad-based reform.[22] Their primary demands focused on human rights, free elections and constitutional amendments designed to weaken and dilute the dominant position of the SED. More importantly, these opposition groups collectively expressed little interest in a full-scale regime change in Eastern Germany. Moreover, there seemed to be a consensus among opposition groups, as well as political elites, about preserving the independence of the country through the demanded and prescribed Roundtable Talks.[23]

As symbolically significant and politically important as they may have been, the Roundtable Talks between opposition groups and the old political elites could not have any legal institutional authority.[24] From the outset, this undermined the very legitimacy of the talks. Indeed, after the first free election in the GDR on 18 March 1990, the Roundtable lost its influence in controlling the process of democratic transition. At this point, the opportunity to preserve any symbols of eastern identity through political institutions consistent with its national identity were lost. The 1990 election underscored in vivid terms the stark reality of 'the relation of forces' among different political actors with the unified Germany. The result was the victory of CDU-led 'Alliance for Germany', and an array of allied groups of right-centre parties.[25] Any hopes of the Roundtable, as well as of the Modrow government, for slowing unification in order to preserve some sense of legitimate national identity in the minds of Easterners was lost at this juncture. Essentially, therefore, the 'third way' alternative to unification was eliminated with the outcome of the election of March 1990. Democratic socialism, in effect, was no longer a real alternative to Eastern Germany. Without this alternative, any links to a national identity built on common symbols and shared citizenry obligations in the East were rendered illegitimate and irrelevant to the course of unification now proposed by the balance of forces demanding a more rapid unification via simple imposition and adoption of Western institutions in the East.[26]

Przeworski's analysis of democratic transition seems instructive here, as well. In the process of transition to democracy, he argues, the constitutional choice of new institutional arrangements is determined by two conditions: (1) 'whether the relation of forces is known to the participants when the institutional framework is being adopted and, if yes, (2) whether this relation is uneven or balanced'.[27] During periods of critical junctures and historical moments which propel authoritarian states toward democratic transition, if the relation of forces among society's major politically contentious groups is uncertain and unsettled and, more importantly, if the choice of new institutional agreements is made *before* the relation of forces is known, then new institutional arrangements would be determined by the very uncertainty of the relations of force. That is, new institutions would be based on important considerations of 'checks and balances' among competing political forces, the maximisation of political influence of minorities, and the provision of 'political guarantees against temporary political adversity, against unfavorable tides of opinion, against contrary shifts of alliance'.[28] Therefore, the timing of constitutional choice, relative to the balance of forces within society at the critical juncture, subsequently influences the nature of new institutions.

In the context of German unification after 1990, timing of constitutional choice was *after* the relation of forces was already known through the result of the March election. The overwhelming victory of the CDU in the election reinforced Kohl's strategic choice to seek 'the fast-track' to unification controlled by West Germany. It also served to encourage East German citizens so inclined to pursue a collective preference for acquiring access to West German prosperity, held out as the plum to be plucked from the tree of rapid unification. Therefore, both Western and Eastern Germans were caught in an atmosphere which increasingly narrowed the options after March 1990 to that of rapid unification, an option which at least was in part politically orchestrated. The first step of unification was economic and monetary union in July 1990. This greatly accelerated the pace of unification by effectively disintegrating the political economy of the GDR.

However, the immediate effect included extensive economic dislocation in the eastern states of Germany. By October 1990 the choices open to Germans were so constrained by the decisions following the outcome of the March 1990 elections that all that remained was the formal ratification of the Unification Treaty. In theory, in October 1990 there remained two options open to German politicians. The first was through Article 146 of the Basic Laws of the FRG, which would serve to 'request' the replacement of the West German Basic Law with a newly negotiated constitution of the reunited Germany. This was the pathway to consolidation via integration. The second option was through Article 23, which would have specified the continuity of the West German political system and called for its simple extension to the East. This second option dictated a consolidation strategy which precluded the integration of both German political systems through the constitutional agreement between West and East Germans fashioned through consensus and negotiation. Following the outcome of the March 1990 elections, the second option was the most politically feasible and most consistent with the resulting balance of political forces in both East and West Germany.

EXIT, VOICE AND LOYALTY: IN SEARCH OF A NEW GERMAN IDENTITY

There are still two unanswered questions. First, why did East Germans seem collectively to prefer rapid unification (the 'exit' option) over their own independent political project, which might have developed a more social democratic GDR (the 'voice' option)? And, second, what is the political consequence of the choice? Clues to the answers of these two questions may be gleaned by considering the nature of exit, voice and loyalty in the last days of the GDR.

Hirschman interprets the collapse of the GDR as the result of 'the collaboration of exit and voice'.[29] Unlike his original proposition articulated in his classic *Exit, Voice, Loyalty*, which posits that exit grows in an inverse relation to voice, one finds in the GDR during the period 1989–90 a positive relationship emerging between exit and voice within East Germany – both grew in tandem. The exit option as a private activity was rapidly transformed into voice as a public choice within a climate characterised by only latent and weak loyalty across the population. According to Hirschman, 'loyalty holds exit at bay and activates voice'.[30] However, in the absence of loyalty within the East, voice was not an effective and realistic option as a tool for repairing the political regime of the GDR.

Offe offers further insight of relevance when he reminds us that the legitimacy of the political regime of the GDR was built on a foundation of identity strongly attached to the culture of a command economy. What identity across the populace there was with social democracy and a command economy could not, therefore, be effectively transferred to the resulting new democracy following unification in 1990.[31] Such a transfer was all the more difficult in that East Germans frequently compared their command economy unfavourably with the far wealthier West German market capitalist system, thus making loyalty even weaker among Easterners. While wholesale and rapid unification may not have been the route preferred by all Easterners in 1990, the lack of loyalty and the emerging advantage which therefore was afforded to voice and exit left the doorway open to rapid unification through the adoption of the West German constitutional system, and effectively precluded a more balanced integration of the East into the West.

These clues suggest yet another question. What is the political consequence of a united Germany driven by exit and voice, yet having little effective loyalty? For both Western and Eastern Germans, unification was essentially an economic transformation of the East. Nothing of the old system was either legitimate or salvageable within the context of the rapid unification chosen after March and later, in October 1990. Therefore, without sufficient loyalty, and with exit and voice working in tandem, the effect for unification was the complete rejection of the Eastern political culture and the replacement of a Western set of symbols and values as the boundaries of institutional authority within the newly united Germany.

In addition, the failure of any debate of the legitimacy of the Eastern political culture and the ensuing rapid unification deprived West Germans of a sense of choice, or derived consensus, on the matter of unification. Costs were imposed to cover the unification and transition of the East to a capitalist economy, but the process was driven by a clear agenda, and was not subjected to the normal tug and pull of the extensive checks and balances commonly at work within the polity of the FRG. In retrospect, it appears to be the result of a primordial nationalism mobilised by the recall of shared history, memory and culture.[32] Of course, time will tell whether economic practicality and nationalism can sustain a tolerance for the increasing costs of unification, and not give way to the deeper fractures separating the two parts of Germany.

For Habermas, the issue is clear. Citizens of the FRG have already transformed their mentality from that of 'the Volk as a historical community of fate, the nation as linguistic and cultural community' to the mentality of 'constitutional patriotism' based on the public pride of their economic performance and democratic institutions.[33] When we combine this fact with the telltale signs of lack of political trust toward institutions among Eastern Germans, we can begin to see the outline of a fractured political community lacking a common identity, and, worse, a sufficient degree of loyalty across the two recently united parts.[34] Hirschman would hold that voice is the avenue toward deepening loyalty and achieving a more unified political community. However, voice requires, according to Hirschman, that members in a political community enjoy full political and social citizenship. This assuredly requires more than merely civic rights, personal freedoms and political privileges. It also requires a sense of legitimate identity and role within the political community.[35] Thus, the problem of loyalty in the newly united Germany reflects a far more fundamental problem of political integration based on the development of citizenship. This was exactly Rokkan's theoretical implication with regard to nation-state development.

Thus, we may conclude here that, based on different perceptions of the responsibility of the citizen and the state which gave rise itself to differing perceptions of nation identity in the two parts of Germany, East and West Germany during the first decade of unification have held divergent perceptions both of what unification means, and of what it can deliver. Eastern Germans desire the benefits of wealth and prosperity associated with a social market system of economy found in Western Germany, while Western Germans see unification as a vindication of their national pride in the Federal Republic. There is nothing to suggest in history that these two motivations cannot be assimilated into a foundation from which to build and sustain a cohesive and coherent political community. Yet the choice of rapid unification in an atmosphere of exit and voice (and very weak loyalty) in the East has denied both Western and Eastern Germany an opportunity to forge a coherent new basis of loyalty founded on anything other than national pride and economic practicality. Failure to achieve growth and prosperity levels over a defined period of time, with its attendant affect on pride, are certainly not unlikely scenarios as Germany faces the prospects of an expensive and fiscally demanding period of EU enlargement, growing social benefits associated with an ageing population, and the unrelenting demands of globalisation.

CONCLUSIONS AND IMPLICATIONS

German unification in 1990 was yet another example within Europe's long history of territorial consolidation, with significant implications for state- and nation-building in the heart of the continent. While Rokkan and other students of comparative European history may offer insights into how such a consolidation was achieved, and why it attains its level of significance within the broader perspective of European history, the more immediate task before students of German and European politics is to understand the constraints on nation-building facing the German democracy in a crucial period of pan-European reform and transformation. Thus, the broader implications of German unification can be better appreciated by addressing two challenges emerging from the process of German state and nation consolidation during the past decade: (1) how to overcome the path-dependent constraints imposed by the process of unification itself; and (2) what kind of national identity is desirable in the context of the united German society and the politics of the European Union?

Overcoming the path-dependent process will realistically be achieved only within the constitutional framework of the Federal Republic. Radical change is not in the political culture of the German democracy of the Federal Republic era. Indeed, as we have seen, the process of consolidation via the Unification Treaty in October 1990 (following the political realities imposed by the March 1990 elections in the East) in accordance with Article 23 of West German Basic Law meant the loss of historical opportunity of a new constitutional reform that might have effectively achieved consolidation through a multi-cultural model[36] of political and social citizenship based on the idea of diverse society and social justice rather than the concept of citizenship based on economic pragmatism, or 'constitutional patriotism'. In fact, after unification, there was the effort for constitutional reform through reform through the Joint Constitutional Commission of the Bundestag and Bundesrat. This was dictated by the fact that the Unification Treaty specified certain amendments to the Basic Law in order to achieve unification. Through the Commission, two issues received special attention from the democratic GDR government: (1) the introduction of broader basic social rights and the specification of particular state objectives into the Basic Law, and (2) direct democracy through referendum.

However, the primary goal of West German Basic Law of 1949 was to establish political stability and effective representation in the wake of World War II and the disaster of National Socialism. Therefore, the constitutional principles of the Basic Law are built on the presumptions of caution and political temperance. It is a conservative philosophy which delivers an effective brake on political impulse and drama via direct and democratic participation and popular consultation.[37] Consequently, constitutional reform after unification could reasonably be expected to result in only limited reform centring on the relationship between the German federal government and the Länder.

It is doubtful if the legal, economic and political frameworks defined by the Basic Law 50 years ago can be still effective and desirable in the situation of consolidating two parts of Germany with such divergent national and political identities. Of course, this is an open question, and to date the record of unification suggests the strategy has not been an outright failure. Yet it is also clear that in the united Germany of today the question of national identity, and, to a lesser extent, institutional identity, lies at the roots of post-unification dissatisfaction in the East and is linked to a feeling of isolation from the newly created German political community. In effect, the constitutional formula selected for the purpose of achieving consolidation in 1990 seems to have delivered to the doorstep of Germans a 'denial of the democracy and self-determination' throughout the East.[38]

What kind of national identity is desirable in the context of the united German society and the politics of the European Union? Is it preferable from the standpoint of Europe to have a unified Germany with a clear and healthy sense of national identity, or would it serve the longer-term goals for Europe to allow the status quo to persist well into the period of the EU's planned major expansion to Eastern and East-Central Europe? To begin, even to the casual observer, there are interesting and important similarities between the united Germany of 2002 and the European Union of 2002. United Germany was not constructed around a constitutional moment, *per se*, and neither is the European Union – at least not yet. That is, the political community of both have been forged by treaty, not an explicit, constitutional convention designed to incorporate competing and complementary visions of representation, democracy and citizenship. And this common feature has certainly been at least partly responsible for claims of a 'democratic deficit' and a lack of collective identity found within both Germany and the EU.

When considering the broader pattern of European integration in recent years, these similarities between the unified Germany and the EU are more than a mere coincidence. 'Europeans' writes Schmitter, 'feel themselves, rightly or wrongly, at the mercy of a process of integration that they do not understand and certainly do not control – however much they may enjoy its material benefits.'[39] This description aptly underscores the frustration of many Germans following their national unification in 1990.

Yet does such a similarity matter? In the face of growing immigration pressures, labour reform, and the heightened demand of fiscal responsibility in the era of a common European currency and the challenge of expanding EU membership to increasingly poorer regions of Europe, underdeveloped national identity may deny both Germany and Europe a confident and clear voice of leadership to deal with the genuine challenges of an increasingly pan-European Union. It appears that the day is fast approaching when European pressures will force German politicians and citizens to openly confront their ideals of political representation, citizenship, and democratic decision-making in their society from the perspective not merely of efficiency and stability, but of political community. Following Schmitter's analysis of 'the Euro-democracy', it seems reasonable to conclude that, at a minimum, the process of German unification now needs to move beyond its initial phase of being an economic strategy of integrating East Germany, and a celebration of German national success, to an enterprise devoted to creating a common German political community which is justified and legitimated by something other than national pride and constitutional patriotism. Europe's continued success as a venture on democratic and economic development seems to 'request' this historical challenge. If achieved, Germany's consolidation and unification will have proved to be more than a political strategy for Germans, but a visionary and strategic stroke for European security and prosperity.

NOTES

1. Max Kaase and P. Bauer-Kaase, 'German Unification 1990–1997: The Long, Long Road', in Guy Lachapelle and John Trent (eds.), *Globalization: Governance and Identity* (University of Montreal, 2000), pp.153–86; Russell J. Dalton, 'Communists and Democrats: Democratic Attitudes in the Two Germanies', *British Journal of Political Science*, 24 (1994), pp.469–93; Russell J. Dalton, *Germans Divided: The 1994 Bundestag Elections and the Evolution of the German Party System* (Oxford: Berg, 1996); Dieter Fuchs, 'The Democratic Culture of United Germany', in Pippa Norris (ed.), *Critical Citizens: Global Support for Democratic Government* (New York: Oxford University Press, 1999), pp.123–45; and Rolf Steininger, 'The German Question 1945–1995', in Klaus Larres (ed.), *Germany Since Unification: The Domestic and External Consequences* (New York: Macimillan Press, 1998), pp.9–32.
2. Grzegorz Ekiert and Jan Kubik, 'Contentious Politics in New Democracies: East Germany, Hungary, Poland, and Slovakia, 1989–93', *World Politics*, 50 (1998), pp.547–81.
3. See Thomas Christensen, *Eurobarometer 55.1, April – May 2001: Globalization and Humanitarian Aid* (Ann Arbor, MI: Inter-university Consortium for Political and Social Research, 2002). The eight institutions covered (and the respective percentages of Western and Eastern Germans responding that they tended to trust the particular institution) were: national government in general (47% v. 41%), national parliament (52% v. 39%), political parties (20% v. 15%), police (81% v. 70%), the justice system (68% v. 48%), the army (75% v. 66%), the civil service (57% v. 46%), and unions (47% v. 44%). For a more thorough analysis, see Robert Rohrschneider and Rüdiger Schmitt-Beck, 'Trust in Institutions in Germany: Theory and Evidence Ten Years After Unification', this volume; and Robert Rohrschneider, *Learning Democracy. Democratic and Economic Values in Unified Germany* (Oxford: University of Oxford Press, 1999).
4. Sven Seinmo and Kathleen Thelen (eds.), *Structuring Politics* (New York: Cambridge University Press, 1992).
5. See Victor Nee and Paul Ingram, 'Embeddedness and Beyond: Institutions, Exchange, and Social Structure', in Mary C. Brinton and Victor Nee (eds.), *The New Institutionalism in Sociology* (New York: Russell Sage Foundation, 1998), pp.19–45, and Colin Hay and Daniel Wincott, 'Interrogating Institionalism Interrogating Institutions: Beyond "Calculus" and "Cultural Approaches"', *Columbia International Affairs Online Working Papers*: www.ciaonet.org/wps/wid01/.

6. Colin Hay and Daniel Wincott, 'Structure, Agency and Historical Institutionalism', *Political Studies*, 46/5 (1998), pp.951–7. For their more extended discussion, see Hay and Wincott, 'Interrogating Institutionalism Interrogating Institutions'.
7. Kathleen Thelen, 'Historical Institutionalism in Comparative Politics', *Annual Review of Political Science*, 2 (1999), 369–404 at p.384.
8. Hans Kohn, 'Western and Eastern Nationalism', in J. Hutchinson and A.D. Smith (eds.), *Nationalism* (Oxford: Oxford University Press, 1994).
9. Peter Flora, Stein Kuhnle and Derek Urwin (eds.), *State Formation, Nation-Building and Mass Politics in Europe: The Theory of Stein Rokkan* (Oxford: Clarendon, 1999).
10. For this argument of the formation of collective social political identities, particularly national identity, see Benedict Anderson, *Imagined Communities* (London: Verso, 1983); Eric Hobsbawm, *The Age of Revolution: Europe 1789–1848* (London: Abacus, 1986); Eric Hobsbawm, *Nations and Nationalism since 1780* (Cambridge: Cambridge University Press, 1990); Ernest Gellner; *Nations and Nationalism* (Oxford: Blackwell, 1983).
11. For the discussion of symbolic boundaries, see Michele Lamont and Virag Molnar, 'The Study of Boundaries in The Social Science', *Annual Review of Sociology*, 28 (2002), pp.167–95.
12. John Breuilly, *Nationalism and the State* (Chicago: University of Chicago Press, 1985).
13. Stein Rokkan, 'The Survival of Peripheral Identify', in Flora *et al.* (eds.), *State Formation, Nation-Building, and Mass Politics in Europe*, p.208.
14. Erik Ringmar, *Identity, Interest, and Action: A Cultural Explanation of Sweden's Intervention in the Thirty Years War* (New York: Cambridge University Press, 1996). He defines this concept as the following: 'Formative moments are characteristically periods of symbolic hyper-inflation-times when new emblems, flags, dress codes, songs, fetes and rituals are continuously invented', p.85.
15. John Borneman, *Belonging in the Two Berlins* (New York: Cambridge University Press, 1992); Heinrich August Winkler, 'Rebuilding of a Nation: The Germans Before and After Unification', in Michael Meters, Steven Muller and Heinrich August Winkler (eds.), *In Search of Germany* (New Brunswick: Transaction Publishers, 1996), p.69.
16. Andreas Glaeser, *Divided In Unity* (Chicago: University of Chicago Press, 2000).
17. For this point, particularly, see Winand Gellner and Gerd Strohmeir, 'The Double Public: Germany after Reunification', in this volume; and Felix Philipp Lutz, 'Historical Consciousness and the Changing of German Political Culture', in this volume.
18. Thelen, 'Historical Institutionalism in Comparative Politics', p.388.
19. Hay and Wincott, 'Structure, Agency and Historical Institutionalism', p.955.
20. Samuel P. Huntington, *The Third Wave: Democratization in the Late Twenties Century* (University of Oklahoma, 1991). Huntington's classification of the type of democratic transition is basically focused on 'the relative importance and power between the elites in power and opposition groups' in the process of democratisation. That is, if the elites in power played a decisive role in bringing about democracy and changing the old authoritarian regime, whereas opposition groups were weak, democratic transition is classified as *transformation*. More importantly, in this case, 'the emergence of reformers' within the old authoritarian regime is a necessary condition (p.129). In the case of *replacement*, opposition groups are stronger than reformers within government, or there is a dominance of 'standpatters' within government. Furthermore, the process of democratic transition starts from the anti-authoritarian movement under the political leadership of opposition groups. *Transplacement* is a mix of *transformation* and *replacement* in that a balance of power exists between reformers and standpatters within the old regime, thus the democratic transition is achieved by the negotiation between elites in power and opposition groups. In this case, the opposition groups are 'strong enough to prevail over antidemocratic radicals, but they are not strong enough to overthrow the government' (p.151). Finally, *intervention* occurs when transition is achieved by 'foreign imposition' and 'declononisation' (p.112).
21. Huntington, *The Third Wave*, p.144.
22. Chris Flockton and Eva Kolinsky, 'Recasting East Germany: An Introduction', in Chris Flockton and Eva Kolinsky (eds.), *Recasting East Germany: Social Transformation after the GDR* (London: Frank Cass, 1999), pp.1–13; Ulrich K. Preuss, 'The Roundtable Talks in the

German Democratic Republic', in Jon Elster (ed.), *The Roundtable Talks and Breakdown of Communism* (Chicago: University of Chicago Press, 1996), p.100.

23. Preuss, 'The Roundtable Talks in the German Democratic Republic', pp.99–134.
24. Daniel V. Friedheim, 'Accelerating Collapse: The East German Road Form Liberalization to Power Sharing', in Yossi Shain and Juan J. Linz (eds.), *Between States: Interim Governments and Democratic Transition* (New York: Cambridge University Press, 1995), pp.160–78.
25. David Childs, *The Fall of the GDR* (Essex: Pearson Education, 2001); Charles S. Maier, *Dissolution: The Crisis of Communism and the End of East Germany* (New Jersey: Princeton University Press, 1997); Kurt Sonthemer, 'United Germany: Political Systems Under Challenge', *SAIS Review*, Special Issue (1995), pp.39–54.
26. For more detail on the political events and decisions of the period November 1989–October 1990, and an assessment of the various positions of the political groups within East Germany, see Timothy Garton Ash, *In Europe's Name: Germany and the Divided Continent* (New York: Vintage Books, 1994), pp.343–56. Also see Gordon A. Craig, 'The New Germany', in Gordon A. Craig, *Politics and Culture in Modern Germany: Essays from the New York Review of Books* (Palo Alto, CA: Society for the Promotion of Science and Scholarship, 1998), pp.344–56.
27. Adam Przeworski, *Democracy and the Market* (New York: Cambridge University, 1991).
28. Ibid., p.87.
29. As Hirschman himself notes, many studies have employed his concept of exit, voice, and loyalty in explaining the collapse of the GDR in 1989. See Albert O. Hirschman, 'Exit, Voice, and Fate of the German Democratic Republic: An Essay in Conceptual History', *World Politics*, 45 (1993), pp.173–202.
30. Albert O. Hirschman, *Exit, Voice, and Loyalty: Responses to Decline in Firms, Organizations, and States* (Cambridge: Harvard University Press, 1970), p.78.
31. Claus Offe, *Varieties of Transition: The East European and East German Experience* (Cambridge: MIT Press, 1997).
32. Heinrich August Winkler, 'Rebuilding of a Nation: The Germans Before and After Unification', in Mertes *et al.* (eds), *In Search of Germany*, pp.59–78.
33. Jurgen Habermas, 'Yet Again: German Identity – A Unified Nation of Angry DM-Burghers?' *New German Critique*, 52 (1991), pp.84–101.
34. See Robert Rohrschneider, *Learning Democracy. Democratic and Economic Values in Unified Germany* (Oxford: University of Oxford Press, 1999).
35. Hirschman, *Exit, Voice, and Loyalty*, p.80. 'Loyalty or specific institutional barriers to exit are therefore particularly functional whenever the effective use of voice requires a great deal of social inventiveness while exit is an available, yet not wholly effective, option'.
36. Peter van Ham suggested the multicultural model as an alternative of civic nationalism and ethic nationalism in the context of European integration. According to his definition, in the multicultural model, 'the nation does allow scope for the maintenance of cultural and ethnic differences. This would make full citizenship relatively easy without the requirement of cultural assimilation'. See Peter van Ham, 'Identity Beyond The State: The Case of the European Union', *Columbia International Affairs Online Working Papers, 2000.* For Habermas' criticism of civic patriotism, see Habermas, 'Yet Again: German Identity – A Unified Nation of Angry DM-Burghers?'; Ciaran Cronin and Pablo De Grief (eds.), *The Inclusion of the Other: Studies in Political Theory* (Cambridge: MIT Press, 1998), pp.105–27.
37. Gert-Joachim Glaeβner, 'Government and Political Order', in Gordon Smith, William E. Paterson and Stephen Padgett (eds.), *Developments in German Politics 2* (Durham: Duke University Press, 1996), pp.14–34.
38. Patrick Stevenson and John Theobald, 'A Decade of Cultural Disunity: Diverging Discourse and Communicative Dissonance in 1990s Germany', in Patrick Stevenson and John Theobald (eds.), *Relocating Germanness* (New York: St. Martin's Press, 2000), pp.1–22.
39. Phillippe C. Schmitter, *How to Democratize the European Union and Why Bother?* (Lanham: Rowman & Littlefield Publishers, 2000), p.116.

Historical Consciousness and the Changing of German Political Culture

FELIX PHILIPP LUTZ

Historical consciousness in unified Germany 13 years after the fall of the German Democratic Republic is undergoing a profound change whose direction is not yet clearly visible. The following describes the status and content of historical consciousness in the period from autumn 1989 until the end of the twentieth century. However, during the 1990s, in the aftermath of unification, and following revolutionary-like changes and adjustments in different fields such as foreign policy and the changing international role of united Germany, a gradual change in political culture is occurring. This change is occurring parallel with the demise of the last generations of Germany who witnessed the Third Reich – either as victims or as perpetrators.

Ambivalent signals indicate change – but in which direction? In a survey comissioned by the weekly magazine *Der Spiegel* in summer 2001, a representative sample of German people were asked about their knowledge of what had happened on 17 June 1953. Overall, only 43 per cent of all Germans were able to answer correctly.[1] The numbers indicate a loss of knowledge about recent history which is remarkable. Also, differences between East and West Germans are still enormously high with regard to judging the GDR and views of socialism and capitalism. At the same time, numerous discussions about history which focuses on the Nazi past and the recent era of the GDR have been part of the unification debate within the Federal Republic. The former Federal Republic has become the subject of numerous debates concerning the significance and evaluation of particular aspects of its history. These include, for example, the *Ostpolitik* advocated by Western German political parties and governments, the inner-German policies pursued in the post-war era, and methods of assessing the way in which German citizens have come to terms with the National Socialist past.

The GDR's self-rightous claim that it was an anti-fascist state allowed citizens to avoid an understanding and reconciliation with the National Socialist past. Whereas the Federal Republic claimed to be the legal successor of the German state and the Third Reich, the GDR did not, and thus offered neither moral nor financial compensation. In practical terms,

Felix Philipp Lutz, Schiller International University, Heidelberg the Nazi past ceased to play a role in the political life of the GDR. Rather, it was externalised and projected onto the Federal Republic. It would be true to say that in a large variety of ways, such as in political education or contemporary history research projects, a real attempt was made over the years in West Germany to understand and come to terms with the National Socialist past. However, the attempt to bring the guilty to justice must be viewed more critically. After the war, many of those responsible for National Socialist crimes were able to secure influential and often prestigious positions, within the legal, medical, higher educational and civil service professions.

The process of addressing the crimes committed by the former GDR regime is still ongoing, while the history of the GDR is being rewritten on the basis of official documents and other material that can now be freely consulted. More than 50 years after the end of the National Socialist dictatorship, and more than 12 years after the collapse of the SED regime, Germans are actively involved more than ever in trying to understand their past.

HISTORICAL CONSCIOUSNESS

The term historical consciousness describes an individual's ability to think about three temporal dimensions – past, present and future – and to order them in a meaningful manner in areas of potential conflict such as the individual versus society, existence and volition, and personal values and wishes on the one hand, and social norms on the other. Historical consciousness is an ongoing achievement of the human intellect. The epitome of cerebral activity, it processes the experience of time in the realm of memory in order to provide orientation in real life. The individual critically evaluates his own position both in the temporal continuum of history and in the social context. Neither the quality of such thinking nor the ability to engage in it is the decisive factor. Rather, an individual's historical consciousness or his or her ability to engage in such thinking is determined by the fact that we can all perceive and process time.

On the personal and the collective level, historical consciousness performs a series of discrete, complementary and specifically related functions. This web of relationships and casuality is characterised by interdependent and hierarchical structures. At the lowest level there are experiential and memory funcions, actions which have to be performed continually. These are followed by functions such as interpretation, orientation, the formation of opinions and values, and action (either in the shape of verbal opinions, or participation in political life). At the top of this structure there is the synthetic product of the various processes and functions. This, ideally, is the stable individual or collective identity, and the practical realisation of the self-image thus created on the level of action. Historical consciousness is a culturally modified, functionally more complex, more diversified, and subjective, value-determined and ideologically enhanced form of consciousness which incorporates the features and functions mentioned above. Thus, historical consciousness signifies the activity or operation of a functional complex consciousness on the factual level of an individual's biography, and historical knowledge of a collective history based on specific social, ideological, practical and personal goals, norms and regulations.[2]

TWO SOCIETIES AND DIFFERENT PASTS

The five new federal states of the Berlin Republic witnessed a striking break with the past. Because of the dramatic changes they were and still are confronted with, the citizens of these five states have a patent need for reorientation. This, in turn, has strongly influenced how they view their individual and collective past. The process of coming to terms with recent history, including the interpretation of the interviewees' own past, had certainly not been completed at the time the data were collected. The survey revealed a deep-seated insecurity among citizens of former East Germany; at times this amounted to a crisis of identity.[3] The following results – insofar as they relate to the new federal states – represent a snapshot of the change of consciousness that is still taking place. They also show the process of reorientation, the insecurity and the contradictory and obviously ambivalent feelings of the interviewees.

The survey at hand revealed that only the two eldest generations in Western Germany – and occasionally members of the 1968 generation – had experienced things that were of existential importance. On the face of it this insight appears to be rather trivial: since 1945 it has been impossible to experience anything like the Third Reich. On the other hand, it is surprising that interviewees find it difficult to relate their own lives to the history of the Federal Republic (with the exception of the post-war years and the period of reconstruction). Thus, events do not really supply the reference points that historical consciousness requires. Rather, the nature of everyday life helps to transmit and internalise events, values and attitudes. In other words, the 'experiential' value systems of the older generation differ from the 'acquired' ones of the younger generation. However, this does not apply to Eastern Germans: conditions in the GDR were of existential importance for everyone.

Anti-Fascism and National Socialism

National Socialism provides West Germans with a negative backdrop for the current situation, and constitutes the origin of the way in which they view the present.[4] In contrast to former East Germany, they do not have to justify the existence of the Federal Republic, which continues to determine their day-to-day existence. The Federal Republic represents the antithesis of the latter, and is a historical object-lesson. The reconstruction period of the 1950s in particular has become a part of people's historical consciousness, and, on account of what has been achieved, it is a source of pride and satisfaction. In contrast to this, the historical consciousness of citizens of former East Germany is far more process-related. They are confronted with a need to justify and explain themselves which exceeds that of West Germans. In order to rescue at least a part of their biographies and personal identities in the face of the downfall of the GDR, they have tried to extrapolate positive elements from its history. In the main, these are anti-fascism and the idea of socialism. National Socialism and the Holocaust do not play the same kind of role as in the West. In fact, they are fairly insignificant as reference points for the present.[5]

Anti-fascism[6] made it seem legitimate to believe that there was something essentially positive about East Germany. The GDR was seen as the country which was the direct result of the resistance movement, and which had made a clean break with the National Socialist past. This, it was believed, had not happened in West Germany. The other (and indeed the 'better') Germany, which was symbolised by resistance to National Socialism, supposedly became a reality when the GDR was founded. It differed profoundly from the 'FRG', it was thought, because of its thorough de-nazification programme, the permanent provision of information about fascism and its causes, and the anti-fascist education of children. Although many interviewees expressed their disappointment at the extent to which anti-fascism had been misused as an advertising gimmick, the extent to which the government had betrayed its own declared anti-fascist ideals, and, as time went on, the growing credibility gap, they continued to believe in the positive anti-fascist myth on which the GDR was founded. And anti-fascism also stood in the way of a more profound understanding of the nature of National Socialism.[7]

Political Upheaval and Unification

The changes on the international level as a result of Gorbachev's policies led people to hope that change would also become possible in the GDR. However, the speed with which it finally arrived and the political upheaval itself came as a surprise. People were overwhelmed by the developments. The vast majority of East Germans welcomed the demise of the old system, though not all were unreservedly in favour of reunification with the Federal Republic. Conversely, a considerable number of West Germans stated that they were not interested in German unity.[8] The reason for the demise of the GDR was almost unanimously considered to be the mismanagement of the economy. Other reasons adduced were developments in the Soviet Union, in Hungary and in Poland. Furthermore, after Gorbachev's meeting with President Reagan, there was a new relationship between the USA and the Soviet Union. Against this background, 'one could risk going on demonstrations without having to be afraid that the Soviet Army would become involved'. Up to the moment of reunification, people had a great deal of faith in the economic power of the Federal Republic, which, it was thought, would simplify the transition. Those who were able to conceive of a reformed GDR saw reunification as a straitjacket, and considered Hans Modrow's idea of a federation to be a better alternative. Many people saw reunification as a 'hostile takeover' and a relapse into the kind of capitalism which, it was thought, had already been overcome.

Many people who were not supporters of the former GDR were disappointed that the state disappeared so quickly and without much ado, leaving nothing behind. All in all, however, reunification was seen in a positive light because there was a positive image of the Federal Republic.

Generations in East and West

Karl Mannheim's generation-based approach[9] takes as its starting point the notion that in a certain age group shared formative historical experiences lead to stable and long-term attitudes and behavioural patterns. Within the lifetime of the present generations in Germany there has been a series of events which, going by Mannheim's theory, have had a socialising influence of this kind on the various age groups. Thus, events such as the Second World War, the end of the war, the currency reform, the establishment of the GDR tend to appear in the answers given by the interviewees. How the individual is affected by such experiences or insights depends on the extent to which history or historical events have intruded into his biography. Thus, the immediacy of personal experience is of decisive importance for an individual's historical consciousness and the relationship between value and behaviour.[10]

Generations in the New Federal States

East Germans who belong to the war generation felt that the historical events of the twentieth century have had an unduly adverse effect on their lives. As they look back, they resign themselves to their fate, and many, having lived through or experienced three or four completely different periods of German history (the Weimar Republic, the National Socialist regime, the GDR, and, finally, reunited Germany), lack the willpower to reorientate their lives yet again. Their historical recollections are strongly influenced by recent events, and they remember earlier processes of adjustment as they experience another period of radical change.

The founding of the GDR was the formative experience of the post-war generation, whose conscious perception of history begins immediately after the war. In addition to this, there are childhood memories of the war, such as the bombing of Dresden or the arrival of Soviet troops. These are events which interviewees remember to this day. Participation in the process of reconstruction and the notion that the GDR, at least at the time of its foundation, represented an attempt to improve on the past, at first led people to have some faith in the new social order. In retrospect, the founding of the GDR is seen as an attempt to draw certain lessons from National Socialism and to establish a new kind of society which would 'make a recurrence of war and fascism impossible in the future'. Negative memories usually have something to do with the presence of Soviet troops, who are often held responsible for the fact that these promising beginnings evaporated and came to nothing. Virtually all of the interviewees stressed their own contribution to reconstruction in the GDR, the difficulties that had to be overcome, and the effort, sacrifice and self-denial that all this necessitated.

This generation finds it hard to adjust to the new conditions in the Federal Republic, and particularly painful and difficult to come to terms with the GDR past. The GDR generation was the first to grow up exclusively in the former GDR. At the heart of its involvement with history are experiences in the GDR. As people recall their childhood and youth, they often recollect their gradual alienation from the GDR. They remember the normality of everyday life in the GDR, the Young Pioneers and the FDJ. They also recall the experience of being told what to do, the feeling of being 'steered and manipulated from above'. Career choices were influenced by government stipulations and politically motivated decisions. For this generation, the reorientation process was and still is more difficult than for the other generations. Biographies were unavoidably interlinked with the SED state, a fact which creates serious problems with regard to people's sense of identity.

The young generation in particular feels that it has been betrayed by its parents, its teachers and the system. Again, this generation is clearly unsure of itself. The events that marked the reunification process made it necessary to embark on a process of total reorientation. At the same time, the collapse of the old regime was felt to be something positive. It signified the end of being 'told what to do', of state intervention, of attempts to manipulate educational choices and career prospects. And, finally, it also put an end to the omnipresent indoctrination which this age group considered especially hypocritical and lacking in credibility. Within this generation, people undoubtedly perceive the political upheaval (*die Wende*) as a liberating experience. They wish to get to know the world, to travel, to enjoy new experiences. And they are full of confidence, for they still have all of their lives to look forward to.

Generations in the Old Federal States

In the old federal states, people from the war generation most frequently refer to events that radically changed their lives and which were of existential importance. A few aspects of National Socialism, such as solving the problem of unemployment, building the *Reichsautobahnen*, and the alleged existence of a community spirit, are considered to be ambivalent and were described in positive terms, though negative experiences and assessments clearly predominate.

Interviewees often described their experiences during the Third Reich as 'the best time of their lives'. These included experiences in the Hitler Youth or in the League of German Girls (BDM or Bund Deutscher Mädel), when they were away from home for the first time, or time spent with the German air force in occupied Paris. However, such experiences do not necessarily lead people to idealise National Socialism. The lessons people learned from their experiences during the Nazi period are summed up in statements such as 'No More War' and 'No More Dictatorship'. The generation has a positive view of the late 1940s and the 1950s, Germany's period of reconstruction, although it is also recalled as a time of deprivation that was not always easy. To this day, the achievements of this era are seen as a cause for pride, and they are considered to be the underlying reason for the success of the Federal Republic.

The formative experiences of the post-war generation were the presence of Allied troops and the obvious sacrifices that had to be made, such as food shortages and hard work. The generation learned the lesson of democracy from the historical consequences of National Socialism, for to some extent it had to pay for the misdeeds of the previous generation. Many people have the impression that they missed out on something in their youth, particularly when they compare themselves with the younger generation. On the other hand, this has led to a special kind of self-confidence built on the knowledge that one can get by with fewer possessions than people now consider necessary. In this age group, people's personal involvement in the reconstruction of the 1950s, and their negative experiences under the National Socialist regime or in the war, are the reasons for a specific and very noticeable pride in the Federal Republic. For this generation, the immediate post-war period (with the exception of the question of reunification) came to an end with the treaties dealing with the German question that were concluded at the beginning of the 1970s, when Germany recovered its ability to engage in a political discourse with the states to the east.

The '1968' or 'Federal Republic' generation sees the period since the mid-1960s as a time of awakening and upheaval which witnessed societal changes that are still being felt today. This epoch, which had a formative influence on the interviewees, was characterised by events and concepts such as existentialism, the Beatles, the Vietnam War, the student and feminist movements, and *Ostpolitik*. Coming to terms with National Socialism continues to play an important role in historical consciousness as a result in part of the debates on the subject which took place within the family. They make a point of emphasising that, as Germans, they have a sense of responsibility, especially in view of what happened in the past. It is seen to constitute an obligation that applies to all Germans equally. This attitude to National Socialism has also had a strong influence on their collective identity.

The generation has an ambivalent attitude to the founding of the Federal Republic. On the one hand, after the experience of dictatorship and war, it was a precondition for the attainment of freedom, prosperity and peace. On the other hand, it is seen as the root of many evils. Up to the disintegration of the Eastern bloc, these were considered to be the systemic confrontation of the two military blocs, the Federal Republic's dependence on the superpowers in general (and the USA in particular), environmental pollution and the ostensibly inadequate implementation of social justice.

The youngest generation of West Germans takes its political bearings mainly from the National Socialist regime and the Second World War (as do the other age groups). In terms of historical consciousness, this era, together with the obvious success of the post-war reconstruction period, forms the youngest generation's most important reference point. However, people reject the notion of personal guilt, and at times there are signs that they are tired of talking about National Socialism. In this generation in particular, German unity has considerably altered the significance attached to certain important events. Unification may lead to a host of new experiences, and for this age group it represents a greater potential for change than for the other generations.

PATTERNS OF HISTORICAL CONSCIOUSNESS IN THE WEST

In 1991, five clearly separate groups of people in the western federal states[11] could be distinguished on the basis of the way in which they dealt with the past.[12] The groups were identified by the predominant method of each for dealing with the past, in conjunction with current orientations, and on the basis of the strongest factor loadings. Furthermore, the typology was verified by additional correlation analysis. The complexity and diversity of the data base, which is characteristic of every individual group, is important for the evaluation of the statements that were made.[13]

Repression

In the first group[14] the past is primarily dealt with by means of 'repression'.[15] The people in this cluster – who in fact constitute 23.4 per cent of the total interviewed – no longer want to hear about the National Socialist past and 'resent the fact that Germans continue to be held responsible for the crimes of the Nazis'.[16] There is also a tendency to play down the crimes of the Nazis and the Holocaust by placing them in a larger context, which does not, however, lead to a positive view of National Socialism. The refusal to accept responsibility for the past is understood in a collective and in an individual sense. Considerable support for the 'seduction theory' exists only in this and the second group: 'Hitler's public persona and his rhetorical gifts deceived most people as to his true intentions'. However, this group rejects any attempt to idealise National Socialism.

People in this group take a great deal of pride in economic performance, in particular that of the post-war period. Their systemic patriotism is based on two elements that are inextricably linked: the certain knowledge that they 'are living in the most liberal state in the history of Germany', and the insight that 'German citizens have a better life than people in most other countries'.

However, the notion of 'repression' does not wholly suffice to explain this category. The reasons given for refusing to think about the Third Reich or the Holocaust within this group can be rather diverse. There are older people who no longer want to discuss the subject due to personal experiences or complicity in certain actions or crimes, or simply because they were fellow-travellers. However, repression can also derive from a feeling that the subject of National Socialism has been overdone.

Conformity

The second group[17] sees Germans in a historical perspective as fated to be victims. This is mirrored in statements such as 'Under the Nazi regime, the Germans themselves suffered more than anyone else'. As in the first group, people believe that the Germans were seduced by Hitler, though there is a slight measure of agreement with regard to the factor 'responsibility for the past'. Thus, the crimes of the Nazis are not repressed to the extent described in the case of the first group. Of particular interest in this group are the attitudes to National Socialism. Idealisation, the corresponding factor, includes a fundamental tendency to play down the importance of National

Socialism by placing it in a wider context, and to see it in a positive light. This leads to statements such as 'I do not believe that everything about National Socialism was bad' and 'National Socialism was the reason why things began to get better in Germany after 1933'.

However, the interviewees in this cluster are neither Nazis nor radical right-wingers. They include a number of people who had positive experiences in the Third Reich. These interviewees are generally very conservative and proud to be German. At the same time, they display a strong systemic patriotism with regard to the Federal Republic. The responses of this group display a strong desire for harmony and consensus, which leads to contradictions in the views and attitudes expressed.

Historical Pessimism

The third group is characterised by a sense of responsibility toward the history of National Socialism and ways of dealing with the recent past. Thus, group 3 closely resembles the predominant method of dealing with the past in group 4.[18] They recognise individual and collective responsibility for the problematical aspects of German history and therefore take for granted that political asylum should be a basic right, and favour an open society in which foreigners, ethnic Germans from Central-Eastern Europe, refugees from the Third World, and so on, can live harmoniously and peacefully with Germans.

Two characteristics distinguish these interviewees from all the others. First, there is the profound pessimism which characterises their attitudes towards history and politics. 'I do not believe that people will ever learn anything from history.' Thus, with regard to Germany, they reject the assertion that 'Germans have now demonstrated that they have learned something from the past'.

The second characteristic, which also has historical origins, is a distinct discontinuity in their feeling of identity,[19] both with regard to their self-image as Germans and the political system of the former and now enlarged Federal Republic. Criticism is levelled at the way in which the values and freedoms laid down in the Constitution (*Grundgesetz*) materialise in the parliamentary system, the political institutions and everyday political reality.

This group might be defined using the term 'post-materialists'; their value system takes its bearings from individual freedom, equal opportunities and individual self-realisation. The response rate to the question about national pride was not merely the lowest; it was also rejected in a most emphatic manner within this group. The self-image among 'Historical Pessimists' is especially negative. Thus, at the time of the survey, the Germans were considered to be xenophobic and ready to do what they were told, and to lack self-confidence and *joie de vivre*.

Furthermore, they were thought to be authoritarian and opinionated. When asked which of these characteristics had a negative influence on German history, almost all were mentioned a second time round. In other words, the Germans have not changed, and for this reason it is right to be pessimistic.

This group experienced the greatest change during the past ten years of unification. While the Social Democrats together with the Green Party came to power in 1998, the war in former Yugoslavia and in Kosovo forced the political leadership of the Green Party to face *Realpolitik*. Now those people, who originated in the pacifist and environmental movement of the 1970s, had to lead the Federal Republic in its first war since WWII.

Responsibility

The fourth group is characterised by a feeling of responsibility and changes in value.[20] The crucial difference between groups 3 and 4 is the presence of political attitudes that support the system, and these lead to a strong identification with the German state, the Federal Republic. In this context, responsibility for the past contains elements that not only refer to National Socialism, but also to the *Ostpolitik* of the SPD–FDP coalition, which is considered to have been the right thing to do under the circumstances. Attitudes towards National Socialism and the ways of coming to terms with it closely resemble those of the pessimists, though in some respects they are even more critical and negative with regard to the phenomenon. The knowledge that one is living in an economically successful state and a liberal democracy, and the approval of this kind of social and political structure, were termed 'systemic patriotism' in the relevant factor of the data analysis. However, in the case of group 4 the term 'constitutional patriotism' would be more appropriate, because the level of participation in the political system is very high, and the types of participation are conventional. Support for a united Europe and an open society is even more pronounced than approval of statements that might be subsumed under the heading 'systemic patriotism'. Those conscious of their responsibilities represent the system-supporting 'value-oriented conservatives' (*Wertkonservative*) in the total sample. It is very clear that people are proud to be German (64.8 per cent), and is based on a pronounced confidence in the Federal Republic.

Idealisation

The fifth and last group[21] clearly has a positive view of National Socialism and is very critical of the Federal Republic, or, to be more precise, of everyday life in the Federal Republic. Responsibility for the German past is rejected, both on an individual and on a collective level. They wish to have nothing more to do with the National Socialist crimes. Indeed, they do not even want to talk about them. In contrast to all other interviewees, the 'idealisers' do not have a negative view of National Socialism, and are in agreement with statements such as 'I do not believe that everything about National Socialism was bad', 'If it had not been for the war, Hitler would have become one of the greatest German statesmen', and 'National Socialism was the reason why things began to get better in Germany after 1933'. Thus, this group has the smallest number of people who agree with the following statement: 'Hitler's public persona and his rhetorical gifts deceived most people as to his true intentions.' The potentially dangerous aspect of these attitudes and the crucial difference between group 5 and group 2 is the combination or the coincidence of a kind of 'chauvinism of affluence' that verges on racism. In other words, they are likely to agree with such assertions as: 'We Germans should take care to maintain the purity of our race' or 'The large number of refugees from the Third World is developing into a serious threat for our country'. They are also likely to hold an attitude to the political system of the Federal Republic that is either very critical or which rejects it altogether. Furthermore, in response to questions concerning the form of government (democracy or dictatorship), this group recorded the highest percentage expressing a favourable attitude toward authoritarian-type regimes. All in all, the idealisers hold rather negative views of Germans, though in a fashion that differs from that of the 'pessimists'. However, these patterns of thought do not necessarily lead to support for undemocratic or extremist partiesor movements.

CONCLUSION: SYNDROMES OF CHANGE AND PERSISTENCE

Foreign Policy and War

There are important lessons that Germans in both east and west have taken to heart. For the vast majority of people war is not seen as a political means to an end. This was shown during the Gulf War, for example, when the strongest criticism of UN military involvement was voiced in the Federal Republic. The rejection of military force is still at the heart of the historical consciousness of all Germans, whatever their age, political allegiance or level of education. However, aspects of this 'culture of reticence' are slowly being eroded, and this is a sign of gradual and inexorable change in German political life. When, for the first time after 1945, a German Foreign Minister sent combat troops into an armed conflict in 1998, he did so by emphasising the morale of the mission with reference to the Holocaust in German history. However, the participation of the German Air Force and ground troops was more a result of a change in the attitudes and expectations of the NATO Allies towards Germany, and the resulting pressure on the German government, than a profound change in attitudes and values of the Germans themselves. There was and still is (even after the terrorist attacks of 11 September 2001) a clear split within the population, dividing the majority of the German population from the elites and also dividing East and West Germans. This is an ongoing top-down process in the Federal Republic, which finds elite opinions on Germany's future role in international security being passed down to the 'general' public.

Prussia's Past and Aesthetics of the 'New Germany'

Until well into the 1990s, the topic of Prussia produced numerous controversial debates concerning its values and political culture, the meaning of Prussia and its significance to the ideological origins of the Third Reich, and Prussia's architectural legacy for Germany after 1945. However, the recent debate about the resurrection of the City Palace of the Hohenzollern Dynasty, the 'Stadtschloss' in Berlin, shows that old fears and prejudices against Prussia and its symbolic representations (authoritarian rule, *Militarismus*, *Untertanenmentalität*) are about to disappear. The building was destroyed by the communist regime of the GDR in 1950. The commission on the resurrection of the *Stadtschloss* concluded in spring 2002, after many years, that the only solution in regard to the overall architectural and aesthetical design and setting of the location was to rebuild the *Stadtschloss* with its original structure and façade.

The Return of the SED?

A fundamentally positive view of the idea of socialism is still a powerful force in the five new federal states. Together with the myth of anti-fascism and other aspects of SED ideology, it stands in the way of a comprehensive debate about National Socialism. Anti-fascism was even able to conceal the communist idea in the idea of democracy.[22] There is also a tendency to look back at the SED regime with nostalgia.

The legacy of the SED state includes interpretative patterns[23] and concepts embedded in people's minds that derive from socialist ideology, and these will continue to have an influence on German political culture for a long time to come.

There was a significant difference between the SED's understanding of history[24] and the historical consciousness of the citizens of the former GDR. Current fears and prejudices, and the way in which Germans in east and west see each other, tend to encourage a situation in which Eastern Germans identify more strongly with the former GDR than with the Federal Republic. This has an influence on people's historical consciousness, and leads to attempts to attribute something positive to the former GDR.

In addition to such differences in meaning, there are diametrically opposed evaluations in east and west of certain historical events and individuals. This becomes particularly obvious in the case of Konrad Adenauer. In the old federal states his name is synonomous with reconstruction, firm integration into the West and the German economic miracle, whereas East Germans consider him an unpatriotic individual who sacrificed unification for the sake of capitalism.[25]

Various surveys show that Germany is still a divided country when it comes to historical consciousness. Asked about the importance of German unification in 1990 in German history, more than 29 per cent of East Germans consider unification the most important event in history, whereas only 13 per cent of West Germans share this opinion.[26] This pattern holds true for other topics and opinions as well and will continue to mark the cultural and political landscape for the duration of another generation to come.

NOTES

1. See *Der Spiegel*, 25/2001.
2. See Joern Ruesen, *Historische Orientierung. Ueber die Arbeit des Geschichtsbewußtseins, sich in der Zeit zurechtzufinden* (Koeln/Weimar/Wien, 1994), and Felix Ph. Lutz, 'Geschichtsbewusstsein', in W. Weidenfeld and K.-R. Korte (eds.), *Handbuch zur deutschen Einheit 1949–1989–1999* (Frankfurt/New York, 1999), pp.392–402.
3. The data presented in this essay come from two empirical surveys conducted in 1989 and 1991. A total of about 250 people in the new and old federal states were interviewed applying qualitative methodology, both in focus groups and individually. In addition to this, a representative survey of 2,000 people was carried out in the old federal states on the basis of the qualitative data thus obtained. Part III briefly describes some of the results of the qualitative research carried out in East and West Germany. In abbreviated form, Part IV provides an empirical map of historical consciousness in West Germany based on multivariate data analysis of the material of the representative survey. The data have been complemented by the results of similar surveys from 1991 to 2001.
4. See Joern Ruesen and Friedrich Jaeger, 'Erinnerungskultur', in Karl-Rudolf Korte and Werner Weidenfeld (eds.), *Deutschland-Trendbuch. Fakten und Orientierungen* (Bonn: Bundeszentrale für politische Bildung, 2001), pp.397–428.
5. See Christiane Lemke, *Die Ursachen des Umbruchs 1989. Politische Sozialisation in der ehemaligen DDR* (Opladen, 1991), p.270.
6. See Raina Zimmering, *Mythen in der Politik der DDR. Ein Beitrag zur Erforschung politischer Mythen* (Opladen: Verlag Leske und Budrich, 2000).
7. See Juergen Habermas, 'Bemerkungen zu einer verworrenen Diskussion. Was bedeutet "Aufarbeitung der Vergangenheit" heute?', *Die Zeit*, No.15, 3 April 1992.
8. See surveys in *Der Spiegel*, 44 (1984), 47 (1989) and 22 (1990); Harro Honolka, *Schwarzrotgruen. Die Bundesrepublik auf der Suche nach ihrer Identität* (München, 1987); Willi Herbert and Rudolf Wildenmann, 'Deutsche Identität. Die subjektive Verfassung der Deutschen vor der Vereinigung', in R. Wildenmann (ed.), *Nation und Demokratie. Politisch-strukturelle Gestaltungsprobleme im neuen Deutschland* (Baden-Baden, 1991), pp.71–98.
9. Karl Mannheim, 'Das Problem der Generationen', *Kölner Vierteljahreshefte für Soziologie*, 7/2–3 (1928), pp.157–85; and Helmut Fogt, *Politische Generationen* (Opladen, 1982).

10. See Howard Schuman and Jacqueline Scott, 'Generations and Collective Memories', *American Sociological Review*, 54 (1989), pp.359–81.
11. It seemed logical to limit the survey to West Germany, because attitudes in the new federal states had not yet, at the time of the survey (Jan.–Feb. 1991), attained the kind of stability characteristic of the old Federal Republic. The qualitative survey conducted in the old federal states after 1989 revealed a remarkable stability and continuity in people's historical consciousness, despite the demise of the GDR and unification. However, it was impossible to assume this in the case of the former GDR, where the changes were of existential importance for everyone and affected the lives of all of its inhabitants. For a detailed account of the results, see Felix Ph. Lutz, *Das Geschichtsbewusstsein der Deutschen. Grundlagen der politischen Kultur in Ost und West* (Koeln/Wien: Boehlau-Verlag, 2000).
12. The survey made use of questions that were based on the results of the narrative interviews. They were presented to the interviewees in the form of statements with which, on the basis of a six-point scale, they were able to agree or disagree. The factor and cluster analyses which were then carried out are described in the typology that follows. The representative survey was carried out by the Institut für Demoskopie Allensbach. The qualitative surveys had been polled by the SINUS-Institute and by ZUMA-Mannheim.
13. The five clusters presented and described below are based on c. 100 detailed statements concerning the past and the present, attitudes towards democracy, policies on Europe, values, future expectations, etc.
14. The socio-demographic data for type 1 include size (23.4% of a total of 2,000); party allegiance (50% CDU/CSU compared to a total average of 42.7% CDU/CSU; average support for SPD and FDP; little support for the Greens); education (little higher education).
15. The description of a predominant way of dealing with the past in one category does not mean that another category cannot make use of a very similar or indeed identical pattern. The difference lies in the factor loadings, i.e. the strength of a group's agreement or disagreement with a certain pattern and/or a type-specific combination of factors running in the same political direction.
16. The statement comes from the standardised questionnaire, in which interviewees were able to express disagreement or agreement on a six-point scale. The following statements in inverted commas also come from the standardised questionnaire.
17. The data for type 2 include size (21.4%); age structure (significant above average proportion of people over 60); religion (more Catholics than Protestants, significantly more regular church-goers than in the other groups); education (least formal education of all types). This cluster represents a response set. People in this group generally tended to agree with all positively formulated statements.
18. The data for type 3 include size (17% of the population of the western federal states); party allegiance (CDU/CSU, 11.4%; SPD, 45.4%; Greens, 33.4%). This group has the highest percentage of people who have completed higher education courses.
19. See Dirk Berg-Schlosser, 'Entwicklung der Politischen Kultur in der Bundesrepublik Deutschland', *Aus Politik und Zeitgeschichte*, B 7/90 (1990), pp.30–46; Max Kaase, 'Bewusstseinslagen und Leitbilder in der Bundesrepublik Deutschland', in W. Weidenfeld and H. Zimmermann (eds.), *Deutschland-Handbuch. Eine doppelte Bilanz 1949–1989* (Munich, 1989), pp.203–21.
20. The data for type 4 include size (22.1%); party allegiance (CDU/CSU, 49.8%; SPD, 32.5% [compared to a total average of 37.5%], the Greens, 5.4% [compared to a total average of 10.4%]); occupational structure (28% managerial or freelance [compared to a total average of18%]).
21. The data for type 5 include size (14%); age (6% more over 60, but 6% fewer under 34); education (54% without or with elementary education certificate compared to a total average of 44%).
22. See Francois Furet, 'Jenseits der Jahrestage. Eine weltgeschichtliche Betrachtung', *Frankfurter Allgemeine Zeitung*, 8 May 1995.
23. For an overview see recent data in Elisabeth Noelle-Neumann and Renate Koecher (eds.),

Allensbacher Jahrbuch der Demoskopie 1998–2002. Balkon des Jahrhunderts (Allensbach am Bodensee/München: K.G.Saur/Verlag für Demoskopie, 2002).

24. See Wolfgang Protzner, Alexandra Neubauer and Christel Schuster, 'Der Geschichtsunterricht in der DDR als Instrument der SED-Politik', *Aus Politik und Zeitgeschichte*, B 29 (1993), pp.42–51.

25. See 'Adenauer als Denkmal. Eine Allensbacher Umfrage zum 25. Todestag', *Allensbacher Berichte* 7, ed. Institut für Demoskopie (Allensbach, 1992). The quantitative Allensbach survey lends support to these findings.

26. See Wilhelm Buerklin and Christian Jung, 'Deutschland im Wandel. Ergebnisse einer repräsentativen Meinungsumfrage', in Korte and Weidenfeld (eds.), *Deutschland-TrendBuch*, pp.675–711.

Trust in Democratic Institutions in Germany: Theory and Evidence Ten Years After Unification

ROBERT ROHRSCHNEIDER and RÜDIGER SCHMITT-BECK

In their investigation of the political cultures of five nations in the late 1950s, Almond and Verba argue that the stability of political systems is increased if they are based on a reservoir of good will among citizens.[1] This presumably helps regimes to weather times of poor performance. To democratise a society thus not only requires the establishment of democratic rules but also that citizens agree with the general values upon which a framework is based. Moreover, citizens ideally believe that political institutions and incumbents do not ignore their interests, and do not abuse their privileged positions of power.

These insights are behind this article. We examine Germans' confidence in the core institutions of the democratic state and the rule of law a decade into Germany's unification: the federal government, the national parliament, the constitutional court, and the legal system. These are familiar institutions to most citizens in the West because most West Germans experienced only one political order – the democratic regime established by Germany's constitution (the Basic Law). In contrast, most East Germans have lived under at least two regimes. The development of East Germans' trust in these institutions thus constitutes an important component of democratic consolidation in East Germany. We therefore begin by describing the development of East and West Germans' confidence in core institutions of the German polity between 1984 and 2000.

Beyond this descriptive goal, our theoretical interests lead us to test the predictive power of three models of institutional trust. First, is confidence in institutions rooted in individual predispositions, especially political values?[2] Second, is institutional trust mainly rooted in the system's perceived performance? Third, is institutional trust rooted in a public's social capital generated through inter-personal relationships? By examining the empirical validity of these models in Eastern and Western Germany, we not only test the predictive power of each model at the micro-

Robert Rohrschneider, Indiana University; Rüdiger Schmitt-Beck, Center for Survey Research and Methodology (ZUMA)

level, but also consider whether the age of a democratic regime mediates these linkages.

We address these questions using data from the German General Social Survey – the 'Allbus' (*Allgemeine Bevölkerungsumfrage der Sozialwissenschaften*). We mainly rely on the most recent wave, conducted in 2000, with occasional usage of data from previous Allbus waves; and we occasionally use the 1995–97 World Values Surveys.

TRUST IN INSTITUTIONS

The early debates in the US-based trust literature focus on the systemic implications of institutional distrust. Some analysts initially viewed institutional trust as an expression of strong support for a regime,[3] whereas critics viewed institutional distrust as a more ephemeral expression of low incumbent evaluations.[4] During the 1970s, the comparative politics literature broadened the discussion to include several advanced industrialised democracies where an important study diagnosed a 'crisis of democracy'.[5] And more recently the collapse of communist systems has spawned a revival of analyses of public trust in new institutions.[6]

Despite the long-term presence of this concept in the academic literature, it is plagued by a surprising degree of imprecision.[7] To some degree, the earlier US-based debates foreshadow a problem that currently exists in magnified form: despite nearly three decades of analyses, the conceptual meaning of trust remains ambiguous. This assessment is exemplified by a recent collection of leading analysts of the institutional trust literature.[8] After noting that public attitudes toward democracy can be assessed at various levels of abstraction, the study continues that:

> public commitment to democracy per se has risen in the last half century. At the other extreme, our study is not concerned with day-to-day evaluations of specific leaders, policies, and governments. ... Thus, this book is about neither a "crisis of democracy" as such. ... Rather, our concern is with popular confidence in the performance of representative institutions.[9]

Despite the study's claim not to examine the 'crisis of democracy' argument, the authors present convincing evidence a few pages later that trust in institutions has declined in 14 'Trilateral Democracies'.[10]

This juxtaposition is not meant to dispute the argument and findings – we concur with most of the conclusions. But it does highlight one problem in the trust literature: the concept of public trust in institutions is rarely conceptualised systematically and its utility seldom (if at all) compared to conceptual relatives. Other publications follow this pattern.[11] Even when trust in institutions is discussed in some detail,[12] the usefulness of this concept is not assessed by linking it to similar concepts of regime evaluations. Thus, studies typically conclude with a declaration that trust matters somehow but leave ambiguous its precise conceptual value.

Conceptualising Institutional Trust

Our first task, therefore, is to provide a conceptual anchor that positions the meaning of trust in the academic literature. Figure 1 highlights several important categories of regime evaluations that have been used by various analysts.[13] The figure begins at the top with evaluations of citizens' democratic ideals. By following the categories downward towards the polar end of democratic reality, evaluations increasingly focus on the existing system and, at the most concrete level, consist of appraisals of the performance of public officials. Each of these levels targets a different aspect of a regime; and evaluations of each level reflects a different aspect of a regime's acceptance among citizens.

Let us start with citizens' constitutional ideals. This is the most general level of evaluating a regime because citizens evaluate the principles of different regime forms. They do not simply appraise whether the existing system is desirable. Neither do they focus on the performance of the system. Instead, they indicate whether they endorse, in principle, a democracy or its alternative, usually an autocratic regime. Low support for a democratic regime at this normative level would indicate a severe crisis of legitimacy which we define as a preference for another regime.[14]

FIGURE 1
CONCEPTUALISING INSTITUTIONAL TRUST

1. **Constitutional Ideals**: Is *some* form of democracy preferred over other forms of governance?

2. **Constitutional Reality I**: Is another Constitutional Regime preferred over the *existing* constitution?

3. **Constitutional Reality II**: Is the existing Constitution viewed positively?

4. **Trust in Institutions**: Do institutions work well in the long run?

5. **Satisfaction with Democracy**: Does the current system work well?

6. **Evaluation of Governments**: Does the current Government perform well?

At the level of constitutional ideals, there is a widespread consensus across advanced democracies – indeed, across the globe – that democracies are desirable over other regime types.[15] The same pattern holds in East and West Germany.[16]

At the second and third level, citizens appraise the existing regime. The second level requires an explicit comparison of the existing constitution to an alternative regime. Given the strong support for democratic regimes at the level of constitutional ideals, the comparison is most likely between the existing democratic regime and another democratic framework. A rejection of the present system, as on the first level, would suggest a crisis of legitimacy of the existing framework. At the third level (constitutional reality II), citizens evaluate whether they view a system positively or negatively *without* comparing the current regime with another one. It is quite conceivable that one views a democratic regime critically and, at the same time, does not consider an alternative regime preferable. Just as Churchill considered a democracy the worst regime except for its alternatives, citizens may prefer a democracy *and* view it sceptically.

Whereas the top three levels are primarily concerned with individuals' constitutional preferences, the fourth level – institutional trust – begins to focus increasingly on the long-term performance of a regime. Institutional trust means two basic things. Trust implies a broad confidence that an existing regime is a desirable regime. And it represents a generalised tally of a regime's capacity to deliver what citizens want, both in the economic and political domain. Economically, citizens expect a regime to produce affluence. Politically, citizens expect a regime to produce procedural goods.[17] Procedural fairness, representation and political freedoms especially emerge as the most important sources of institutional support, in both Central Europe[18] and the EU.[19] Thus, trust in institutions essentially means that citizens accept the existing framework and view its long-term performance positively.

The fifth level – satisfaction with a democracy – moves even closer to the performance end. These evaluations contain a clear performance component, both in terms of its conceptualisation and in terms of how the concept is usually operationalised ('Are you satisfied with how the democracy works in your country?'). At the same time, it does not focus on the performance of incumbents, even though their performance influences how content publics are with the existing regime.[20] Furthermore, this level is removed a considerable distance from the level of constitutional ideals. That is, dissatisfaction with the current performance of a regime does not convey much information about the constitutional preferences of mass publics.

Finally, the sixth level – evaluations of a government – are located at the most specific level. Citizens evaluate the performance of specific office holders, not the regime. Poor performance ratings of officials in all likelihood have little bearing on how citizens evaluate the desirability of a regime type. Of course, in the long-term, disastrous policy performance is likely to move 'upward' to affect appraisals of the regime itself.

In sum, on this 'ladder of abstraction', institutional trust is located at the intersection between regime evaluations that are primarily performance-oriented to appraisals that are mainly derived from one's constitutional ideals. As such, institutional trust contains a significant performance component over the long term; and it most likely reflects individuals' appraisals of a nation's regime.

The Empirical Meaning of Institutional Trust

Do mass publics make the distinctions suggested in Figure 1? In order to address this question, we require indicators for mass trust in institutions, along with appraisals of political regimes. The World Values surveys 1995–97 contain several measures that permit a preliminary examination of the meaning of institutional trust.

The trust measure in the World Values surveys (WVS) 1995–97 is based on the following question: 'I am going to name a number of organisations. For each one, could you tell me how much confidence you have in them: is it a great deal of confidence, quite a lot of confidence, not very much confidence, or none at all?' Respondents evaluated the parliament, the government and the legal system.[21] We created an additive indicator based on these three items and correlated it with indicators for several regime dimensions outlined in Figure 1.

Two indicators in the WVS gauge an aspect of constitutional ideals. One question asks respondents to evaluate the Churchill hypothesis (strongly agree–strongly disagree): 'Democracy may have many problems but it's better than any other form of government.' Another question also focuses on the desirability of having a democracy: 'I'm going to describe various types of political systems and ask what you think about each as a way of governing this country. For each one would you say it is a very good, fairly good, fairly bad or very bad way of governing this country?' Respondents evaluated the statement 'Having a democratic political system is good'. Both indicators are located at the level of constitutional ideals because they do not focus on the existing system. And both indicators focus on the desirability of each system in general, not their capacity to perform well in specific policy domains (the top level in Figure 1).[22]

The relationship (Pearson's r) between institutional trust and these two indicators is quite weak both in the East and the West (Table 1). While the coefficients are statistically significant due to the fairly large sample size, the magnitude suggests that distrust in institutions has little to do with a

TABLE 1

SYSTEMIC AND PERFORMANCE CORRELATES OF INSTITUTIONAL TRUST.

	East	West
Constitutional Ideals		
To have a Democracy is good	.10	.17
Democracy is the best system	.04*	.17
Constitutional Reality II		
Present system is good	.42	.47
Evaluation of Incumbents		
Satisfied with incumbents	.42	.49

Note: Entries are Pearson's r. * indicates insignificance at the .05 level. Minimum N=1017 and
            1009 in the West and East, respectively.

Source: World Values Survey 1995–1997. The trust indicator is additive (parliament,
            government, judicial system), ranging from 3 (distrust) to 15.

rejection of a democratic regime as an ideal-typical system. As Figure 1
suggests, one may distrust a range of existing democratic institutions and
simultaneously value democracy as an ideal.

A third indicator measures mass evaluations of the constitutional reality
II: 'People have different views about the system for governing this country.
Here is a scale for rating how well things are going: "one" means very bad
and "ten" means very good. Where on this scale would you put the political
system as it is today?'

This indicator gauges how respondents appraise the current
constitutional arrangements.[23] The introductory wording also anchors the
measure at the systemic level, not merely at the level of public officials.
Respondents are thus encouraged to think of the desirability of the regime
as a whole; and they may consider its long-run performance. The
relationships are substantially stronger than for the level of constitutional
ideals, both in the East (r=.42) and the West (r=.47). As our discussion
suggests, institutional trust correlates substantially with evaluations of the
current regime type when these evaluations do not involve a comparison to
other regime forms.

A final measure asks respondents to evaluate the performance of
incumbents (the sixth level).[24] Again, we find a strong relationship between
trust and the performance of public officials, both in the East (r=.42) and the
West (r=.49).

In sum, these analyses examine the conceptual context and empirical
correlates of institutional trust. We argued, and provided initial support, that
institutional trust represents individuals' evaluations of the performance of

the current officials as well as the regime as a whole. It thus adopts a medium position in the ladder of abstraction in Figure 1: it is not solely a performance measure, nor entirely a regime-support measure. Rather, it represents the locus where the performance of a regime intersects with broad-based public support for the constitutional foundation of a regime.

Institutional Trust 1984–2000

How much confidence do East and West Germans have in various public institutions? One indicator has been asked in the Allbus 1984, 1994 and 2000 surveys and thus allows us not only to assess levels of trust (or distrust) but also to compare trust over time. The Allbus survey asks respondents: 'I am going to name several public institutions and organisations. Please tell me for each one, how much trust you have in them. Please use this scale: 1 means no trust at all; 7 means completely trust.'

We used the respondents' assessments of the parliament, government, constitutional court, and the judicial system for conceptual and empirical reasons. Conceptually, these institutions represent the major representational organisations (parliament and government) as well as the main judicial institutions. Empirically, a factor analysis produces only one factor[25] indicating that evaluations of one institution are linked to appraisals of the other three institutions.[26]

Table 2 shows that the trajectory of trust in institutions in West Germany was one of monotonous decline. Especially during the late 1980s and early 1990s institutional confidence declined in the West. The sharp decline that took place in the West between 1984 and 1994 concerned especially the 'partisan' institutions – the national government and parliament. In contrast, in the East confidence slightly increased during the 1990s, but starting from a very low level, and not reaching a level comparable to that of the West. In 1984 majorities of Germans in the West of the country still displayed a fairly high level of confidence in the major institutions of liberal democracy. Substantial majorities have little trust in the parliament, national government and the judicial system, especially in the East. The constitutional court is evaluated more positively, especially in the West. Even here, however, considerable distrust exists among a substantial minority (in the West) and a small majority in the East. Also note that the improvements in the East are fairly limited. This suggests that the rather negative appraisals in the East cannot simply be explained by the lack of familiarity of Eastern Germans with democratic institutions.

The summary index – an additive scale based on the four institutional evaluations – documents the degree to which citizens in Germany distrust these institutions. Only a quarter falls into the trusting camp in the West (25.2 per cent); an even smaller proportion trusts institutions in the East

TABLE 2

TRUST IN INSTITUTIONS, 1984–2000

| | East | | West | | |
	1994	2000	1984	1994	2000
Constitutional Court[1]	34.8	49.4	69.8	61.5	58.4
Judicial System	26.7	27.5	55.1	47.8	45.8
National Parliament	14.9	17.7	50.0	28.4	25.7
National Government	21.7	22.6	48.3	26.9	23.7
Trust (Index)[2]	12.9	16.9	43.9	26.1	25.2

Notes: Minimum N in 1984=2943 in the West; in 1994, minimum N=2142 and N=1073 in the West and East, respectively; in 2000, minimum N=800 and N=464 in the West and East, respectively.
1   Percentage of respondents who trust institutions (5 6 7 on a seven point scale)
2   Index ranges from 4–28. For this table, trust represents respondents who have a score of at least 20.

Source: Allbus surveys 1984, 1994, 2000. Non-German nationals are excluded.

(16.9 per cent). And these overall evaluations remain largely stable between 1994 and 2000. In contrast, the corresponding proportion reached almost 44 per cent in 1984 in the West.[27]

Overall, then, trust in institutions has been low throughout most of the 1990s. Given the correlates of trust to evaluations of a nation's constitutional reality, the lack of trust is alarming, especially in the eastern part of Germany.

Naturally, to assess the constitutional implications of distrust, it would be desirable to examine the relationship of institutional trust with other regime indicators. Unfortunately, however, the Allbus survey does not contain a direct measure of citizens' appraisals of Germany's constitutional reality; neither does it gauge how citizens evaluate constitutional ideals. We are, however, able to provide indirect evidence of an important East–West difference regarding the constitutional implications of low institutional trust. The Allensbach institute periodically asks whether citizens can think of a better system than the existing one. Note that this question is located at the level of constitutional reality I (because it asks respondents directly to think of an alternative).

Figure 2 conveys a clear message: the low trust in the East coincides with a highly ambivalent view about Germany's existing constitution. In contrast, the fairly high degree of distrust in the West apparently does not coincide with a preference for a different regime.[28]

In sum, trust in Germany's institutions is a scare commodity, especially in the East. Because trust is correlated with negative evaluations of the current system, these results may, in the long run, entail that citizens not only evaluate the current constitution negatively, but also believe that there is a better regime (as does a sizeable proportion in the East). To some degree, the exact implications depend on why citizens distrust institutions, and this topic is taken up in the next section.

FIGURE 2

SUPPORTING THE POLITICAL SYSTEM

'Do you think that the existing system in Germany is the best system, or is there a better one?'

Eastern Germany

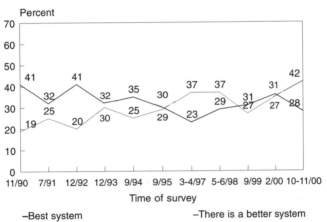

Western Germany

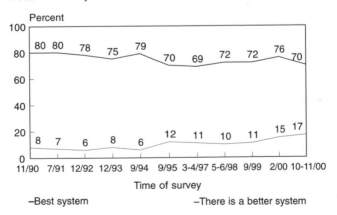

Source: Allensbacher Institut für Demoskopie

Explaining Institutional Trust

We develop three groups of predictors of institutional trust (Figure 3). First, we argue that institutional trust is influenced by individual predispositions, especially one's ideological values (a political values approach). Second, we suggest that the perceived performance of institutions shapes institutional trust (a performance model). Third, we maintain that relationships with other citizens affect institutional trust (a social capital approach).

POLITICAL VALUES

The premise of the value-based approach is that value predispositions of an individual affect his/her views on existing institutions. This approach stands in the tradition of the *Civic Culture* study published nearly 40 years ago.[29] The so-called congruence postulate developed by Almond and Verba stipulates that individuals hold political values – defined as deeply rooted preferences for an ideal-typical order – which citizens like to see implemented by a regime. When individuals perceive a mismatch between the type of regime they prefer and the existing regime, they are less likely to endorse that order because it does not realise their political ideals. All else

FIGURE 3

DETERMINANTS OF INSTITUTIONAL TRUST

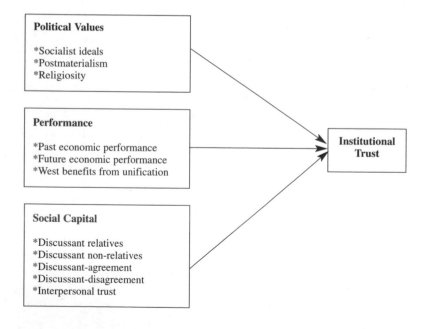

being equal, in turn, when a person's ideals are congruent with an existing order, support for institutions is likely to increase. Here we consider citizens' socialist ideals, their post-material values and their religiosity.

Socialist Ideals

During Germany's division, Eastern and Western Germans were exposed to two different regimes. They exposed citizens to different forms of socialisation, and to different opportunities and restrictions in the political process. It is well established that these different experiences left their mark on how citizens think about a range of democratic values and ideals.[30] While there is a widespread consensus to secure basic democratic rights – the right to free speech, freedom of movement and a free press, for instance – diverging visions exist over a range of central democratic ideals. For instance, Eastern Germans are substantially more likely to value socialism as an ideal when the term 'socialism' is separated from the collapsed GDR. That is, while many citizens in the East did not support the existing system of the GDR, socialism continues to be widely accepted.

These differences are reflected in respondents' evaluations of the statement: 'Socialism is a good idea that was poorly implemented' (Table 3). About 75 per cent agreed with this proposition in the East in 1991; and the proportion remained virtually unchanged. The proportion was substantially lower in the West in 1991, although it did increase to over 50 per cent by 2000. Detailed analyses based on different data suggest that citizens in the West do not associate the term 'socialism' with a different form of democracy whereas many Eastern Germans connect it with a different form of democracy.[31] This interpretation is consistent with the pattern that evaluations of the current regime are substantially more negative in the East than the West (see Figure 2).[32]

TABLE 3

POLITICAL VALUES, 1991–2000

	East		West	
	1991	**2000**	**1991**	**2000**
Socialism is a good ideal[1]	75.6	76.2	39.6	51.4
Postmaterialism[2]	14.5	16.1	30	28.5
Religiosity[3]	6.8	4.4	24.4	20.5

Notes: in 1991, minimum N=1329 and N=1415 in the East and West, respectively; in 2000, minimum N=520 and N=796 in the East and West, respectively.
   1   Percentage of respondents agreeing with the statement (fully or somewhat)
   2   Percentage of post-materialists on Inglehart index
   3   Percentage attending church 1-3 times a month or more often

Source: Allbus 1991, 2000. Non-German nationals are excluded.

Overall, these patterns suggest that socialist values continue to play an important role in the minds of citizens in Germany. Given the role of political values in affecting evaluations of institutions, we hypothesise:

Hypothesis 1: Support for socialism as an ideal decreases public trust in Germany's institutions.

Post-materialism

The theory of post-material value change was developed by Ronald Inglehart in a series of writings.[33] The theory suggests that economic affluence and stability in the post-war decades in advanced democracies led to the formation of post-material values. When in conflict, post-materialists provide higher priority to such non-economic goals as environmental protection and gender equality. Materialists, in contrast, give greater priority to such policy domains as economic growth and domestic stability. Another characteristic of post-materialists rests with their emphasis on direct democratic procedures with which they would like to supplement representative procedures.

The rise of a post-material generation has fundamentally affected German politics, especially in the West where several of the conditions stipulated by Inglehart's theory (that is, affluence, domestic and international stability) are common. The fact that the Green party is now a junior partner in the SPD-led government appeared unthinkable when the first Green deputies took their seats in the newly elected parliament in 1983. In addition, environmental issues are important to a fairly large number of voters. By now, nearly one-third of the West German population holds post-material values in the West (Table 3). The proportion is lower in the East. This is consistent with the premise of post-material theory that suggests these values should emerge primarily in contexts with economic affluence. Given the emphasis of post-material values on direct-democratic procedures, we hypothesise:

Hypothesis 2: Post-material values decrease public trust in Germany's institutions.

Religious Values

Religious values are less central to our concern. But we consider them here because religious values are usually associated with a host of moderate to conservative views on a range of dimensions. This includes the degree to which citizens are willing to support a fundamental regime change.[34] Consequently, the decreasing proportion of citizens who continue to attend church regularly may also trust existing institutions more than those who do not engage in religious practices. Given the low religiosity of East Germans, brought about by decades of anti-religious rule of the Socialist government in the GDR, this relationship could be a possible explanation for the lower levels of trust in institutions in that part of the country. Thus:

Hypothesis 3: Religious values increase public trust in Germany's institutions.

Performance

Our conceptualisation of institutional trust also suggests that economic assessments affect institutional trust. There is a long theoretical tradition in considering such appraisals, starting with Almond and Verba's *Civic Culture*, and Easton's[35] concept of specific support (institutions are supported when the economy functions well). Recently, empirical studies of democratic transitions point to both economic and political performance as a central source of approval for institutions in Central Europe,[36] the EU,[37] or emerging regimes in Africa.[38] The same basic patterns also emerge in Western Germany.[39] As Table 4 shows, Eastern Germans were quite optimistic about the economy shortly after unification. This no doubt reflects economic hopes as much as realistic assessments of future economic developments because many Eastern Germans supported unification, in part because they wished to improve their economic situation. However, over the following decade this has given way to a similar level of pessimism as in the West as the Eastern economy collapsed.

A second performance factor focuses on the perception among Germans that unification evolved in such a way as to systematically disadvantage Eastern Germans and primarily benefit Western Germans.[40] This argument is not restricted to the economic domain but also includes a range of subjective perceptions of the fairness of the unification process. From this perspective, one would predict that institutional trust is lowered when East German citizens perceive the West to be the primary beneficiary of the unification process. In the West, in contrast, perceptions that the West benefited should, all else being equal, increase institutional trust.

Table 4 suggests that these performance evaluations are comparable by 2000 in the two parts. In 1991, however, appraisals of who benefited from Germany's unification were lopsided. Together, the economic and benefits arguments predict that:

Hypothesis 4: Poor performance appraisals reduce trust in institutions.

Social Capital

In recent years, the relationships among citizens are viewed as another important antecedent of support for institutions in addition to governments' performance and people's values. Echoing Tocqueville's classic statements about the importance of civic associations for American democracy in the

TABLE 4

PERFORMANCE EVALUATIONS, 1991–2000

	East		West	
	1991	2000	1991	2000
Past economic performance[1]	a	37.4	a	27.9
Future economic performance (good)[2]	65.9	22.4	36.8	24.2
West benefits[3]	77.7	77.4	33.5	32.8
East benefits[4]	33.9	60.5	71.8	84.7
Unification good for West only[5]	60.5	48.1	12.4	7.4

Note: a indicator not available. Minimum N 836 in the West; 530 in the East in 2000; in 1991, minimum N=1329 in the West and N=1415 in the East.
  1 Percentage of respondents agreeing with the statement (fully or somewhat).
  2 Percentage of respondents agreeing with the statement (fully or somewhat).
  3 Percentage of respondents agreeing with the statement (fully or somewhat).
  4 Percentage of respondents agreeing with the statement (fully or somewhat).
  5 Percentage of respondents who believe that the West only benefited from unification (2-4 on the additive index ranging from 2-8).

Source: Allbus surveys 1991, 2000. Non-German nationals are excluded.

nineteenth century, authors like Putnam[41] developed the notion of 'social capital' to characterise this relational underpinning of a democratic political culture. According to this approach, the private is political, and '[t]he prospects for a democracy in which men do not get along well with one another, do not trust one another, and do not associate with one another is uncompromising'.[42] While much of the recent writing on the political role of social capital has concentrated on civic activism and citizens' membership in voluntary associations, other manifestations of social capital can be expected to be at least as important. This article concentrates on two of these: individuals' ties to fellow citizens, and their mutual trust.

Interpersonal Trust

According to Almond and Verba's study of the 'civic culture',[43] democratic support rests mainly with a pervasive trust among citizens. If people do not trust their fellow citizens, Almond and Verba asked, how can they be faithful to elites that are endowed with considerable power to affect their lives in vital aspects, and in the institutions that embody that power? After all, a liberal democracy as a system of checks and balances of power institutionalises distrust in officeholders. Almond and Verba believed that confidence in politicians and in the institutions of democracy represents a special case of a more general 'faith in people'; a theme echoed by Inglehart,[44] who registered strong correlations between levels of interpersonal trust and the duration of democracy in many societies across the world.

Overall, however, evidence in support of the social capital argument remains mixed. Some studies observed substantial relationships between social and political trust,[45] but others were unable to demonstrate substantial correlations. They thus concluded that social and political trust belong to different realms of social life, rather than being two sides of the same coin.[46]

We measure respondents' amount of trust in other people with an index combining responses to two items. One is the classic indicator of 'faith in people', developed by Almond and Verba: 'Some people say that most people can be trusted. Others say you can't be too careful in your dealings with people. How do you feel about it?'[47] The second item is taken from an instrument designed to measure individuals' isolation: 'Most people don't really care what happens to the next fellow.'[48] Our prediction is:

Hypothesis 5: The higher citizens' trust in other people the higher their confidence in political institutions.

Judging from the percentages given in Table 5, social trust is not particularly high in Germany, and even decreasing over time; a pattern that does not differ much across the East–West divide.

Personal Networks

In a recent study of Russian voters, Gibson[49] also suggests – and provides evidence – that the *linkages* of interaction among people affect their institutional trust. In a mass society of atomised individuals, citizens are isolated from each other and hence vulnerable.[50] According to this view, people's embeddedness in social networks is an important prerequisite of political support. While some authors argue that ties to relatives are the central source of confidence – because they mediate between individuals and the more distant world of politics[51] – others maintain that it is rather the weak ties that are essential for democracy. Such loose ties between mere acquaintances (and not relatives) affords opportunities for 'cross-cutting exposure', providing citizens with experiences of political diversity and debate.[52] In a very practical sense they can thus learn that in a democracy conflict is a normal and non-threatening part of social and political life, thus increasing their confidence and support in democratic institutions.[53] From these considerations two competing expectations can be derived:

Hypothesis 6a: The larger citizens' networks of strong ties the higher their confidence in political institutions.
Hypothesis 6b: The larger citizens' networks of weak ties the higher their confidence in political institutions.

To operationalise the structures of our respondents' primary environments we rely on data that reflect ego-centred friendship networks

TABLE 5

SOCIAL CAPITAL

	East		West	
	1990/91	**2000**	**1990/91**	**2000**
Friends-relatives	a	0.92	0.73	0.74
Friends-non-relatives	a	1.1	1.5	1.4
Friends-same party preference	a	0.32	0.69	0.43
Friends-different party preference	a	0.25	0.48	0.32
Trust other people	17.6	13.40	18.50	15.30

Notes: Entries are mean values of the number of individuals with whom respondents discuss politics, except for 'Trust other people' which reflects the proportion trusting other people (categories 1 and 2 on the index ranging from –2 to 2). a indicator not available.

Source: Allbus 1990 (network variables; minimum N 2959 (West only)), 1991 (interpersonal trust; N 1456 in the West, 1526 in the East), in 2000, minimum N=1847 in the West; N=1068 in the East). Non-German nationals are excluded.

of respondents. The Allbus survey provides data on up to three friends for each respondent. We use two indicators to measure whether these ties are strong or weak: whether relationships are between relatives (strong ties) or non-relatives (weak ties), and whether the dyads of respondents and each of their friends are characterised by agreement (strong ties) or disagreement (weak ties) in terms of party preferences.

Table 5 indicates that German voters' friendship networks contain more non-relatives than relatives. This pattern is more pronounced (and more stable) in the West than in the East. (No comparable longitudinal measures are available for Eastern Germany.) Further, more people agree than disagree with each other concerning their partisanship. However, over time, at least in the West, a trend toward more partisan heterogeneity within individuals' personal lives becomes visible. This may, in part, result from the growing fragmentation of the German party system so that there is a greater chance for each individual to meet people with political loyalties different from their own.

MULTIVARIATE ANALYSES

To what degree do these factors influence institutional trust? In order to answer this question, we conducted several multivariate analyses, paying particular attention to respondents' values, performance evaluations and networks. We also included standard control variables, such as age, education, left–right ideology and whether respondents supported the current parties in government in the last election.

TABLE 6

PREDICTING INSTITUTIONAL TRUST (OLS)

	East	West
Political Values		
Socialism as an ideal	−.42 (−.11)*	−.32 (−.11)**
Post-materialism	−.20 (−.04)	−.43 (−.10)**
Religiosity	.72 (.13) **	.13 (.03)
Performance		
Unification good for the West	−.23 (−.07)	.24 (.09)*
Past economic performance positive	.83 (.16)**	.64 (.14)**
Future economic performance positive	.76 (.10)	.91 (.14)**
Social Capital		
Discussants relatives	−.42 (−.09)	−.10 (−.03)
Discussants non-relatives	−.54 (−.12)*	−.13 (−.04)
Agreement with discussant	.01 (.01)	.54 (.11)**
Disagreement with discussant	.20 (.02)	.68 (.11)**
Trust in people	.28 (.07)	.55 (.16)**
Demographics/Political Controls		
Age	.01 (.03)	.01 (.04)
Left self-placement	−.09 (.06)	.30 (.12)**
High-school ('Abitur')	1.5 (.11)*	1.2 (.11)**
Supported government in past election	.23 (.03)	−.23 (−.04)
R-Square	.15	.20
N	381	654

Notes: Entries are unstandardised regression coefficients (OLS); standardised coefficients appear in parentheses. *, ** denotes significance at the p=.05 and p=.01 level, respectively.

Source: Allbus 2000. Non-German nationals are excluded.

Several patterns deserve to be highlighted (Table 6). Political values have the predicted effect on institutional trust. Socialist ideals reduce trust in institutions by a significant margin, both in the East (b= -.42) and the West (b= -.32). It is remarkable that socialist ideals continue to inhibit the development of trust in the East ten years after unification. However, we find a similar effect in the West. Given our earlier interpretation of the differences in specific meaning of the socialism indicator, we would argue that the effect in the West does not represent a rejection of the existing system. One possibility is that among Western citizens support for socialism reduces evaluations of Germany's regime at the third level in Figure 1, but not the first and second level. In contrast, in the East, our interpretation suggests that socialist ideals reduce support for Germany's constitution at the third *and* second level. We acknowledge, of course, that this must remain speculation as long as we lack the indicators to establish the precise correlates of institutional distrust.

Post-materialist values partially exhibit the expected patterns. In the West, post-material values significantly reduce trust in institutions (b= -.43). Just as Inglehart predicts, supporting a set of value priorities that conflicts with the dominant economic and political arrangements reduces individuals' trust in these institutions. In contrast, in the East, this effect does not emerge as a significant predictor (b= -.20). This is expected given that Eastern Germany did not meet the theoretical requirements (especially affluence) of the theory of value change.

The reverse pattern characterises the religiosity variable: significant in the East and insignificant in the West. The fact that freedom of religious conscience is enshrined in Germany's constitution undoubtedly contributes to the fact that religious convictions increase trust in Germany's institutions among religious Eastern Germans.

Moving on to the group of performance variables, note that trust in institutions is affected by the three variables in the West: lower economic expectations and the perception that the West primarily benefited from unification decreases trust. In contrast, performance-based expectations are less important in the East; only assessments of past negative performance evaluations lower institutional trust. Especially important is the statistical insignificance for the West – benefits – variable; it conflicts with accounts that East Germans' distrust results from their perceptions as being treated as 'second-class' citizens in the unified Germany.[54] The remaining economic variables have essentially the same effect (as measured by the unstandardised regression coefficients) but fail to reach statistical significance because of the fairly small number of cases in the East. All in all, performance variables have the expected influence on institutional trust.

The social capital variables, in turn, reveal intriguing patterns. For one, their importance is different in the two regions of Germany. In the East, only one of the social capital variables appears important, and the direction of the effect conflicts with our expectations. Respondents with many ties to non-relative individuals display lower, not higher, levels of political trust than those with fewer such contacts. This finding seems at first sight to be a paradox. However, it can be interpreted in view of the pervasive distrust in institutions in the East. As we have seen above (Table 2), a large majority of East Germans either rejects the existing institutions directly, or is at least ambiguous about it. Thus, if people discuss their situation after unification, they are likely to focus on problems resulting from Germany's unification. Consequently, to the degree that one is embedded in a larger network of weak ties, the pervasive scepticism resulting from unification is reaffirmed if the topic emerges among citizens. And the likelihood that it does emerge is greater in larger networks. In contrast, in the West, levels of trust are higher, and – especially important – the commitment to the existing democratic regime is substantially stronger. Consequently, the odds of encountering institutional criticism during routine interactions with fellow citizens are much lower, thus reducing the odds that negative views about the existing system are reinforced by how many people are known beyond the family.

In contrast, the extent of agreement or disagreement on the partisanship variable does not affect institutional trust in the East, yet, as it does in the West. Two hypotheses that we assumed to be competing are both supported by our findings for West Germans. If citizens have among their friends many people with whom they disagree politically, they are more trusting. However, this is also the case if they agree with their friends. This suggests that what matters is not the experience of agreement or disagreement within friendship networks, but whether a network is politicised or not. In the West, these 'politicised' networks have a 'healthy' effect on trust: they increase trust as the give-and-take in discussions nurtures an appreciation of diversity. Importantly, it does not matter whether someone agrees or disagrees with their discussion partner on partisanship – they are friends after all. What does matter is whether politics is discussed at all – and such discussions boost trust in the West.

Finally, we note that the generalisation of interpersonal trust to the political realm does seem to be an important source of trust in institutions. Yet this applies only to the West; in the East, the coefficient has the right sign but is too small to attain statistical significance. This finding resembles the pattern found by Almond and Verba in their comparison of old and new democracies in the 1950s:[55] in established democracies like Britain and the United States, personal trust was generalised to the political realm, but not so in the new democracies, like West Germany. This suggests that social capital in the form of personal trust may not be such a valuable asset for the cultural consolidation of new democracies. Perhaps personal trust feeds into political trust only under conditions that are usually not present in a new democracy. Personal trust may by a valuable underpinning of democracy once a certain level of democratisation is reached, but it does not contribute to attaining that level.[56]

CONCLUSION

This article has examined Germans' confidence in the core institutions of the democratic regime: government, parliament, constitutional court and the legal system. In our conceptualisation, trust represents an intermediate level of political support, more general than the level of office-holders, but more specific than the level of the regime and its constitutional ideals. Although trust in institutions, especially in the constitutional court, has somewhat increased over recent years, a decade after unification East Germans' trust in the institutions of the Basic Law is still considerably lower than in the West – despite the fact that it has been declining in the West for more than a decade.

Citizens' political values, evaluations of the system's economic performance, and specific aspects of social capital all affect institutional trust. Most notably, in both the East and the West, citizens who see positive sides in socialism are less favourable towards the institutions of the German political system. In contrast, higher levels of education contribute to a more favourable view of the institutions.

Apart from these similarities, the different influence of networks on institutional trust reflects the different regime experience across the East–West divide. In the East, ties to other citizens *reduce* institutional trust, in part because larger networks provide more occasions to grumble about the desolate situation for many East Germans. In the West, in contrast, what matters is that the networks are politicised, which they surely are when individuals are aware of their partisanship. In that case, networks function as predicted – they increase trust in institutions because the give-and-take of politicised discussions, on the whole, nurtures confidence in the existing institutions. To us, this is the most intriguing result of this study: networks in an established and a new democracy have a substantially different effect on how citizens view their regime.

These individual-level patterns point to one important reason why trust is lower in the East. Our research shows that socialist ideals continue to be widely held. In turn, socialist values substantially reduce mass trust in Germany's liberal democratic institutions, *especially* among eastern Germans. Further, other research found that the meaning of the term 'socialism' differs across the East–West divide:[57] in the East, it is linked to systemic alternatives; in the West, it is primarily linked to the welfare state. Given the East–West differences in the precise meaning of the term and the fact that a large proportion of Eastern Germans adheres to socialist values, citizens' institutional trust is significantly lower overall in the East. In short, the legacy of socialism continues to exert a disturbing effect on the current institutional framework.

Another reason why trust is lower in the East is related to the age of the regime. Cross-national research shows that the duration of a regime affects popular trust in it.[58] Since Western Germans were exposed to the liberal-democratic constitution since 1949, whereas Eastern Germans had barely ten years to become accustomed to it, trust is lower in the East than the West regardless of individual-level differences. For example, when we included all individual-level variables from Table 6 and included an East–West variable in a pooled analysis of the model, the East–West variable remained highly significant – the mere fact of residing in the East substantially reduces trust in institutions independently of all the other indicators.[59]

We are not arguing, of course, that the regime in the East is about to collapse. But we do suggest that, in the long run, low levels of trust may reduce the effectiveness of bureaucratic procedures, citizens' willingness to accept binding decisions by policy makers, and their motivation to participate in democratic processes. Neither are we suggesting that Eastern Germany is to be 'blamed' for the decline in trust among Western Germans. After all, the 'crisis of democracy' is a phenomenon widely diagnosed for decades in most mature democracies. What we do suggest is that Germany's unification contributed to the decline in the West which, for reasons discussed elsewhere, had begun much earlier across a range of industrialised democracies.[60] One way to think about this aspect is to envision Germany's unification representing two rivers merging at a slight angle: institutional trust was declining in the West already, but with Germany's unification it accelerated. This may arguably be the most troublesome aspect of unification: it reinforces a pre-existing trend towards institutional distrust, with consequences which are difficult to anticipate at this point.

APPENDIX

This appendix presents variable information not described in the main text.

Age: in years

Education: Dummy variable indicating whether respondents have the *Abitur*.

Left-right: ten-point self-placement indicator.

Network variables: 'We now have a few questions about those individuals with whom you spend a fair amount of time together privately. Would you please think of the three people with whom you spend the most time together. You may include relatives and non-relatives.' Respondents were also asked to indicate whether these individuals are relatives or non-relatives; and whether they could indicate friends' partisanship. Based on this information, along with respondents' own partisanship, we constructed four variables:
  Network relatives: number of friends who are relatives.
  Network non-relatives: number of non-relative friends
  Discussant agreement: Number of friends who have the same partisanship as respondent.
  Discussant disagreement: Number of friends who have a different partisanship.

Postmaterialism. Inglehart's four-item index which distinguishes the 'mixed' category depending on whether the post-materialism or materialism item is mentioned first.

Religiosity: 'How often do you attend church?' More than once a week; one a week, one to three times a month; several times a year; rarely; never.

Trust other people: Based on two indicators. One asks: 'Most people can be trusted.' ('No' coded –1; 'Depends' 0; and 'Yes' coded 1).
  A second indicator asks: 'Most people don't care what happens to other people.' ('1' if respondents disagree; '0' don't know; '-1' if they agree.) The additive index ranges from 2 (trusting) to –2 (distrusting).

West Benefits: An additive index of two indicators. One asks respondents whether: 'Unification created more advantages than disadvantages for the West.' Another indicator focuses on the East: 'Unification created more advantages than disadvantages for the East.' Response categories range from 'agree completely' to 'disagree completely'. After the polarity of the second indicator was reversed, we created an additive indicator ranging from 2 (East benefits) to 8 (West benefits).

NOTES

1. Gabriel Almond and Sidney Verba, *The Civic Culture* (Princeton: Princeton University Press, 1963).
2. Ibid.
3. Arthur H. Miller, 'Political Issues and Trust in Government, 1964–70', *APSR*, 64 (Sept. 1974), pp.951–72.
4. Jack Citrin, 'Comment: The Political Relevance of Trust in Government', *APSR*, 68 (Sept. 1974), pp.973–88; and Jack Citrin and Christopher Muste, 'Trust in Government', in Roy Jenkins (ed.), *Measures of Political Attitudes* (New York: Academic Press, 1999), pp.465–532.
5. Michel Crozier *et al.*, *The Crisis of Democracy: Report on the Governability of Democracies to the Trilateral Commission* (New York: New York University Press, 1975).
6. William Mishler and Richard Rose, 'Trust, Distrust, and Skepticism: Popular Evaluations of Civil and Political Institutions in Post-Communist Societies', *Journal of Politics*, 59 (1997), pp.418–51; William Mishler and Richard Rose, 'What are the Origins of Political Trust? Testing Institutional and Cultural Theories in Post-Communist Societies', *Comparative Political Studies*, 34/1 (2001), pp.30–62; Robert Rohrschneider, *Learning Democracy. Democratic and Economic Values in Unified Germany* (Oxford: Oxford University Press, 1999).
7. See Citrin and Muste, 'Trust in Government' for similar argument.
8. Susan J. Pharr and Robert D. Putnam, *Disaffected Democracies* (Princeton: Princeton University Press, 2000).
9. Robert D. Putnam, Susan J. Pharr and Russell J. Dalton, 'Introduction. What's Troubling the Trilateral Democracies', in Susan J. Pharr and Robert D. Putnam (eds.), *Disaffected Democracies* (Princeton: Princeton University Press, 2000), pp.3–27 at pp.7–8.
10. Ibid., p.20.
11. E.g. Marc J. Hetherington, 'The Political Relevance of Political Trust', *APSR*, 92/4 (1998), pp.791–808.
12. E.g. Mishler and Rose, 'What are the Origins of Political Trust?'.
13. E.g. Russell J. Dalton, 'Political Support in Advanced Industrial Democracies', in Pippa Norris (ed.), *Critical Citizens: Global Support for Democratic Government* (Oxford: Oxford University Press, 1999), pp.57–77.
14. Juan Linz and Alfred Stepan, *The Breakdown of Democratic Regimes* (Baltimore: Johns Hopkins University Press, 1978); Rüdiger Schmitt-Beck, 'Kulturelle Aspekte demokratischer Konsolidierung in Osteuropa: Bulgarien und Ungarn in vergleichender Perspektive', in Oskar Niedermayer and Bettina Westle (eds.), *Demokratie und Partizipation. Festschrift für Max Kaase* (Wiesbaden: Westdeutscher Verlag, 2000), pp.384–403.
15. Richard I. Hofferbert and Hans-Dieter Klingemann, 'Remembering the Bad Old Days: Human Rights, Economic Conditions and Democratic Performance in Transitional Regimes', *European Journal of Political Research*, 36 (1999), pp.155–74.
16. Dieter Fuchs and Robert Rohrschneider, 'Der Einfluss politischer Wertorientierungen auf Regimeunterstuetzung und Wahlverhalten', in Hans-Dieter Klingemann and Max Kaase (eds.), *Analysen zur Bundestagswahl 1998* (Opladen: Westdeutscher Verlag, 2001), pp.245–82.
17. Geoffrey Evans and Stephen Whitefield, 'The Politics and Economics of Democratic Commitment: Support for Democracy in Transition Societies', *British Journal of Political Science*, 24 (1995), pp.485–514.
18. Mishler and Rose, 'What are the Origins of Political Trust?'.
19. Robert Rohrschneider, 'The Democracy Deficit and Mass Support for an EU-wide Government', *American Journal of Political Science*, 46 (2002), pp.463–75.

20. Harold Clarke, Nitish Dutt and Allan Kornberg, 'The Political Economy of Attitudes toward Polity and Society in Western European Countries', *Journal of Politics*, 55 (1993), pp.998–1021.
21. In the mid-1990s, when these surveys were conducted, confidence in the government and parliament were quite low, both in the West (24% and 28% respectively) and the East (16.6% and 16.2% respectively). Trust in the legal system is considerably higher in the West (53.4%) and the East (32.2). Other data (see below) also indicate that the legal system is trusted by more citizens than political institutions.
22. A vast majority agrees with the first statement in both East (89%) and the West (92%). There is a nuanced – but we think important – East–West difference: over 48% chose the 'strongly agree' category in the West but only 24% in the East did. A majority agrees with the second statement in the West (56%) but the proportion is lower in the East (39%). Together, these patterns hint at the equivocal support for a democratic regime at the level of constitutional reality; a pattern that emerges more clearly in additional analyses (see below).
23. Only a minority evaluates the current system positively (39% in the West and 37% in the East).
24. Unfortunately, there is no appropriate indicator for the fifth level (satisfaction with democracies) in the WVS.
25. The battery of items includes those mentioned in the text, plus administrative institutions, the army, the police, public and private institutions, such as the welfare system and labor relations, churches, and the mass media. These institutions are evaluated independently of evaluations of the political institutions analysed here: they form separate dimensions in a factor analysis (varimax rotation).
26. We conducted all multivariate analyses (see below) for each separate institution. These analyses produce essentially identical conclusions.
27. Another indicator from the Eurobarometer series shows a similar decline in satisfaction with Germany's democracy since unification.
28. In the language of Figure 1, there are clear East–West differences at constitutional reality I. Unfortunately, the WVS surveys lack appropriate indicators for this level to examine whether the correlation between institutional trust and level I differs across the East–West divide as our argument predicts.
29. Almond and Verba, *The Civic Culture*.
30. Werner Weidenfeld and Karl-Rudolf Korte, *Die Deutschen: Profil einer Nation* (Stuttgart: Klett-Cotta, 1991); Dieter Fuchs, 'The Democratic Culture in Unified Germany', in Pippa Norris (ed.), *Critical Citizens. Global Support for Democratic Governance* (Oxford: Oxford University Press, 1999), pp.123–45.
31. Fuchs and Rohrschneider, 'Der Einfluss politischer Wertorientierungen auf Regimeunterstuetzung und Wahlverhalten'.
32. Fuchs and Rohrscneider use a FORSA survey which contains several detailed indicators for individuals' values and institutional preferences. The study shows that socialist values affect the expectations eastern Germans have for the regime as a whole. In the West, in contrast, socialism-derived expectations affect regime dimensions less strongly.
33. Ronald Inglehart, *Modernization and Postmodernization* (Princeton: Princeton University Press, 1997); Ronald Inglehart, *The Silent Revolution* (Princeton: Princeton University Press, 1977).
34. Seymour Lipset, *Political Man* (Baltimore: John Hopkins University Press, 1959).
35. David Easton, *A Systems Analysis of Political Life* (New York: Wiley, 1965).
36. Evans and Whitefield, 'The Politics and Economics of Democratic Commitment'.
37. Rohrschneider, 'The Democracy Deficit and Mass Support for an EU-wide Government'.
38. Michael Bratton and Robert Mattes, 'Support for Democracy in Africa: Intrinsic or Instrumental?', *BJPS*, 31 (2001), pp.447–74.
39. Kendall Baker, Russell J. Dalton and Kai Hildebrandt, *Germany Transformed* (Harvard: Harvard University Press, 1999).
40. Detlef Pollack, 'Das Bedürfniss nach sozialer Anerkennung', *APuZ*, B13 (1997), pp.3–14; Detlef Pollack and Gert Pickel, 'Die ostdeutsche Identitaet-Erbe des DDR-Sozialismus oder Produkt der Wiedervereinigung?', *APuZ*, B41–42 (1998), pp.9–23.
41. Robert D. Putnam, *Making Democracy Work. Civic Traditions in Modern Italy* (Princeton:

Princeton University Press, 1993).
42. Robert E. Lane, *Political Life. Why and How People Get Involved in Politics* (New York: Free Press, 1959), p.163.
43. Almond and Verba, *The Civic Culture*.
44. Inglehart, *Modernization and Postmodernization*, ch.6.
45. Richard L. Cole, 'Toward a Model of Political Trust: A Causal Analysis', *AJPS*, 17 (1973), pp.809–17; John Brehm and Wendy Rahn, 'Individual-Level Evidence for the Causes and Consequences of Social Capital', *AJPS*, 41 (1997), pp.999–1023.
46. Max Kaase, 'Interpersonal Trust, Political Trust and Non-Institutionalised Political Participation in Western Europe', *WEP*, 22/1 (1997), pp.1–21; Kenneth Newton, 'Social and Political Trust in Established Democracies', in Norris (ed.), *Critical Citizens*, pp.169–87.
47. Almond and Verba, *The Civic Culture*.
48. Leo Srole, 'Social Integration and Certain Corollaries: An Exploratory Study', *American Sociological Review*, 21 (1956), pp.709–16.
49. James L. Gibson, 'Social Networks, Civil Society, and the Prospects for Consolidating Russia's Democratic Transition', *AJPS*, 45/1 (2001), pp.51–69.
50. William Kornhauser, *The Politics of Mass Society* (New York: Free Press, 1959).
51. Elihu Katz and Paul F. Lazarsfeld, *Personal Influence. The Part Played by People in the Flow of Mass Communication* (Glencoe: Free Press, 1955); Almond and Verba, *The Civic Culture*.
52. Robert Huckfeldt and John Sprague, *Citizens, Political, and Social Communication* (New York: Cambridge University Press, 1995); Ronald L. La Due and Robert Huckfeldt, 'Social Capital, Social Networks, and Political Participation', *Political Psychology*, 19 (1998), pp.567–84.
53. James L. Gibson, 'Social Networks, Civil Society, and the Prospects for Consolidating Russia's Democratic Transition'; Stephen E. Bennett, Richard S. Lickinger and Staci L. Rhine, 'Political Talk Over Here, Over There, Over Time', *BJPS*, 30 (2000), pp.99–119; Robert O. Wyatt, Elihu Katz and Joohan Kim, 'Bridging the Spheres: Political and Personal Conversation in Public and Private Spaces', *Journal of Communication*, 50 (2000), pp.71–92; Michael Schudson, 'Why Conversation is Not the Soul of Democracy', *Critical Studies of Mass Communication*, 14 (1997), pp.297–309; Diana C. Mutz and Paul S. Martin, 'Facilitating Communication across Lines of Political Difference: The Role of Mass Media', *APSR*, 95/1 (2001), pp.97–114.
54. For this argument, see, for instance, Pollack, 'Das Bedürfniss nach sozialer Anerkennung'.
55. Almond and Verba, *The Civic Culture*.
56. The same patterns emerge when earlier Allbus surveys are used. See also James L. Gibson, 'Social Networks, Civil Society, and the Prospects for Consolidating Russia's Democratic Transition'; Stephen E. Bennett, Richard S. Lickinger and Staci L. Rhine, 'Political Talk Over Here, Over There, Over Time', *BJPS*, 30 (2000), pp.99–119.
57. Fuchs and Rohrschneider, 'Der Einfluss politischer Wertorientierungen auf Regimeunterstuetzung und Wahlverhalten'.
58. Edward N. Müller and Mitchell A. Seligson, 'Civic Culture and Democracy: The Question of Causal Relationships', *American Political Science Review*, 88/3 (1994), pp.635–52.
59. The standardised coefficient is beta=.12 (p>.01).
60. Putnam *et al.*, 'Introduction. What's Troubling the Trilateral Democracies'.

The 'Double' Public:
Germany After Reunification

WINAND GELLNER and GERD STROHMEIER

During the process of reunification, it seemed clear to West German elites that the internalised political behaviour and culture of East Germans would wear off quickly in a reunified Germany. The idea was widespread that East Germans could be educated in the same way West Germans were after World War II – but in a far shorter period. This idea was supported by political scientists – often with reference to established theories of political culture.[1] However, since this assumption was obviously wrong, frustration about the persistence of a 'double German public', that is, the continuing split into two German sub-publics,[2] was high.

A fundamental impact on the development of this double public can be attributed to the mass media. It is surprising, though, that the role of the media after German reunification has hardly ever been studied. Whereas there are many studies on the influence of the mass media on the process of reunification in 1989/90, the assumption was that after reunification a fast normalisation of the relationship between media and politics in East Germany would take place. Ten years later, we must ask how and why the mass media have promoted the inner-German process of reunification only very modestly, why the media might even have slowed down or blocked the process and, why we have to realise that Germany still has two different publics? The following analysis addresses these questions from a historical-descriptive and an empirical-analytic perspective, referring to a theoretical approach which emphasises the impact of political culture on political communication processes.

THEORY

In several of his publications, Karl Rohe pointed to the importance of drawing the distinction between 'socio-culture' (*Soziokultur*) and 'interpretational culture' (*Deutungskultur*). Whereas socio-culture reflects the latent part of political culture and the undisputed conclusions of a cultural collective respectively, interpretational culture is characterised by a character which permanently questions foregone conclusions through

Winand Gellner and Gerd Strohmeier, University of Passau

cultural discourse. Rohe sees a tense and critical exchange relationship between the two levels of political culture.[3] If the political, interpretational culture is able to support or change socio-culture and hence the complete political culture, the question at centre-stage of political culture studies is who *will* or *can* offer *which* political interpretations to *whom* in *which way*.[4] The stability and sheer existence of political socio-culture depends on the continuous symbolic visualisation and validation of basic political rules through interpretational culture. In a modern mass democracy, symbolic interpretations have largely replaced traditions and individual experience as factors of political socio-culture. Thus, political culture is closely connected with political communication, being an instrument of interpretational culture. Eventually, the submission of interpretations is only possible through political communication, channelled by the mass media. If interpretations *can* be conveyed and if they are *accepted* by the society (that is, whether they really become an internalised scheme for action in socio-culture) depends decisively on their reference to socio-culture and their validation through the mass media. Only if interpretational culture sufficiently elucidates socio-culture and hence embeds it in a basic idea or concept, can successful political communication and incremental opportunities for change within socio-culture be expected.

Obviously, relations between socio-culture and interpretational culture in East and West Germany are different.[5] The assumption that West German patterns of interpretational culture could easily be transferred to the East Germans was thwarted by the East German socio-culture and its defective representation in Western interpretational culture, which in effect ignored specific East German values and beliefs. Hence, East Germans were left out of all-German interpretational culture, dominated by the West. Despite strong Eastern efforts to participate in German political communication, the 'Western Lords of the Discourse' denied access.[6]

West German interpretational culture could not relate to the existing socio-culture in the East. Hence, the hope for a rapid development of a civic culture did not come true. Instead, a contrasting East German political culture stabilised, based on the cultural programme of the former GDR.[7] Finally, there are fundamental differences both on the level of socio-culture and interpretational culture. Whereas the fear of unemployment and the general feeling of being disadvantaged after reunification prevails in the East, there are still very diverse 'lifestyles' and ideas in the West. Lifestyles themselves result from the diverse social cleavages. In West Germany, traditional social cleavages have been weakened and have partly been overlapped by new cleavages in recent decades.[8] Especially in the late 1970s and early 1980s, the emergence of new social cleavages could be observed. Post-material values replaced materialism more and more: 'Whereas the core of the Old Politics concerned the conflict between haves and have nots, the New Politics are about the conflict concerning a new set of political demands – environmental care, alternative lifestyles, sexual freedom, minority rights and political participation.'[9] Looking at the multitude of basic views – especially including goals in life, personal values and personal strength[10] – and views concerning central areas of life – among other things professional life, family and leisure time[11] – a multitude of different individual lifestyles can be observed. Gluchowski distinguishes different types: the post-industrial, left-alternative young person; the left-liberal, integrated post-materialist; the unobtrusive, rather passive employee; the dutiful employee driven by norms; the open and flexible average citizen; the upper-class conservative; the integrated senior citizen; the isolated senior citizen.[12] In West Germany, these individual lifestyles have been – similar to a generally favoured view of Western democracy – generated through discourse and conflict and, so to speak, have been traded over the decades, whereas East German political culture was shaped by continuing hierarchical and collective patterns. Typical middle-class values, a positive view of the future, increasing individualisation have been developed and learned only in West Germany, due to economic development (*Wirschaftswunder*) and the strong, well-established ties to the West.[13]

By contrast, in the former GDR, there was an immense loss of middle-class norms in favour of proletarian and petty bourgeois ones, not least due to the throngs of refugees before the creation of the Wall and the general lack of means.[14] That is the main reason why East German society is still far less differentiated than West German society. The specific process of political socialisation in the former GDR has caused a relatively homogeneous social structure. Even functional elites and newly educated Easterners have almost exclusively emerged from the petty bourgeois classes in which they were moulded by the 'mass culture' of workers, farmers and low-level employees: 'Egalitarian cultural principles which are connected to this fact are diversely embodied in everyday life and affect all areas of life.'[15] As a result, East Germans have created a stronger sense of community and are less belligerent than West Germans, who can be described as strongly individualistic, self-confident and even confrontational.[16] These different self-images and 'ways of life' in the two publics correspond to patterns of interpretational culture which might be labelled as more 'dogmatic' in East Germany and more 'liberal' in West Germany.[17]

Our central argument is that due to these different constellations, citizens in East Germany and West Germany have developed both a different 'political interest' and different 'patterns of political communication'. The relationship between those two elements of political culture can be presented in a simplified form (see Figure 1).

FIGURE 1

POLITICAL CULTURES IN GERMANY

		Political Communication	
		Passive	Active
Interest in Politics	High	hierarchical/collective	liberal/competitive
	Low	isolated/fatalist	populist/dogmatic

The low interest in politics in the GDR corresponded with a passive style of political communication which resulted in a sort of a fatalist/alienated political culture. In the final stages of the GDR there was high interest in politics which, however – due to external forces – went along with a still passive pattern of political communication. At this time, the SED tried to use the existing high interest in politics for their purposes. Therefore, this relationship leads us to the assumption of a politicised, but still controlled, political culture. A typical characteristic of developed mass democracies is the relatively high interest in politics among citizens, together with a strong, participatory and articulate political communication. At least in the early stages of German reunification in 1990, this pattern which has been a typical trait of West German society since the late 1960s could also be observed in the GDR – even if only for a short while. However, with the experience of Western 'carpet-bagging' and an overwhelming feeling of inferiority, many citizens of the former GDR turned away from this Western-style political culture. It was made much easier by a strong supply of entertainment-oriented media which may in fact represent a high interest in communication, and, at the same time, a rather low interest in politics. We therefore call this political culture not just populist, but dogmatic, because a heavy diet of entertainment programmes, being easily exploited by populists with their often dogmatic answers to critical political questions, leads to uncritical political behaviour. Hence, communication behaviour in West Germany and East Germany diverged substantially during the course of the 1990s, although communication patterns in the Western states also indicate a growing trend towards this populist/dogmatic pattern.

To recap, our central argument can be summarised as follows. In West Germany, a liberal/competitive political culture, with growing populist/dogmatic tendencies, developed due to an *evolutionary* process, whereas, during the process of reunification, there was an erratic *revolutionary* change of paradigms in East Germany from a hierarchical/collective political culture (showing only infrequent traits of liberal/competitive culture) to a more populist/dogmatic political culture.

The main reasons for this development into a double German public can be found in the respective political communication structures and processes. These structures and processes are themselves determined by three factors: (1) the organisation of the mass media, (2) the role of journalists and (3) the communication behaviour of citizens. Within the scope of our theory, we may formulate the following propositions:

1. The organisation of the mass media in East Germany and the re-structuring of the East German press and broadcasting market, respectively, promoted the decline of political interest and simultaneously led to a strong entertainment-oriented media supply for East Germans. Such media structures, shaped by the West, have widely failed in promoting integration. Private company structures – due to their requirement for profit-maximisation – have not been contoured to the existing political socio-culture which would have been necessary to promote the integration of East Germans through a working and effective interpretational culture.
2. The origins, views and working methods of East German journalists did nothing to promote the acceptance of the political media in East Germany, or to increase the East German audience's interest in politics. Instead, the development of a liberal/competitive pattern of political culture in the East has been blocked. Hence, East German journalists have promoted the strengthening of a more traditional Eastern socio-culture, according to their own long-established interpretations.
3. Media use of East Germans has promoted the emergence of a populist/dogmatic pattern of political culture in East Germany. The overwhelming sense of inferiority, caused mainly by economic circumstances, resulted in escapism, and gave vent to the wide use of light media entertainment, accompanied by political alienation and atomisation.

EMPIRICAL ANALYSIS

We now turn our attention to empirical evidence which supports our propositions. In this section we will try to explain the existence of the two German publics in light of our theoretical framework. The empirical analysis is based on the so-called East–West study by the two nationwide TV channels, ARD and ZDF, data from studies on mass communication, as well as various documents and reports on user experiences.

Changes in Company Structures

Very soon after German reunification, Western institutional structures expanded to the East. In general, instead of careful evaluation and efforts to restructure and integrate Eastern and Western press and broadcasting, the existing structures in the East were captured and overlaid by exclusively Western ones. Top management positions were almost entirely recruited from the West, with a few cosmetic concessions to Easterners. Below the top levels, however, the old structures persisted.

The Press Market

Already in January 1990, the old GDR district newspapers – with the exception of *Neues Deutschland* – freed themselves from their editors, the Socialist Unity Party (SED) or the Party of Democratic Socialism (PDS), respectively. Based on the decision of the GDR People's Parliament 'concerning the guarantee of the freedom of thought, information and media', from 1990 the Media Control Council was founded, consisting of representatives of the parties, mass organisations and several other democratic groups. Consequently, the press was liberalised: the sale of Western press products was permitted and commercial organisation was introduced. Restructuring of the East German press market proceeded, according to Schneider,[18] in several stages. First, the West German publishing companies started to deliver newspapers from the FRG to the GDR. Then they began editing local editions of their papers. Later, a vast number of publishing companies were established in East Germany, mostly founded and financed by West German companies. In the course of 1990, these newly formed companies edited print media in the GDR which contributed to an enormous quantitative diversity in the East German press market. After reunification, the *Treuhandgesellschaft* (Trust Company) became the transitional new owner of newspapers in East Germany and had sold all former SED district newspapers to large West German publishing companies by May 1991. As a consequence, the majority (about 90 per cent) of the East German newspaper market fell into the hands of a few West German publishing companies. Thus, through the assistance of the *Treuhandgesellschaft*, West German publishing companies could create Eastern monopolies.[19] The newly established companies and the newspapers of the bloc parties, already at a disadvantage within the GDR, had no real chance for survival.[20] From mid-1991 onwards, a massive process of concentration led to a drastic decrease in the East German press market. Whereas in 1991 there were 40 independently owned press units in East Germany, only 23 survived until 1993. The process of concentration and the decline in the number of newspapers affected almost all newspapers – with the exception of the former SED district newspapers. National newspapers were particularly affected.[21] It is almost ironic that after nearly ten years following reunification there are

fewer publishing companies and editorial offices than in the former GDR –
34 and 21 respectively.[22]

The revolutionary processes of adjustment and change in the first half of
the 1990s was followed by a period of stabilisation in the East German press
market. In spite of being owned by Western companies, the Eastern press
market is now entirely dominated by former SED district newspapers,
whose share of the market is on an even higher level than during the GDR.
Furthermore, the former SED district newspapers have newspaper
monopolies in most East German districts.[23] The press landscape resembles
less the new federal states and more the former SED districts.[24] The
psychological effect of this development on the East German press market
cannot be underestimated. The specific structures that had already created
identitics in the former GDR remained and thus prevented the emergence of
a new process of identity creation.

A slightly different picture shows the East German magazine market
which developed – largely without the intervention of the
Treuhandgesellschaft – by supply and demand.[25] Most former GDR titles had
to be dissolved, and also many West German magazines had immense
problems in becoming accepted in the East. In order to survive, West German
magazines sold at low prices, filled the supply gaps of the former GDR,
offered specific services, or were especially designed for the East German
magazine market. These magazines are, as the example of *Super-Illu* shows,
colourful and sensational, similar to US supermarket tabloids like *The
National Enquirer*. Western political news magazines, representing the
typical Western interpretational culture, have never been equally accepted in
the East: until 1995, *Spiegel* and *Focus & Co*. had only sold between four per
cent and six per cent of their copies in East Germany.

The restructuring of the East German newspaper and magazine market
had a strong effect on the behaviour of political communication of East
Germans. Given the 'restoration' of the old SED structures in the press
market with the help of big West German publishing companies, East
Germans could not develop an acceptance of the new/old communication
processes. Therefore, there was a decline in the interest afforded political
content. Indeed, a decline of interest in political content is followed in the
entertainment-dominated magazine market and prevented the emergence of
an East German news magazine market.

The Broadcasting Market

Whereas an asymmetrical relation emerged in the press market in West and
East Germany, there was a strict assimilation in the broadcasting market, as
the reorganisation of broadcasting in East Germany followed very much the
media laws of the Federal Republic of Germany.

The decision of the GDR People's Parliament 'concerning the guarantee of the freedom of thought, information and media' initially intended the creation of a new public broadcasting system in the GDR independent of the state. In accordance with Article 36 of the unification agreement, the 'Rundfunk der DDR' and the 'Deutscher Fernsehfunk' (DFF) were first turned into a joint independent institution of the five new federal states and East Berlin, which dissolved after a transitional period lasting until 31 December 1991.[26] From December 1990, the West German ARD used the frequencies of DFF 1, whereas the ZDF started to experiment on previously unused frequencies. After a successive 'regionalisation' of TV programmes, the broadcasters of the federal states were officially established on 1 July 1990. Soon it became clear that the establishment of a channel for each of the five East German federal states could not be financed. Thus, only two new broadcasting companies emerged: the Mitteldeutscher Rundfunk (MDR) for Saxony, Saxony-Anhalt and Thuringia, and the Ostdeutscher Rundfunk Brandenburg (ORB) for Brandenburg; Mecklenburg-Pomerania joined the Norddeutscher Rundfunk (NDR). Consideration was given to the creation of Nordostdeutscher Rundfunk for Berlin, Brandenburg and Mecklenburg-Pomerania, but this came to nothing.[27]

Eventually, the 'Treaty concerning broadcasting in unified Germany' of 31 August 1991 created the basis for a dual broadcasting system in East Germany, following the lines of the already established Western model. Similarly, with regard to the structures of public broadcasting, the private broadcasting media which was created in the new federal states came to resemble the Western system.[28] Given the wide circulation of satellite receivers in East Germany, West German private broadcasters could be viewed at a very early stage. Due to their specific entertainment programmes, those private TV channels effectively managed to conquer East Germany without having to adjust programme content (at least in part) to the special needs of East Germans. Thus, RTL, followed by SAT.1, established themselves as market leaders in East Germany. Not even one national channel was licensed in East Germany and local/regional private TV companies did not emerge for some time, but private radio did manage to develop rapidly.[29]

Results

The restructuring of the East German press market led to a consolidation of the old GDR structures. After a short period of diversity on the East German press market, the sale of the old SED district newspapers to big West German publishing companies by the trust company caused major concentration. Due to this process, the former SED district newspapers still dominate the press landscape in East Germany, arguably more than during the era of the former GDR. Therefore, East Germans could not develop acceptance of the new communication processes and thus no (all-German) process of identity creation could emerge. Instead, there was a decline of interest in political content, caused by a magazine market dominated by entertainment-oriented titles.

Whereas an asymmetrical relation between West and East Germany developed in the press market, there was an absorption of East by West on the broadcasting market. The reorganisation of broadcasting in East Germany essentially followed the lines of the media laws of the Federal Republic of Germany. Western-based national private broadcasters with their huge number of entertainment programmes 'colonised' the new federal states.

The restructuring of the East German press and broadcasting markets occurred through (1) the consolidation of the old GDR structures in the press market, (2) the flood of entertainment on the magazine market, (3) the missed chance of restructuring the national public broadcasting system and (4) the 'colonisation' of East Germany by Western private broadcasters. This in turn promoted a decline of interest in politics and at the same time encouraged a turn toward entertainment-oriented media in East Germany.

THE JOURNALISTS: KEEPERS OF INTERPRETATIONAL CULTURE

Journalists who had previously worked in the GDR were widely integrated into the new structures and companies. Contrary to academic disciplines, like the social sciences, which were severely evaluated and regulated, many journalists who had been faithful to the GDR regime could establish themselves permanently in the new Eastern Germany, especially in the press. Along with this followed the consolidation of stereotyped patterns of thought.

The Role of Journalists in the Process of Reunification

In the autumn of 1989, the editors of all media in the GDR were still firmly on the side of the political leaders. Though they distorted protests against the SED regime in late 1989, these editors tried to help stabilise the old system by the *mise-en-scène* of the ceremony on the fortieth anniversary of the GDR, acting according to their role as propaganda tools of the party.[30]

Only when Erich Honecker began to lose his power did journalists begin to change their minds. First, journalists working at the broadcasting companies gradually freed themselves from state patronage and reported more and more about the 'crisis', even allowing representatives of oppositional groups to speak. Furthermore, the TV channels, followed by the radio stations, started to replace executives officially employed by the SED.[31] A similar development could be observed in the press market.

Suddenly, the GDR journalists found themselves in a situation of complete freedom from any control. 'In autumn of 1989', wrote Rosi Ebner, former *Prisma* editor of GDR Television, 'a paradise-like period began for journalists. There was absolute freedom; we were only responsible to ourselves and our judgment of right.'[32] This situation, however, lasted only a few months.

The Role of Journalists After Reunification

In spite of the professional socialisation of GDR journalists and their utilisation by the SED, many West German publishers decided to employ the East German editors. These editors seemed to be qualified and young enough for a fresh start.[33] Basically, the import of West German top journalists only reached the upper levels of editorial positions. Therefore, East German journalists predominate throughout at the level of department heads and heads of editorial offices, and are composed primarily of those employed within the GDR media. Schneider *et al.* assume that three-fifths of the journalists in East German editorial offices had been working for these organisations.[34] The new federal broadcasting companies and the private newspaper publishers in East Germany employed about 3,500 former GDR journalists.[35] In the editorial offices of the former SED district newspapers, the share of journalists who had been working for GDR media before is extraordinarily high (71 per cent). Even after 1989, the still influential former SED district newspapers, sold by the *Treuhandgesellschaft* to big West German publishing companies, were widely edited by the same people who had been working for these papers in the GDR.[36] The proportion of journalists who had been working for GDR media was even higher in East German magazines (82 per cent). In the East German radio and television organisations, the proportion of former GDR journalists was a little lower, but with more than 50 per cent it was still quite high.[37]

Views of East German Journalists

Within the former GDR journalists had very low social prestige, viewed by the public as a 'mouthpiece for the rulers'.[38] They only achieved credibility among the population of the East when SED censorship ended. It is conspicuous, though, that there have only been a few former GDR journalists who have to date come to terms with their past or appear to judge their career from a critical perspective. Suppression and denial may be a pattern.[39]

Former GDR journalists working in East Germany after reunification differ distinctly from their West German colleagues.[40] The reason for this lies not only with the rudimentary competence in research attributed to low journalistic education standards in the East, or with the separation of information and opinion, or even the extreme time pressures affecting journalism in the East. To these reasons must be added the moral standards of former GDR journalists.

Basically, East German journalists have developed a completely different relationship to their profession than their West German colleagues. East German journalists, having grown up in the GDR, have a far more idealistic view of their profession and are far more inspired by their job than West German journalists. Journalism offers them an opportunity to promote values and ideals and affords them the means of sharing their views with others.[41] These attitudes show that East German journalists, having been socialised in the former GDR, have not been able to create a normal relationship with their professional tasks. Instead, they feel a strong need to publish their subjective views and to proselytise. This radical reorientation can be seen when looking at their views concerning the prestige of their profession. Whereas East German journalists had very low prestige in the GDR, after reunification they were far more convinced of their value than West German journalists. Equally apparent is the conviction that journalists must and can influence political decisions (see Table 1).

It is evident that East German journalists who grew up in the former GDR have a far more complete and dedicated view of their professional responsibilities. Much more than West German journalists, East German journalists believe that they must offer advice, and convey certain principles, but they should also entertain. Furthermore, East German journalists have more desire to act as educators/interpreters for society, and even as 'politician[s] by other means', than their West German colleagues. (see Table 2)

East German journalists' idealistic view of their profession does not go along with a greater carelessness concerning controversial methods of research. East German journalists judge the legitimacy of methods of research even more critically than West German journalists (see Table 3). Furthermore, East German journalists also differ fundamentally from West German journalists as regards their textual method. This can be clearly seen

TABLE 1

VALUED ASPECTS OF JOURNALISM (%)

	Western journalists	Eastern journalists (GDR residents before 1989)
Discover and criticise mismanagement	67	93
Promote values and ideals	49	81
Share their views with many others	34	61
Influence decisions	30	47
Prestige of journalists	10	42

Source: Beate Schneider, Klaus Schönbach and Dieter Stürzebecher, 'Journalisten im vereinigten Deutschland. Strukturen, Arbeitsweisen und Einstellungen im Ost-West-Vergleich', *Publizistik*, 38 (1993), p.368.

TABLE 2
GERMAN JOURNALISTS' VIEW OF THEIR ASSIGNMENTS (%)

	Western journalists	Eastern journalists (GDR residents before 1989)
Help and advise people	64	89
Entertain people	77	87
Convey principles	59	74
Act as an educator	13	25
Act as a politician with other means	11	25

Source: Beate Schneider, Klaus Schönbach and Dieter Stürzebecher, 'Journalisten im vereinigten Deutschland. Strukturen, Arbeitsweisen und Einstellungen im Ost-West-Vergleich', *Publizistik*, 38 (1993), p.371.

in their respective journalistic styles: East German journalists tend much more toward a dogmatic style, expressing clear black and white thinking, whereas West German journalists have a more liberal or discursive style. For example, studying 261 *Neues Deutschland* and *Frankfurter Allgemeine Zeitung (FAZ)* newspaper articles of 1989/90, Berth and Romppel proved that, on average, the degree of dogmatism in *Neues Deutschland* is much higher than in *FAZ*.[42]

Journalists in East Germany form an astonishingly homogeneous group as regards their attitudes and their view of their professional responsibilities and role. This is a result of the far less sophisticated media system in the former GDR, where most of them were socialised.[43]

East German journalists do not differ distinctly from West German journalists in their attitudes toward political parties. West German journalists have a much more negative view of the PDS than East German journalists, although even East German journalists judge the PDS as the worst of all political parties.[44] Furthermore, Scherer *et al.* have shown conclusively that even in the editorial offices of the former SED district

TABLE 3

LEGITIMACY OF CONTROVERSIAL METHODS OF RESEARCH (%)

	Western journalists	Eastern journalists (GDR residents before 1989)
Use secret government documents	75	65
Pretend to be of another view or opinion in order to inspire an informer's confidence	39	23
Procure confidential documents through financial support	28	15

Source: Beate Schneider, Klaus Schönbach and Dieter Stürzebecher, 'Journalisten im vereinigten Deutschland. Strukturen, Arbeitsweisen und Einstellungen im Ost-West-Vergleich', *Publizistik*, 38 (1993), p.375.

TABLE 4

GERMAN JOURNALISTS' EVALUATION OF THEIR AUDIENCE (%)

	Western journalists	Eastern journalists (GDR residents before 1989)
Open	54	88
Well informed	49	74
Critical, demanding	49	73
Interested in politics	50	73
Insecure	24	77
Easy to influence	29	46

Source: Beate Schneider, Klaus Schönbach and Dieter Stürzebecher, 'Journalisten im vereinigten Deutschland. Strukturen, Arbeitsweisen und Einstellungen im Ost-West-Vergleich', *Publizistik*, 38 (1993), p.373.

newspapers – with the exception of *Neues Deutschland*, which was established as a PDS paper – there is no party line.[45]

Fundamental differences between West and East German journalists can be detected in their evaluation of the audience. East German journalists have a more positive and idealistic view of their audience than West German journalists. For example, they judge their audience to be open, interested in politics, well-informed and critical. However, to a greater degree than their West German colleagues East German journalists judge the audience to be insecure and easy to influence. In general, East German journalists see themselves as confronted with an audience which is 'extreme' in every respect, and which conforms to their own 'extreme' view of their profession (see Table 4).

Results

Not least due to the media system in East Germany, which is far less sophisticated, East German journalists form an astonishingly homogeneous group as regards their attitudes and views of their assignments. This is no surprise given the fact that most East German journalists were socialised in the former GDR. West German broadcasting or publishing companies were happy to fill only the top positions in East German editorial offices with Westerners, widely employing East German editors for the rank-and-file.

The views and working methods of East German journalists have two consequences for the East German audience. First, the fact that not much changed in East German editorial offices after the Wall came down has not improved East Germans' acceptance of the media or increased their interest in politics. Second, in the scope of the audience's rudimentary interest in politics, the more dogmatic style of the journalists has prevented the emergence of a liberal/competitive pattern of political culture.

Communication Behaviour of Citizens

The East German population's communication behaviour differs fundamentally from the West Germans'. For instance, Held notes that 'Journalistically, the two parts of Germany are not unified as yet. Instead, it would appear that the different media supplies consolidate recognisable differences within all types of media'.[46] These different communication styles are evident in a variety of forms. One obvious explanation lies in the fact that the specific media structures mentioned before lead to specific media use. East Germans have surpassed West Germany in several areas of media development, especially television use. The degree to which they have become totally 'Americanised' through an entertainment-based media indicates they may have overtaken the traditional mass media of West Germany.[47] This can be seen especially in the differing quantities and qualities of media use in East and West Germany.

Quantity of Media Use

The reach of traditional mass media also indicates specific differences between East and West in the past ten years. However, these differences have decreased gradually. Still, both the broadcasting media and the daily press have a wider reach in East Germany than in West Germany (see Table 5).

The use of television and radio has increased distinctly compared to the use of daily newspapers in Germany in recent years. It is evident that the use of television and radio has always been greater in the new federal states than in the former states, whereas there is no difference between East and West in the use of daily newspapers or magazines and books (see Table 6).[48]

In general, there is a far higher share of 'long-term audience' in East Germany than in West Germany, regardless of the reach of television (out of 28 time segments, short-term audiences spent from 0 to 9 segments, average audiences from 10 to 14 segment and long-term audiences from 15

TABLE 5

REACH OF DIFFERENT MEDIA (%)

	West	East	West	East	West	East
	1990		1995		2000	
Television	81	90	82	89	85	87
Radio	79	86	74	83	84	88
Daily newspaper	71	78	64	69	54	55

Source: Own compilation, based on Birgit van Eimeren and Christa-Marie Ridder, 'Trends in der Nutzung und Bewertung der Medien 1970 bis 2000', *Media Perspektiven* (Nov. 2001), pp.542ff.

TABLE 6

USE OF DIFFERENT MEDIA (MINUTES PER DAY)

| | West | East | West | East | West | East |
	1990		1995		2000	
Television	135	171	150	191	181	198
Radio	170	182	150	200	181	242
Daily newspaper	28	33	29	32	30	30

Source: Own presentation based on Birgit van Eimeren, Christa-Marie Ridder, 'Trends in der Nutzung und Bewertung der Medien 1970 bis 2000', Media Perspektiven (Nov. 2001), pp.544ff.

to 28 segments watching television). In all age categories, there is more long-term audience in East than in West Germany (see Table 7).[49]

Quality of Media: Dominance of Private Television Broadcaster in East Germany

The quality of media across the two parts of Germany is also high. Due to its uncensored and authentic procurement of reality, television has crystallised as the most credible traditional mass medium in Germany. In terms of credibility, television ranks much higher than daily newspapers and radio in both West and East Germany. However, there are distinct differences between East and West concerning the evaluation of credibility of television and the daily newspapers. For example, television is judged to be much more credible in the new federal states than in the old ones, whereas newspapers are seen as far less credible (see Table 8).

Asked about their preferred TV channel, West and East Germans show relatively asymmetrical views. The public broadcasting channels, with the exception of the ARD's third programmes, are far better regarded in the West than in the East. This is entirely opposite to the situation in the West.[50] Thus, East Germans use private channels much more than West Germans. Along with this goes lower interest in politics and less political participation in East Germany.[51] Schulz shows that the willingness for political

TABLE 7

TYPES OF TELEVISION USERS IN EAST AND WEST IN 1994 (%)

	West	East
Short-term audience	34	24
Average audience	37	35
Long-term audience	29	41

Source: Edith Spielhagen: 'Ergebnisse der Ost-Studie der ARD/ZDF-Medienkommission', Media Perspektiven (Aug. 1995), p.368.

TABLE 8

RELATIVE CREDIBILITY OF THE MEDIA IN EAST AND WEST GERMANY IN 1990
AND 1995: IN WHICH MEDIUM WOULD YOU BELIEVE MORE IN THE CASE OF
CONTRADICTORY REPORTING? (%)

	West	East	West	East
	1990		1995	
Television	63	70	55	61
Radio	14	16	15	16
Daily newspapers	22	15	28	20

Source: Marie-Luise Kiefer, 'Massenkommunikation 1995', Media Perspektiven (May 1996), p.245.

participation correlates negatively with the degree of private channel use. Therefore, long-term private channel audiences show less willingness for political participation than long-term public channel audiences.[52]

West and East German expectations of television are rather similar. For example, interest in news and movies is very high in both parts of Germany. On closer inspection, East Germans show much less interest in political, business and cultural information programmes than Western audiences. East Germans prefer entertaining series and shows.[53]

Although East Germans believe that ARD and ZDF offer the best news, business and political programmes, and political and business reports, they are far less convinced of this perspective than audiences in West Germany. However, private broadcasters' political and business news and information programmes do better in Eastern than in Western Germany: RTL, SAT.1 and Pro 7 are judged in the East to provide better political and business news and information programmes, in contrast to audience attitudes in West. However, ARD's tertiary programmes do better in the East than in the West.[54] This may be a result of the fact that ARD and ZDF are still seen as Western channels by East Germans. For example, in 1994, 70 per cent of East Germans believed that ARD and ZDF had not changed at all after reunification and had basically remained as Western channels.[55] It may be that political scepticism, along with the differing social structures and living conditions, has caused less acceptance of ARD and ZDF in East Germany.[56] Although the East Germans generally desire that their preferences be taken into consideration as a means of achieving a certain identity through television, they do not want to be continually serviced by public broadcasters.[57] The latter would be necessary, though, to realise the first and to overcome the categorisation of 'East vs. West', and thereby create a shared identity (see Tables 9 and 10).[58]

Quality of Media: Entertainment-Orientation of East German Audiences

The decline of the use of information in daily newspapers by the mid-1990s was more rapid in East Germany than West Germany. A similar

TABLE 9

EVALUATION OF TV CHANNELS BY INFORMATION PROGRAMMES:
'WHICH CHANNEL – IN YOUR OPINION – IS BEST FOR THOSE PROGRAMMES?'
(%)

	ARD		ZDF		Dritte	
	West	East	West	East	West	East
News	63.8	52.3	44.3	40.0	9.9	19.7
Political programmes	61.6	51.0	52.2	52.1	10.7	14.4
Business programmes	53.0	40.7	56.9	51.5	9.5	12.4

Source: Wolfgang Darschin and Camille Zubayr, 'Warum sehen die Ostdeutschen anders fern als die Westdeutschen?', *Media Perspektiven* (June 2000), p.251.

TABLE 10

EVALUATION OF PRIVATE TV CHANNELS INFORMATION PROGRAMMES:
'WHICH CHANNEL – IN YOUR OPINION – IS BEST FOR THESE KINDS OF
PROGRAMMES?' (%).

	RTL		SAT.1		Pro 7	
	West	East	West	East	West	East
News	20.9	28.1	11.7	12.4	7.5	10.9
Political programmes	13.7	17.6	10.4	13.2	5.7	6.9
Business programmes	11.2	13.4	8.4	9.8	5.4	7.3

Source: Wolfgang Darschin and Camille Zubayr, 'Warum sehen die Ostdeutschen anders fern als die Westdeutschen?', *Media Perspektiven* (June 2000), p.251.

development can be observed with regard to television and radio, where entertainment programmes replaced political information. In East Germany, the use of entertainment programmes has increased most dramatically at the expense of political information programmes.[59]

Both the ARD/ZDF media commission study on the East[60] and the long-term study on media use and media evaluation[61] reveal a distinctly higher demand for entertainment programmes in the new federal states than in the former East German states. The long-term study on media use and media evaluation confirms that the share of entertainment consumers in 1995 was 85 per cent higher in East than in West Germany (73 per cent). Obviously, five years after reunification, Easterners consumed entertainment programmes to a greater extent than in 1990, whereas in West Germany there was a decline (see Table 11).[62]

The audiences of private TV stations are much less interested in political information and have declined substantially in the new federal states, whereas the decline of interest in entertainment has been insignificant. The

TABLE 11

USE OF TELEVISION PROGRAMMES IN 1990 AND 1995 (%)

	West	East	West	East
	1990		1995	
Political information	81	84	72	72
Entertainment information	78	82	73	85

Source: Marie-Luise Kiefer, 'Massenkommunikation 1995', Media Perspektiven (May 1996), p.240.

TABLE 12

USE OF PRIVATE CHANNEL TELEVISION PROGRAMMES IN 1990 AND 1995 (%)

	West	East	West	East
	1990		1995	
Political information	74	81	68	70
Entertainment information	93	95	83	89

Source: Marie-Luise Kiefer, 'Massenkommunikation 1995', Media Perspektiven (May 1996), p.240.

TABLE 13

USE OF PUBLIC CHANNEL TELEVISION PROGRAMMES IN 1990 AND 1995 (%)

	West	East	West	East
	1990		1995	
Political information	84	88	81	71
Entertainment information	76	80	70	82

Source: Marie-Luise Kiefer, 'Massenkommunikation 1995', Media Perspektiven (May 1996), p.240.

audiences of private TV stations in the old federal states show similar tendencies. However, the decline of interest in entertainment is far higher than the decline of interest in political information (see Table 12).[63]

The audiences of public broadcasting stations in East Germany are also far less interested in political information programmes than in the West.[64] There has been a sweeping decline of interest in political information and a slight increase of interest in entertainment in East Germany. The audience of public broadcasting stations in the old federal states shows a slight decline of interest in both political information and entertainment.

In East Germany, there is a strong desire for programmes in which people can 'escape' through entertainment and/or fiction.[65] This need for a

TABLE 14

SATISFACTION WITH LIFE IN EAST AND WEST IN 1994 (%)

	West	East
General situation in life	82	66
Financial situation	62	43
Leisure time	70	63
Living situation	83	70
Relationship with friends, acquaintances, neighbours	87	82

Source: Edith Spielhagen: 'Ergebnisse der Ost-Studie der ARD/ZDF-Medienkommission', *Media Perspektiven* (Aug. 1995), p.385.

TABLE 15

SATISFACTION WITH DEMOCRACY IN GERMANY (%)

	West	East
Very/rather satisfied	40	20
So/so	39	44
Very/rather dissatisfied	15	25

Source: Wolfgang Darschin and Camille Zubayr, 'Warum sehen die Ostdeutschen anders fern als die Westdeutschen?', *Media Perspektiven* (June 2000), p.255.

TABLE 16

EXPECTATIONS FOR THE FUTURE IN EAST AND WEST IN 1994 (%)

	West	East
Optimistic	56	48
So/so	33	40
Pessimistic	10	12

Source: Edith Spielhagen: 'Ergebnisse der Ost-Studie der ARD/ZDF-Medienkommission', *Media Perspektiven* (Aug. 1995), p.388.

TABLE 17

LONG-TERM AUDIENCE'S FATALISTIC-PESSIMISTIC VIEW OF LIFE (%)

	Approval by short-term audience	Approval by long-term audience
Most things in life depend on coincidences	15	23
One can hardly influence his or her fate	22	32
Everything changes so quickly these days that one can hardly follow	39	51
There are more bad and sad than beautiful and good things in this world	27	34
In order to succeed in life one mainly needs luck and connections	53	64

Source: Winfried Schulz, 'Vielseher im dualen Rundfunksystem', *Media Perspektiven* (Feb. 1997), p.97.

TABLE 18

FUNCTIONS OF TELEVISION FOR SHORT- AND LONG-TERM AUDIENCE (%)

	Approval short-term audience	Approval long-term audience
Television helps people to find their way in this world	16	32
Television makes a contribution to finding out about the sorrows and problems of other people	34	50
Television offers relaxation and stimulation	52	71
Television sets someone thinking	34	48

Source: Winfried Schulz, 'Vielseher im dualen Rundfunksystem', Media Perspektiven (Feb. 1997), p.97.

pseudo-world can also be deduced from the East Germans' general attitude towards life. After all, in East Germany far fewer people are satisfied with their life than in West Germany (see Table 14). Equivalent to this is the satisfaction with democracy, which is far lower in East than in West Germany (see Table 15). Furthermore, West Germans see their future much more optimistically than East Germans (see Table 16).

The share of East Germans who were satisfied with their lives and expected a positive future was only 40 per cent in 1994, and the share of those who were dissatisfied with their lives and expected a negative future was 30 per cent, twice the level of West Germans. Moreover, the long-term audience in East Germany is the strongest segment of this dissatisfied group.[66] Schulz has shown, for instance, that the long-term audience in East Germany tends toward a fatalistic-pessimistic view of life. Therefore, long-term audiences, more than short-term audiences, believe that their lives are 'determined by anonymous forces' and that people can hardly influence their own fates (see Table 17).

Long-term audiences believe that they can find help for relaxation and orientation on private television.[67] To a much greater degree than short-term audiences, long-term audiences believe that television does provide general orientation and offer relaxation and stimulation (see Table 18).[68] Thus, private television has an important function for the psycho-social balance of the East Germans: Darschin and Zubayr conclude that 'people in East Germany have a higher feeling of powerlessness than those in West Germany and ... this feeling is connected with the preference of private channels'.[69]

Following from the specific situation in West Germany and views of life of the East Germans, there is a preference for tabloid formats and less complexity in media reporting. Many people in the new federal states, including people with higher formal education, can only be reached through 'infotainment formats'. The strong tendency towards entertainment, fiction and 'infotainment' may also explain the great success of private channels – RTL, SAT.1 and Pro 7 – in East Germany. Thus, 'colourful private TV, brought into the new federal citizens' houses through satellite receivers, filled the entertainment vacuum'.[70] East German audiences spend about three-quarters of their entire television consumption on movies, series, entertainment, sport and commercial shows.[71]

The press market shows similar trends. The only Western newspaper which established itself in East Germany was *Bild*, with a share of 12 per cent. In the magazine market, low-quality West German tabloids have reached the same circulation level.[72]

Results

This analysis has shown fundamental differences between West and East Germany. These differences are strongest with regard to the quantity and quality of media use. Thus, in East Germany:

- the use of television and radio is far greater than in West Germany;
- the share of long-term audience and the evaluation of the credibility of television are generally higher than in West Germany;
- the use of private channels is higher in East than in West Germany, accompanied by the preference among long-term viewers of private channels for media to facilitate political participation and information;
- people in general show far less interest in political, business and cultural information programmes, as well as a preference for tabloid formats and a reduction of complexity in media reporting;
- the strong desire for such programmes is a result of a desire to escape from the frustration of everyday life and overall feelings of pessimism.

In particular, the vast number of East German long-term viewers have developed a specific fatalistic-pessimistic view of life and seek escape in television. Finally, it can be noted that not only the specific programmes, but also the media consumption of the East Germans have fundamentally promoted the emergence of a dogmatic/populist political culture in East Germany, which differs from the more liberal/competitive culture in the West.

CONCLUSION

In light of our central argument, all empirical data seem to support the assumption that two rather different publics have developed in Germany. The Eastern public is based on a political culture which still resembles the old socio-culture of the GDR. We have labelled this the *dogmatic/populist* culture. In contrast, the Western culture is much more *liberal/competitive*. This can be shown in all three areas we covered: media structure, journalist's attitudes and backgrounds and audience behaviour.

The New Media Structures

The consolidation of the old GDR structures on the press market, the flood of entertainment on the magazine market, the missed chance of restructuring the public broadcasting system and the 'colonisation' of East Germany by Western private broadcasters led to a decline of political interest and a move towards entertainment-oriented media in East Germany. Eventually, the new media structures prevented the integration of East Germans through a working and effective interpretational culture.

East German Journalists

East German journalists did nothing to promote the acceptance of the political media in East Germany or to increase East German audiences' interest in politics. An idealistic view of the profession and their strong need to publish their subjective views, as well as their wish to influence political decisions and to educate people, have combined to prevent the development of a liberal/competitive pattern of political culture in the East.

Media Use of East Germans

The dominance of pessimistic views of life in East Germany resulted in a strong wish to escape from everyday life's frustrations, leading to an excessive use of private channels and a low interest in political, business and cultural information programmes. As a result, political culture in East Germany can be described as dogmatic/populist.

Strong differences in these three dimensions account for the existence of two publics in Germany, which might not be easily integrated. Early hopes that Easterners would quickly adopt the established political culture of West Germany failed because they neglected the fact that mass media represent a strong interpretational factor for everyday socio-culture. This can be held responsible for the fact that people in the East still adhere to a socio-cultural perspective which differs widely from the dominant pattern in the West. Those who give meaning to this culture, the interpreters of life, have not yet been held responsible for their failure to promote the effective integration of the two publics. And it would be naïve to expect any change soon.

NOTES

1. Dieter Fuchs, Hans-Dieter Klingemann and Carolin Schöbel, 'Perspektiven der politischen Kultur im vereinigten Deutschland. Eine empirische Studie', *APuZ*, B 32/91 (1991), p.46.
2. Dieter Stolte and Hansjürgen Rosenbauer, 'Die doppelte Öffentlichkeit', *Media Perspektiven* (Aug. 1995), p.359.
3. Karl Rohe, 'Politische Kultur und der kulturelle Aspekt von politischer Wirklichkeit – Konzeptionelle und typologische Überlegungen zu Gegenstand und Fragestellung Politischer Kultur-Forschung', in Dirk Berg-Schlosser and Jakob Schissler (eds.), *Politische Kultur in Deutschland: Bilanz und Perspektiven der Forschung* (Opladen, 1987).

4. Winand Gellner, 'Das Internet: Digitale *agora* oder Marktplatz der Eitelkeiten?', *forum medienethik*, 1 (2001): e-Demokratie = Ende der Demokratie?, pp.12–19.

5. Laurence McFalls supports a different view, assuming that Germany's cultural unification had already happened a few years ago, but had not been noticed. See Laurence McFalls, 'Die kulturelle Vereinigung Deutschlands. Ostdeutsche politische und Alltagskultur vom real existierenden Sozialismus zur postmodernen kapitalistischen Konsumkultur', *APuZ*, B 11/01 (2001), pp.23–9.

6. Dietrich Mühlberg, 'Beobachtete Tendenzen zur Ausbildung einer ostdeutschen Teilkultur', *APuZ*, B 11/01 (2001), pp.30–38.

7. Horst Groschopp, 'Breitenkultur in Ostdeutschland. Herkunft und Wende – wohin?', *APuZ*, B 11/01 (2001), p.15.

8. Seymour M. Lipset and Stein Rokkan, 'Cleavage Structures, Party Systems and Voter Alignments', in Seymour M. Lipset and Stein Rokkan (eds.), *Party Systems and Voter Alignments. Cross-national Perspectives* (New York, 1967).

9. Wilhelm Bürklin and Markus Klein, *Wahlen und Wählerverhalten. Eine Einführung* (Opladen, 1998), p.96, translated by the authors.

10. Peter Gluchowski, 'Lebensstile und Wandel der Wählerschaft in der Bundesrepublik Deutschland', *APuZ*, B 12/87 (1987), p.20.

11. Ibid.

12. Ibid., p.21.

13. Hendrik Berth, Wolf Wagner and Elmar Brähler, 'Kulturschock Deutschland. Eine empirische Untersuchung zu alltagskulturellen Differenzen von Ost- und Westdeutschen', *Psychosozial*, 23 (2000), p.10.

14. Ibid.

15. Edith Spielhagen, 'Ergebnisse der Ost-Studie der ARD/ZDF-Medienkommission', *Media Perspektiven* (Aug. 1995), p.363 (translated by the authors).

16. Berth *et al.*, 'Kulturschock Deutschland', pp.11ff.

17. These patterns are only roughly compatible with the classical concepts of political cultural studies, i.e. by the study of 'values', see Gabriel A. Almond and Sidney Verba, *The Civic Culture: Political Attitudes and Democracy in Five Nations* (Princeton, 1963).

18. Beate Schneider, 'Pressemarkt Ost: Ein Refugium des "demokratischen Zentralismus"', in W.A. Mahle (ed.), *Medien im vereinten Deutschland. Nationale und internationale Perspektiven* (München, 1991), pp.71ff.

19. Barbara Held, 'Zehn Jahre gesamtdeutsche Presse. Die publizistische Mauer steht immer noch', *Bertelsmann Briefe*, 143 (2000), p.69 (translation by the authors).

20. Schneider, 'Massenmedien im Prozess der deutschen Vereinigung', p.609.

21. Ibid.

22. Ibid.

23. Michaela Glaab, 'Medien', in Werner Weidenfeld and Karl-Rudolf Korte (eds.), *Handbuch zur deutschen Einheit. 1949–1989–1999* (Frankfurt 1999), p.563.

24. Schneider, 'Massenmedien im Prozess der deutschen Vereinigung', p.609.

25. Ibid., p.610.

26. Ibid., pp.612ff.

27. Ibid., pp.614ff.

28. Ibid., p.616.

29. Ibid.

30. Ibid., p.617.

31. Irene C. Streul, 'Die Umgestaltung des Mediensystems in Ostdeutschland. Strukturwandel und medienpolitische Neuorientierung in Rundfunk und Presse seit 1989', *APuZ*, B 40/93 (1993), p.39 (translation by the authors).

32. Quoted in ibid.

33. Ibid., p.45.

34. Beate Schneider, Klaus Schönbach and Dieter Stürzebecher, 'Journalisten im vereinigten Deutschland. Strukturen, Arbeitsweisen und Einstellungen im Ost-West-Vergleich', *Publizistik*, 38 (1993), p.358.

35. Streul, 'Die Umgestaltung des Mediensystems in Ostdeutschland', p.38.

36. Schneider *et al.*, 'Journalisten im vereinigten Deutschland', p.357.
37. Ibid., p.358.
38. Streul, 'Die Umgestaltung des Mediensystems in Ostdeutschland', p.37.
39. Ibid., p.38.
40. In the scope of their study on the presentation of politics in East and West German daily newspapers Scherer et al. come to an opposite result. They note that the differences between West and East German journalists rather level out as East German journalists adjust to the West Germans. However, the study is a selective snapshot from 1994 which does not exclude an opposite development (Helmut Scherer *et al.*, 'Die Darstellung von Politik in ost- und westdeutschen Tageszeitungen. Ein inhaltsanalytischer Vergleich', *Publizistik*, 42 (1997), p.437.
41. Schneider *et al.*, 'Journalisten im vereinigten Deutschland', p.367.
42. Hendrik Berth and Matthias Romppel, 'Darstellung und Erleben der Wende in Massenmedien. Inhaltsanalytische Untersuchungen am Wendekorpus – zehn Jahre danach', *Medienpsychologie*, 11 (1999), pp.185–99.
43. Schneider *et al.*, 'Journalisten im vereinigten Deutschland', p.380.
44. Lutz M. Hagen, 'The Transformation of the Media System of the Former German Democratic Republic after the Reunification and its Effects on the Political Content of Newspapers', *European Journal of Communication*, 12/1 (1997), p.15.
45. Scherer *et al.*, 'Die Darstellung von Politik in ost- und westdeutschen Tageszeitungen', p.436.
46. Held, 'Zehn Jahre gesamtdeutsche Presse', p.70.
47. Ibid.
48. Birgit van Eimeren and Christa-Marie Ridder, 'Trends in der Nutzung und Bewertung der Medien 1970 bis 2000', *Media Perspektiven* (Nov. 2001), pp.544ff.
49. Spielhagen, 'Ergebnisse der Ost-Studie der ARD/ZDF-Medienkommission', p.368.
50. Held, 'Zehn Jahre gesamtdeutsche Presse', p.69.
51. Spielhagen, 'Ergebnisse der Ost-Studie der ARD/ZDF-Medienkommission', p.368.
52. Winfried Schulz, 'Vielseher im dualen Rundfunksystem', *Media Perspektiven* (Feb. 1997), p.95.
53. Wolfgang Darschin and Camille Zubayr, 'Warum sehen die Ostdeutschen anders fern als die Westdeutschen?', *Media Perspektiven* (June 2000), pp.249ff.
54. Ibid., p.251.
55. Spielhagen, 'Ergebnisse der Ost-Studie der ARD/ZDF-Medienkommission', p.364.
56. Darschin and Zubayr, 'Warum sehen die Ostdeutschen anders fern als die Westdeutschen?', p.256.
57. Stolte and Rosenbauer, 'Die doppelte Öffentlichkeit', p.359.
58. Alexander Thumfart, 'Politische Kultur in Ostdeutschland', *APuZ*, B 39–40/01 (2001), p.13.
59. Medienbericht 1998, p.295.
60. Stolte and Rosenbauer, 'Die doppelte Öffentlichkeit', pp.358–61.
61. Marie-Luise Kiefer, 'Massenkommunikation 1995', *Media Perspektiven* (May 1996), pp.234–48.
62. Ibid., p.240.
63. Ibid.
64. Ibid., pp.240ff.
65. Stolte and Rosenbauer, 'Die doppelte Öffentlichkeit', pp.358ff.
66. Spielhagen, 'Ergebnisse der Ost-Studie der ARD/ZDF-Medienkommission', pp.368ff.
67. Schulz, 'Vielseher im dualen Rundfunksystem', pp.96f.
68. Ibid., p.97.
69. Darschin and Zubayr, 'Warum sehen die Ostdeutschen anders fern als die Westdeutschen?', p.255 (translation by the authors).
70. Held, 'Zehn Jahre gesamtdeutsche Presse', p.70 (translation by the authors).
71. Stolte and Rosenbauer, 'Die doppelte Öffentlichkeit'.
72. Held, 'Zehn Jahre gesamtdeutsche Presse', p.70

The Effects of German Unification on the Federal Chancellor's Decision-Making

KARL-RUDOLF KORTE

All federal chancellors juggle with democratic power. Formally and informally they are integrated in the structural features of governance. Denominations within Germany's political system are programmatic: to different degrees, chancellor's dominance, party power, coalition ties, constraints of negotiating and media-targeted political communication characterise governing in Germany. The terms manifest political entanglement as well as the distribution of power in Germany. Governing has become more complex, more dependent on the media, more time-consuming, more demanding and more incalculable. This is due not least to the process of German unification.[1] The old Bonn Republic, however, has not fundamentally changed but enlarged. Western political systems were, to a great extent, transferred to the East. Federal Chancellor Helmut Kohl, who governed the unified Germany for eight years, made use of instruments very similar to those employed by Federal Chancellor Gerhard Schröder.

Gerhard Schröder said in his inaugural speech on 10 November 1998: 'This "neue Mitte" excludes nobody. It stands for solidarity and innovation, for entrepreneurship and citizen spirit, for ecological responsibility and a political leadership, which understands itself as modern opportunity-management.'[2] Does 'modern opportunity-management' stand for the amount of scope available for political decisions and leadership in the new Berlin Republic? Does this phrase, taken from the parlance of the times, stand for controlled and steered governance? Or is this an oblique description of many new ideas and plans which, unfortunately, cannot be translated into government actions?

The following sections provide an interim assessment of the Schröder chancellorship. As the basic constitutional resources of the Chancellor have not changed dramatically (neither before nor since German unification) they are not considered here specifically. Instead, I concentrate on the relevant political resources. Some comparative perspectives are developed where it seems reasonable to highlight the specifics of the Schröder chancellorship.

The German Federal Republic can be characterised as a mixed political system: a combination of parliamentary structures and negotiating systems.

Karl-Rudolf Korte, University of Duisburg

Majority democracy (*Mehrheitspolitik*) and concordant democratic decision modi are both valid. Conflict regulations and strategies for problem solving are the result of the mutual dependency of those affected, which in turn will lead to enforced negotiations with each other. Overlaps will appear on levels of competition, hierarchy and negotiation, which result in the final conclusion that although the so-called 'negotiating state' will be characterised by a clear loss of 'inner sovereignty',[3] it will nevertheless be able effectively to manage the decision-making process. Every federal government is restricted within its political decision-making process by the 'subsidiary governments' (*Nebenregierungen*: the coalition partner, the power of the Land representatives and so on). This fact makes the process more complex and time-consuming. In this context, it has to be noted that the chronological line of development did not run continuously linear, which means that not all of the so-called subsidiary governments have become more powerful at the same time that the federal government has become weaker. The empirical reality, however, resembles a sloping curve of development.

The next part will analyse how the chancellors employed their limited decision-making scope. Examples from Helmut Kohl's tenure as Chancellor (1982–98) and some of the main aspects of Gerhard Schröder's style of governance will be compared and discussed. The comparison, however, would need to be developed from another angle in order to offer a new approach from which to evaluate the position of the Chancellor – including past chancellors.

INSTRUMENTS AND RESOURCES OF LEADERSHIP

Which governmental instruments are filters; which can be employed by the Chancellor to compensate for internal and external loss of control, and thereby to place himself in a better position to take decisions? Seven different answers can be found:[4]

1. centralisation of power;
2. secret governing;
3. corporatist leadership styles;
4. 'matter-for-the-leader' myth;
5. presidentialisation;
6. open chancellorship;
7. charm of the resource called foreign policy.

Centralisation of Power

The formal power of the Chancellor lies within the area of conflict between the Chancellor and departmental and cabinet principles.[5] In view of the fact that the Federal Republic's political history is based on a coalition democracy, we must add the coalition principle. The centralisation of power offers a productive solution to escape the zone of conflict. This can be expressed by applying pressure on the party, or through the expansion of the Chancellor's Office. Within this context, the question must be asked: What was the strategic use of existing institutions preferred by the chancellors? Which of the existing institutions can and cannot be instrumentalised by the chancellors and which institutions were especially created?[6]

All chancellors tried to control and steer politics through expanding the Chancellor's Office and applying pressure on the party – with varying skill, however. Kohl's control and power over domestic politics were secured first of all by his party political mandate. The political support from his party remained a power resource. The party was not the only central agency for securing a power-base and legitimisation. The party committee – especially in the 1980s – also provided a platform for co-operative politics in a large, heterogeneous people's party with many wings. Via his role as the party leader Kohl tried to compensate for the power he had lost. After the attempted and survived coup at the Bremen party conference in 1989, at the latest, Kohl's power was unchallenged. He solved many problems through the party rather than the hierarchy in the Chancellor's Office. Much of the party work in the Chancellor's Office was centralised and co-ordinated. Nevertheless, the expansion of political power in the Chancellor's Office could only be employed systematically when Wolfgang Schäuble took charge at the end of 1984. Schäuble, in contrast to his predecessor, was made Minister of the Chancellor's Office, which emphasised his special role. The centralisation of governmental management even led to the situation that the Chancellor's Office itself began to interfere in the coalition partner's departmental work. One can easily find extreme examples, especially in the area of Germany's foreign policy between the Chancellor's Office (Bitterlich) and the Foreign Office (Kinkel). At that time, the Konrad Adenauer house became a pure service business. The party had lost some of its influence. However, the fear that the Chancellor's Office might become an independent institution was removed during Kohl's tenure in office. Although the Chancellor's Office was important for the co-ordination of governmental and party work, other advisory circles and decision-making meetings (for example, the coalition round) were also of great importance.

Chancellor Gerhard Schröder has sought vigorously to centralise power within the Chancellor's Office. For example, he ensured right from the outset that the manager in the Chancellor's Office who is responsible for economic/finance policy would also be a representative at the World

Economic Summit. This task had been previously assigned to the Secretary of State of the Ministry of Finance. Schröder finds this effort to centralise power both easier and more difficult compared to his predecessor. In view of his Green coalition partner, Schröder can use his concentrated powers very effectively. He can produce a majority in the lower house not only with the Union, but also with the FDP (Free Democrats), whose fraction is smaller than that of the Greens. However, Schröder's concentration of power poses problems in regard to the constellation within the ruling party. Lafontaine, for example, stopped the Chancellor seizing full power of the party until 11 March 1999. Both Schröder and Kohl gave the Minister of the Chancellor's Office a top position in order to concentrate powers and expand the Chancellor's Office.

However, Schröder's decision-making is characterised by reliance upon administrative procedures within the Chancellor's Office and a few external advisors with scientific, economic and media backgrounds. This is in contrast to the Kohl government. Other party resources were generally blocked at the beginning. Within the context of power concentration, the government spokesman plays a vital role. As was the case during Helmut Schmidt's tenure (1974–82), s/he is not only the person who presents all the announcements and reports, but at the same time is a close political advisor. The double structure which was in place in Kohl's era, and in which a 'spin doctor' worked in the Federal Chancellor's Office side by side with the spokesman, who in turn was a Secretary of State with responsibility for the Federal Government's Press and Information Office, led, in the end, to competition which generated friction within the Chancellor's Office.

In addition to the need for power centralisation, Schröder's tenure as Federal Chancellor has seen a concerted effort to redesign the institutionalised nature of federal government, and return its traditional function. The informal, opaque decision-making channels were to lose some of their influence. The redesign also included the establishment of a coalition committee for crisis management, which was formalised in the coalition agreements. However, the shock of this change felt throughout government and the subsequent criticism of the resulting chaos experienced during the first 100 days of Schröder's tenure, prompted the establishment of a Red–Green coalition round for confidential pre-consultation. These were held only irregularly. Moreover, Schröder planned a revaluation of the party committee in order to enhance co-operative politics. This was to be achieved through the advice offered by the committee regarding party political conflict, and for assistance in formulating decision-making processes. He did so because of lasting criticism from the SPD ministerial presidents (for example, nuclear politics and the related 630 DM regulation). However, this move entailed, at least at the beginning, a high risk of losing the leadership of the SPD committee.

In the process of expanding the scope for decision-making, the creation of a counterbalance became important. This can also be seen as an attempt to stem the possible loss of the Chancellor's control in the decision-making process by compensating other loci of power. The creation of such a counterbalance is especially important in Schröder's case, because he was not in a position to complement his primary power resource – the Chancellor's Office – with his secondary power resource, the party, until April 1999.

In this regard, the Chancellor sought to free himself from the party leader (Oskar Lafontaine) by creating a classical power counterbalance. The counterweights were the Chancellor's Office on one side, and appointments to some of the departments, or patronage, on the other. The intended effect is captured by Werner Müller's statement: 'I am not affiliated to any party and I therefore do not have a party leader.' In this context, a sentence in Willy Brandt's 'Memoirs' clearly shows that he believed the party office to be of more importance than the Chancellor's Office itself: 'No social democrat would have been in office as the leader of the government for more than 14 days [here he meant Chancellor Helmut Schmidt], if I – the party leader – thought him intolerable.'[7] Since the change in government in 1998, no *troika* model (Wehner–Brandt–Schmidt) has existed for balancing the decision-making process. What exists instead is an unequal interest community. And, for the first time in the history of the German Federal Republic, someone superior to the Chancellor sat in the cabinet – someone who was both 'system immanent' and 'system adverse'. This was something entirely new and deviated sharply from previous examples of classical subsidiary governments, such as the *Kreßbronner Kreis* or the *Konzertierten Aktion*. Apart from the amount of tension between Chancellor, cabinet, departmental and coalition principles, the party principle had to be added as the fifth variable. When viewed systematically, it looked like the phenomenon of cohabitation: 'President' Schröder and 'Prime Minister' Lafontaine, each of them equipped with other power resources and sources for legitimisation.

Schröder's power centralisation strategy has become more visible since Lafontaine's early resignation in April 1999. He quickly and consequently secured the party power resource when the opportunity presented itself. Following some mismanagement at the beginning, the Chancellor's Office established itself as the governmental centre once again and succeeded in ending the counterbalancing powers of Chancellor of the Exchequer Lafontaine. However, even after having become SPD party chairman, Schröder kept a rather distant relationship with his party, reminiscent of

Helmut Schmidt's relations with the SPD and in contrast to Willy Brandt. The newly created position of SPD Secretary-General, filled by the energetic Franz Müntefering, did not have the effect of binding Schröder closer to his party.

The loss of the Minister of the Chancellor's Office Bodo Hombach (25 June 1999) conforms with the strategy of power centralisation. The co-ordination of the Chancellor's Office and government business is far quieter and more efficient under the leadership of Frank Steinmeier. Schröder offered a clear sacrifice to the SPD by shedding Hombach, which also helped to stabilise his powers within the SPD. The reconstruction of leadership within the Chancellor's Office once again resembles the model of Kohl's chancellorship.[8] After his formal promotion, Steinmeier was judged to have an even stronger position in the core executive than any single cabinet minister.

However, one should be cautious about using analogies. It seems that Schröder is establishing himself as a new type of party leader. He leads his party from the Chancellor's Office as a populist, preferring a certain distance from the party. Routine guidelines are in place to decide programmatic changes within the profile of the SPD. Schröder's approach to organising the core executive has been marked by a high degree of decisiveness. Both administrative and constitutional resources have been used to provide the new government with a new institutional face.[9]

Therefore, in summary, we note that under Gerhard Schröder the Chancellor's power is once again that of party power. This power resource remains an important factor in governing. It has not changed during the process of German unification.

Secret Governing

State control can no longer be carried out through 'sovereign' decision-making processes, because of the previously noted changes in government during Schröder's tenure as Federal Chancellor. State control must now employ much softer techniques, such as negotiation, in order to offer positive incentives, to stimulate, to propose and to co-ordinate policy options. The utilisation of these softer techniques to compensate for the loss of control is expressed in the process of secret governing. Most of the decision-making processes are carried out according to one pattern: political compromises are negotiated at the coalition working group level, which includes the specialists of the faction. This is followed by a transferral to the responsible department and the formulation of the draft legislation. This, in effect, turns the classic legislative path on its head.

Schröder has also tended to adopt a style of pragmatic presentation. At coalition negotiations he mediates within his own party, the SPD.

Participants of the Greens often felt that they had to negotiate with at least three different SPD wings at the same time. In contrast to the assumption made by coalition theory that parties will act as unitary groups, at least for the period of coalition formation, the SPD did not act in a united manner. However, Schröder, as Kohl before him, exhibited a talent for pragmatic presentation, whilst at the same time appearing to be relatively open in regard to factual questions. Target definitions and programmatic statements characterised the coalition agreements. Schröder agrees with binding targets. However, the steps needed to achieve them had not been clearly established. His political style has also been expressed through the fact that he avoided comprehensive, detailed agreements.After the initial formalisation process, the 'informalisation' of governmental work began to spread. An informal agreement system established itself relatively quickly. The group of 'fiddlers', who exercised power from the back room,[10] reappeared.

A more formalised process still exists in parallel to this informal trend in government. These formal structures take the form of new cabinet committees charged with developing clear planning strategies between departments and the Chancellor's Office, as well as the continued role of the party within coalition rounds. Formalisation and informalisation processes are designed to supplement one another and to eliminate co-ordination dilemmas. In the end, both processes are forms of the new 'Schröder system'. Schröder still makes the decisions at the informal or formal level. His political style is not oriented toward allowing the minority position of his coalition partner to be secured, despite all the formally established guidelines in the coalition agreements regarding voting procedures in the case of conflict within the cabinet. Rather, Schröder tends to prefer decisions based on simple power calculations.

To govern in secret, the integration of parliamentary support must be secured. Kohl established a system whereby the parliamentary secretaries, Schäuble, Seiters and Bohl, were promoted to become leaders of the Chancellor's Office, ensuring a strong connection with the parliamentary faction.[11] This also clearly indicates a widening of the scope for decision-making. Schröder's Leader of the Chancellor's Office, Bodo Hombach, did not have any experience in Bonn or with the lower house. The same applies to other state ministers, for example the State Minister for the Chancellor's Office. Additionally, it seems the top posts were not filled according to the wishes of the SPD, due to the stalemate between Schröder and Lafontaine. Because of this constellation of circumstances a broader scope for decision-making is not to be expected in the near term.

On the other hand, the lack of binding working structures reinforces the power concentration within the Chancellor's Office. Schröder discovered how important the fraction thinks itself when he tried to change the 630 DM settlement. The fraction supported the Minister for Work and not the Chancellor. It was not until the Chancellor's Office was reconstructed in summer 1999 and the State Minister Hans Martin Bury, as an experienced fraction member, drove forward the co-ordination with the SPD, that Schröder's scope of action was widened.

Corporatist Leadership Styles

The pragmatic presentation of internal decision-making processes is expressed through a corporate leadership style. Schröder's promise to establish the Round Table demonstrates a corporate leadership style reminiscent of Kohl. This involves the integration of interest groups and the forging of consensus as a means of achieving control over the political decision-making process. Additionally, leadership is carried out from the background by taking preliminary decisions within the coalition round. The result is that principal actors have succeeded in establishing new institutions for the control of decision-making processes and the centralisation of power.

The more difficulties the Chancellor experienced in the decision-making process, the more important it became to anticipate reactions in advance and integrate those reactions into the decision-making process as soon as possible. The institutional result of this corporatist style is a strong system of compromise and consensus negotiations, the so-called 'Chancellor rounds', which have been seen on German television. Virtually no important political decision can be made without the matter being discussed and prepared at the Round Table beforehand. Schröder prefers this approach, as did Konrad Adenauer, as a method of meeting lobbyists without including the relevant departmental specialist in the discussions.

There is significant risk to the authority of the Chancellor when he acts as a mediator in such negotiations and discussions. While he appeases those who value consensus and involves those who might otherwise be excluded, often the pursuit of consensus requires accommodating those who have little at stake in the result of the policy itself. This corporate leadership style is another feature of the German Chancellor system that has not changed with German unification.

Matter-for-the-Leader Myth

Through the utilisation of an 'as-if' strategy, it was hoped to return decision-making competencies and the potential for control. This strategy relies on strict adherence to constitutional guidelines within the decision-making process. However, the 'matter-for-the-leader myth' has become the Chancellor's answer to the 'as-if' strategy. The 'matter-for-the-leader myth' strategy entails a concerted effort to convince the public that political matters are serious because the leader himself has to lend a hand to sort out the problems. The central point is not whether the Chancellor actually has the last word in the matter, but that he should appear to have the option of ultimate control over the decision-making process, if he so desires. The matter-for-the-leader myth is based on the assumption that an increase in competence and control can be achieved via public articulation and presentation. Whenever a political issue becomes a matter of great significance to the public, the matter-for-the-leader approach comes into play. The idea is to convince the public that only when the Chancellor devotes himself personally to this matter can success be achieved.[12] At a minimum, this approach channels voter exceptions in one direction.

Schröder has much to do as regards this approach if he wishes to avoid over-reliance on administrative information and *pro forma* selection mechanisms. This is the reason why the leader of the Chancellor's Office, Hombach, and the Secretary of State, Steinmeier, initiated a planning paper on the topic 'co-ordination', which was meant to push forward the crossing over of powers between executive and legislature, in order to ensure that there would be no surprises from the departments and the fraction in relation to the day-to-day operation of government. The Chancellor's Office occupies the top position within the information hierarchy. The matter-for-the-leader approach makes a hierarchical structure possible once more and helps to streamline the political process.

However, this highly personalised system is not without risks. Bold decisions by the Chancellor taken in the first months of Schröder's tenure were essentially seen as attempts at escape, which served only short-term solutions. The half-life of each of the political decisions is becoming increasingly brief. The altering of previously amended legislation became a characteristic of the Red–Green coalition during its first year in office.

The matter-for-the-leader approach also characterised Helmut Kohl's term of office, even though the extremely close attention to the Chancellor's word, which almost became the rule, was a distinctive element only in the final years of his chancellorship. German unification was certainly the most significant matter for the leader. Gerhard Schröder explicitly declared the reconstruction of Eastern Germany a personal matter for the leader.

The central point here is that it is not important whether the Chancellor actually has the last word in a political matter, but that he appears to have the power to exercise ultimate control over the decision-making process, if he so desires. This style of decision-making is clearly built on a direct link between the Chancellor and the public.

Tele-Politics

Tele-politics is governing a society through publicity. Complicated democratic negotiations seem to be replaced by tele-politics. All in all, the political system becomes more presidential and an open chancellorship shapes the governing style.

The term 'presidentialisation' implies strong personalisation of politics (not only during the election period) and a personal style of government for each office-holder. This style is employed as a compensatory tool for increasing the control by the Chancellor of the decision-making process. An important aspect of 'presidentialisation' requires the Chancellor or decision-maker to cultivate an independent stance on policy, thus allowing the Chancellor or decision-maker to obtain distance between his/her position and that of government in general.[13] The German unification process itself was an example of 'presidentialisation' (the Chancellor as 'President').

Chancellor Schröder exhibits this style, however, on a very different level. He presents himself as the embodiment of change and has stylised himself as the synonym for the new political centre. This is in order to separate himself from political disputes over the future direction of the coalition. Schröder also tries to give the impression that he can act independently from the governmental team as a whole.[14] Thus, the Chancellor might ask: 'Why should it be my fault that the government lost sympathy and support among the voters during the first 100 days in government? I, the chancellor, am still popular.' His popularity secured, presumably, because he did not identify himself with the governmental chaos in the first days, and because he accepted some of the weaknesses and mistakes in a jovial, light-hearted manner.

Apart from the specific leadership techniques and the cultivation of his own authority, 'presidentialisation' is also based on a well-orchestrated strategy of managing public appearances. Political decisions have become dependent on communication. Through the means of an open chancellorship and by going public on political matters, the Chancellor has sought to regain some authority. Public chancellorship means an open political style, transparency of leadership techniques and public-oriented/media-effective political presentation.[15] The scope for action to develop certain political styles on the presentational level is oriented towards the precept of 'going public'. The media has put increased pressure on the chancellorship. Every mistake will be mercilessly registered. Every stage of unpopularity will be established through opinion polls. The retreat of the decision-making process behind the media spotlight into informal terrain is a consequence of strong media presence. When statesmanship is replaced by television dramaturgy, political decisions will consequently be less transparent and open to public scrutiny. Nonetheless, of course, the vast majority of routine political decisions are made without any influence from the mass media.

Instrumentalisation of the Mass Media

This process involves the use of the media as a tool to build and maintain trust in the Chancellor. This is an important aspect of the federal election campaigns. Politics in decision-making are replaced increasingly by 'presidentialisation' politics. This trend has led to the growing dominance of television within election campaigns and has shifted the focus from issues to people. This has now become an institutionalised feature of the system. Controlling the office of the Chancellor now brings with it a high degree of media influence as well.

The instrumentalisation of the mass media has thus also become a tool to employ modern forms of plebiscite and consequently to preserve the personal powers of the Chancellor. Under these conditions, when decisions are made on the basis of popular opinions, concordance among the various formal institutions of German governance become denuded. As his control over his party slips, the Chancellor has increasingly moved to find ways of employing populist voting tactics. This is not new. Helmut Schmidt employed this strategy as well, though he discovered the limits of his media charisma within a party democracy. Helmut Kohl, on the other hand, relied much more extensively on his control of the CDU. Thus, he did not rely on direct plebiscite as a supplement to his power and control resources.

Chancellor Schröder's strategy is quite different from his two immediate predecessors. The lure of plebiscite decision-making is to reduce the latitude of the party committees within the decision-making process. In this way, Schröder succeeded both in becoming candidate for Chancellor, and later in successfully elevating party outsiders into his shadow cabinet. In regard to the primary election, however, he missed his goal.

Spectacularly, Schröder institutionalised the 'Schröder–Blair Document' deliberately at the time of the SPD feud regarding expenditure cuts in the federal budget. On the surface, the Chancellor sought to place his party on a new path of economic success by 'going public'. The limits of this political style could already be seen at the end of the coalition negotiations in autumn 1998, when everything revolved around the design and personnel of the government. This political style derives its legitimisation from the plebiscite and telegenic momentum, which draws the attention of the public directly to personalities and which preferably employs television as the primary channel of communication. Recently, however, the SPD has been able to adjust to the challenge emanating from the Chancellor's efforts to by-pass party control over decision-making power and has exposed the limits of his overstretched media-based political style.

Schröder heralded at the outset of his tenure that he would govern with the media. Opinion polls declared him the first television Chancellor.[16] Schröder effectively used the media to alter the public impression of Oskar Lafontaine as the real power centre of the party. However, as Schröder does not enjoy the same control over the SPD that Kohl did over the CDU before him, he has become dependent on the resource of 'going public'. However, it has become increasingly apparent that building the authority of the Chancellor upon a personal media base carries with it a high price. Media charisma has its limits. Appearances in talk and game shows may exhibit a Chancellor who appears to be of the people, and they relieve the Chancellor of the normal strains associated with the day-to-day demands of the office. However, in a party democracy the Chancellor must ensure that he stays connected to and receives quality feedback from the party. Therefore, using the media as an instrument of personal power is only effective over time if there is also a balance between the media and the Chancellor's party within the decision-making process.

Chancellor Kohl certainly was not as charismatic as Gerhard Schröder and did not enjoy Schröder's media projection. Nevertheless, from the beginning of his tenure as Chancellor, he stressed communication in structuring the chancellery. Kohl did not appear on talk shows before 1994, 12 years into his tenure as Chancellor. However, he never understood the intensity of daily polls as a means to test the political atmosphere. His distrust of opinion research remained a dominant trait of his leadership.

The Charm of the Resource Called Foreign Policy

In the field of foreign policy, decision-making dynamics and authority are weighted heavily to the advantage of the Chancellor. Foreign policy follows its own guidelines. These guidelines are less constrained by the checks and balances of domestic politics, and are tied to the federal matrix of politics to a lesser extent than other policy matters. Rather, foreign policy is far more influenced by the internal policy-making framework within the chancellery and are to a large extent subject to the discretionary power of the executive.

It is therefore understandable that chancellors have declared foreign policy as being their sole domain. The terrain of foreign policy has increasingly become an important area which has absorbed the attention of chancellors, and the field of foreign policy has been expanded with each successive chancellorship.

A particularly important aspect of this expansion has been symbolic foreign policy. This entails the negotiation of multilateral arrangements which have the effect of conveying an impression of great importance, despite the fact that often such multilateral arrangements have little substance or weight in shaping German foreign policy.[17] In many cases, chancellors have succeeded in using their primacy over foreign policy to influence domestic political discourse and bypass normal channels of policy delegation and debate.

By attaching such primacy to foreign policy, the Chancellor effectively mutes criticism and political attacks on his leadership. However, foreign policy does not necessarily have a major impact on federal election results. Indeed, quite the reverse is true. For example, consider the special election year of 1990.[18] From the very outset of this critical period of German elections, Kohl sought to emphasise foreign policy. According to the Chancellor principle, Kohl also succeeded in constructing his own political early warning system within the field of foreign policy. This was important in enabling him to distinguish himself from a Foreign Office that at the time was dominated by his Foreign Minister, Hans-Dietrich Genscher. This was facilitated by the fact that, by the end of the 1980s, Kohl had steadily increased his power through structural opportunities emerging from the targeted expansion of the Chancellor's Office as a foreign political centre, as well as through finesse, state political leadership, comprehensive personal contacts and endless telephone diplomacy.

During the first six months of 1999, in a very early phase of his chancellorship, Schröder was given the opportunity to act as the host for EU and G7/8 meetings before a German audience. This afforded him a chance to establish a strong and positive public media image, consolidating his early gains during the war in Kosovo. During Kosovo, he appeared as the more serious 'war Chancellor'. During the G7/8 meetings, he took on a light-hearted appearance. The 'war Chancellor' image returned with the anti-terror war against Afghanistan in 2001. Decision-making for a limited time became even further concentrated on the Chancellor. However, as shown in the case of Afghanistan, the foreign policy card can be played only before domestic political priorities trump any foreign policy issues. Thus, the lesson here is that foreign policy can only be employed selectively as a control modi.

CONCLUSION

The instruments of governance explained above characterise the scope of action within the governing process in Germany. Twelve years of German unification have resulted in rapid change within Germany. The style of managing the governing process has had to adjust accordingly. There is abundant evidence that a much more informal web of policy entanglements have affected the nature of government. So have the number of actors who now hold effective veto authority within the political process.[19] Yet the governing style continues to be shaped by the Chancellor as the primary policy actor in the system. This style is characterised by the choice of tools, which has continued to evolve and grow irrespective of 12 years of German unification.

What characterises the Chancellor's scope for decisions and political leadership in the new Berlin Republic? The connection between personalisation and the loss of control in politics has been a strong feature of policy during these years, and a direct result of the role played by the German Federal Chancellor. Chancellors have adapted both actively and reactively to the opportunities afforded them in the culture of decision-making. We have noted above seven strategies that have been developed by the federal chancellors in this regard during the period since unification. Although they differ little with respect to the risk of high decision costs within a democracy built on the foundations of complex and pluralistic negotiations, they are all designed to offer the Chancellor's Office solutions to the control dilemma within such a semi-sovereign state.

On the decision-making level, the Chancellor is the central actor, who is in a strategic position to make instrumental certain political institutions and create new ones if necessary in order to expand his power resources. On the other hand, the Chancellor creates complex networks around these institutions which he cannot control as quickly (for example, the lower house) to minimise constraints on his power. The matter-for-the-leader approach is a possible solution designed to break the Gordian knot of political networks and convert a formal hierarchy within the policy process into something approaching a network of consensus decision-making. On the presentational level, the Chancellor is one of the few actors who can make politics visible in a network democracy. This explains the trend towards symbolic political presentation and the preference for high politics. However, every Chancellor must keep some escape routes open, to 'diffuse responsibility', so that he will not be held accountable by the public for all decisions. Kohl assisted this trend by reducing the transparency of the decision-making process, thereby often allowing rapid decisions before public debate could mobilise resistance and slow the process. As long as Schröder stylises himself as the leading figure, he could still fall victim to his strategy of personalising the political process and allowing himself to become its centre.

The formulation of 'modern opportunity management', as expressed in Chancellor Schröder's inaugural speech – especially with its modern cloak of vagueness – seems to leave open all options. This circumscription is an expression of the new culture of decision-making in the parliamentary governmental system of the German Federal Republic. The formulation arises both from the understanding of the limited scope of decision-making processes and the wish not to be held responsible by the public for all decisions made. This fits well within the framework of the public chancellorship. It does not, however, directly depend on the process of German unification.

Governing in Germany does not focus entirely upon the Chancellor. Yet rising political complexity and the mastery of political communication via the German media will increasingly intensify the concentration on the Chancellor's person, regardless of whether we are dealing with the remains of the Bonn Republic or progressing with the development of the Berlin Republic.

NOTES

1. See Werner Weidenfeld and Karl-Rudolf Korte (eds.), *Handbuch zur deutschen Einheit. 1949–1989–1999* (Frankfurt/New York: Campus Verlag, 1999).
2. Inaugural speech by Chancellor G. Schröder on 10 Nov. 1998; see Karl-Rudolf Korte (ed.), *'Das Wort hat der Herr Bundeskanzler'. Die Analyse der Regierungserklärungen von Adenauer bis Schröder* (Wiesbaden: Westdeutscher Verlag, 2002).
3. See Fritz W. Scharpf, 'Versuch über Demokratie im verhandelnden Staat', in Roland Czada and Manfred Schmidt (eds.), *Verhandlungsdemokratie* (Opladen: Leske und Budrich, 1993), pp.25–50.
4. Compare Karl-Rudolf Korte, 'Regieren', in Karl-Rudolf Korte and Werner Weidenfeld (eds.), *Deutschland-Trendbuch* (Opladen: Westdeutscher Verlag, 2001), pp.515–46.
5. See Karlheinz Niclauß, 'Bestätigung der Kanzlerdemokratie?', *Aus Politik und Zeitgeschichte*, B 10/99, pp.27–38.
6. For general information (Kohl era), see Karl-Rudolf Korte, *Deutschlandpolitik in Helmut Kohls Kanzlerschaft. Regierungsstil und Entscheidungen* (Stuttgart, 1998).
7. Willy Brandt, *Erinnerungen* (München, 1986), p.363.
8. See for reconstruction contributions by Mertes and Gros in Karl-Rudolf Korte and Gerhard Hirscher (eds.), *Darstellungspolitik oder Entscheidungspolitik? Über den Wandel von Politikstilen in westlichen Demokratien* (München, 2000).
9. See Ludger Helms, 'The Changing Chancellorship', *German Politics*, 2 (2001), pp.155–68.
10. *Der Spiegel*, 50 (1998), p.44.
11. See also Jürgen Gros, *Politikgestaltung im Machtdreieck Partei, Fraktion, Regierung* (Berlin, 1998).
12. See Karl-Rudolf Korte, 'Kommt es auf die Person des Kanzlers an?', *Zeitschrift für Parlamentsfragen*, 3 (1998), pp.387–401.
13. See Michael Foley, *The Rise of the British Presidency* (Manchester, 1993).
14. This cannot be compared with the instability of the cabinet leadership, see John D. Huber, 'How Does Cabinet Instability Affect Political Performance?', *American Political Science Review*, 3 (1998), pp.577–91.

15. Parallels can be seen in the American presidency, see Charles O. Jones, 'Campaigning to Govern: The Clinton Style', in C. Campbell and B. Rockman (eds.), *The Clinton Presidency* (Chatham, 1996), pp.30–33.
16. *Medien-Tenor*, 77 of 15 Jan. 1998.
17. See Hanns W. Maull, 'Quo Vadis Germania?', *Blätter für deutsche und internationale Politik*, 10 (1997), pp.1245–56.
18. See Karl-Rudolf Korte, *Wahlen in der Bundesrepublik Deutschland* (Bonn, 3rd edn., 2000).
19. See George Tsebelis, 'Decision Making in Political Systems', *British Journal of Political Science* (1995), pp.289–325.

The German Party System – Continuity and Change

THOMAS SAALFELD

Political parties, as Kaare Strøm observes, are generally 'the most important organisations in modern politics. ... Students of political parties have commonly associated them with democracy itself'.[1] The importance of political parties in German politics is undisputed. In his influential account of (West) German politics, Peter J. Katzenstein considers parties not only to be 'an essential institutional node linking state and society', but – aside from co-operative federalism and parapublic institutions – one of *the* three crucial nodes in the (West) German policy network.[2] In German academic and political parlance, the term *Parteienstaat* ('party state') indicates that parties are considered to be one of the defining elements of German political life. Article 21 of the Basic Law and the Party Act of 1967 emphasise their legal recognition in Germany's constitutional framework. Their role is also recognised in the form of generous public subsidies supporting their activities.[3]

The aim of this article is to assess continuity and change in the German party system since unification in 1990. From a methodological point of view, this presents a challenge, because there are at least three kinds of trends which are difficult to disentangle: (1) the direct effects of unification, (2) general longer-term trends independent of, but coinciding with, unification and, (3) indirect effects of unification (that is, for example, general trends accelerated or delayed by unification). In the absence of suitable statistical controls, it is not possible to determine the 'net contribution' of these different effects. Nevertheless, party and party system change in Germany since unification can be assessed against the backdrop of developments in comparable political systems in Western Europe in order to avoid conclusions based on spurious co-variation.

Political parties and party systems in Western Europe have been characterised by complex patterns of persistence and change over the past century. In the research process, stability has often been taken for granted, while the effort has tended to focus on the description and explanation of change. Yet, as Peter Mair contends, in the late 1990s, despite a large body of literature emphasising party-system change, Lipset and Rokkan's famous 'freezing hypothesis' – formulated in the 1960s and suggesting that the West

Thomas Saalfeld, University of Kent at Canterbury

European party systems of the time still reflected, with a few exceptions, the political cleavage structures of the 1920s[4] – 'remains largely valid, at least up to now, with the evidence of long-term continuities in party systems far outweighing the ostensibly more striking and more immediate evidence of change'.[5] Parties and party systems have withstood considerable (social and political) changes in their organisational environment through *adaptation* on the one hand and their *control* of the political agenda and the ubiquity of the principle of party as fundamental organising principle of government on the other.[6] Germany offers a good illustration of this 'continuity hypothesis' and the adaptability of existing parties. A country experiencing several dramatic regime changes since 1870, including the unification of two components with radically different political and economic systems in 1990, and significant socio-economic change, Germany could have been expected to show considerable signs of party-system change. It will be demonstrated, however, that the elements of continuity have remained strong, despite, as we shall see, some significant changes.

There are at least four main propositions in the literature characterising the patterns of persistence and change and offering predictions for future developments: (1) the 're-fractionalisation-and-blockage scenario', (2) the 'complete institutional-transfer scenario', (3) the 'regionally diversified institutional-transfer scenario' and (4) the 'East-as-vanguard-and-catalyst scenario'. The first and fourth interpretations suggest significant change, while the second and third emphasise the ability of political parties to adapt, and party systems to remain stable. I briefly characterise these interpretations in the second section. In the third section, a simple conceptual framework is set out, which informs the investigation. The fourth, fifth and sixth sections discuss some evidence pertaining to the four interpretations or scenarios.

FOUR INTERPRETATIONS OF CHANGE

The literature identifies a number of developments accounting for changes in the German party system in the past two decades. Some are completely independent of unification. As in other advanced industrial societies, socio-economic change, especially during the 1960s and early 1970s, began to affect the link between political parties on the one hand and their voters and collateral groups on the other. Partisan dealignment, increasing electoral volatility and the development of a new 'post-modern' cleavage are but a few examples.[7] With the exception of the advent of the Green party in parliaments and government coalitions at the regional and national levels, these changes in the link between voters and parties cannot be said to have affected the parameters of the party system at the parliamentary and governmental level in any fundamental way. Unlike countries such as Denmark or Italy, Germany did not experience dramatic changes at the parliamentary and governmental level. If socio-economic change did not have strong repercussions for the party system at the governmental level, German unification in 1990 could have been expected to lead to significant changes: The electorate was expanded by approximately one-quarter; a new East–West cleavage emerged; the party system was enlarged by the Party of Democratic Socialism (PDS) as a post-communist party on the left of the political spectrum; the social frictions of unification and the focus on national unity could have been expected to provide an ideal 'breeding ground' for parties of the extreme right. Yet German unification may in fact have further *delayed* the significant effects of socio-economic change and partisan dealignment for nearly a decade. This is due to the fact that national unification increased the salience of a number of traditional issues such as economics, unemployment or foreign and security policy and helped the established parties to mobilise support along traditional party lines. In this view, the dramatic electoral changes of 1998, for example, were a 'catch-up' and 'normalisation' against the backdrop of the delaying effect of unification rather than a direct effect of unification.[8] The developments following unification generated a great deal of academic interest and led to at least four interpretations which are different in their emphasis but not necessarily mutually exclusive.

The first interpretation of changes in the party system following unification is based on a normative concern about the danger of a re-fractionalisation of the party system and an increased scope for *blockage*. In particular, early accounts of German party-system development after unification often reflected concern about the danger of the re-emergence of the kind of party-system fractionalisation and polarisation that had contributed to the 'blockage' of democratic decision-making and eventually the collapse of the Weimar Republic in the early 1930s. Moreau, for example, sees the PDS as a left-wing, extremist anti-democratic party that polarises and destabilises German party politics.[9] The social and economic problems of transformation in Eastern Germany were said to 'have also fuelled debate on the rise of extreme right-wing sentiment, leading to the possibility of the CDU and SPD having to deal with parties on both their left and the right'.[10] Koch-Baumgarten[11] therefore believes that there is a danger of the re-emergence of a party system characterised by 'polarised pluralism', which Sartori found to be typical of the Weimar Republic.[12] Holtmann[13] and Veen[14] discussed similar conclusions, warning of a danger of dysfunctional fragmentation of the party system and political disintegration and ideological radicalisation.

Secondly, there is the view that unification constituted a nearly complete transfer of West German political institutions to the territory of the former GDR including the party system. Significant institutional consequences in the long term are unlikely from this perspective. The interpretation of the future of the PDS is crucial in this argument, because its mere existence would seem to challenge the thesis of a complete institutional transfer without significant consequences as far as the party system is concerned. According to this thesis, the PDS is a transitory phenomenon in the German party system. In one variant of the argument, the survival of the party was a mere protest phenomenon resulting from the feelings of absolute or relative deprivation in the Eastern German federal states.[15] It was expected to wither away as soon as the economy in Eastern Germany improved. The other variant of this view is that the PDS is 'the main political representative of a specific socio-economic and cultural milieu'.[16] Neugebauer, for example, argues that the membership of this milieu stretches beyond the materially disadvantaged and those feeling relatively deprived.[17] In addition to such deprived voters, and this is crucial to the argument, the party represents the founding generation and the inheritors of the GDR system.[18] Hence it would seem likely in this interpretation that the PDS will eventually disappear as a result of demographic change.

Thirdly, there is a view that German unification entailed a far-reaching transfer of West German political institutions to the Eastern German federal states, but that there have remained some regional peculiarities. This view represents arguably the mainstream of the academic literature in the field. Niedermayer, for example, concludes that the all-German party system strongly resembles the Federal Republic's party system before unification, which had already begun to experience a moderate amount of re-fractionalisation from the early 1980s.[19] Nevertheless, there had been a diversification of the party system due to Germany's federal system. A new dimension of party alignment had been introduced between the Western and the Eastern parts of unified Germany. The decisive difference was the position of the PDS as a major player in the East, whereas it remained marginal in the West. This interpretation is consistent with recent research about the role of the PDS as a regional party[20] treating it as an expression of the 'East–West conflict', a conflict that is not predominantly socio-economic but cultural.[21] It also ties in with strategic thinking within the PDS itself, where leading activists have begun to support the notion of a regional party following the model of the CSU in Bavaria.[22]

A fourth and final interpretation of the consequences of unification does not focus on the PDS but on the organisational and electoral strategies of the two major parties in the Federal Republic, the CDU and the SPD. For instance, in an empirical study of the two parties' organisations in Eastern Germany, Grabow[23] shows that both parties cannot rely on a mass membership and a dense network of political associations controlled by, or close to, the parties. Therefore, they have progressed much further in establishing themselves as modern 'electoral-professional' parties[24] than the more traditional 'parent parties' in Western Germany. Grabow predicts that the CDU and SPD organisations in the East are at the vanguard of the development of the two major parties from 'people's parties' to modern 'electoral-professional parties' which are much less reliant on the party membership as a crucial resource and are much more dominated by the parliamentary parties, leading candidates and professional public-relations staff within and without the parties. Grabow's predictions are largely speculative.

It is possible to derive four broad propositions from these accounts that will be 'tested' in the following:

(1) Unification has led to a fragmentation and polarisation of the German party system and strengthened tendencies towards polarised pluralism. In terms of policy-making this would threaten the capacity of the major established parties to 'internalise' socio-economic and other conflicts of interest and their ability to guarantee consensual, incremental policy-making in what Schmidt[25] refers to as a *de facto* 'grand coalition state'.

(2) Unification has led to a transfer of the West German party system to East Germany. The PDS is an atavism, which will gradually disappear. The main parameters of the system are likely to revert to the *status quo ante*. The disequilibrium caused by the system shock of unification is likely to be only a temporary one.

(3) Unification has largely led to a transfer of the West German party system to East Germany, although there is a new East–West cleavage expressing itself in the differential strength of the PDS in East and West. On the national level, the changes will have minimal impact.

(4) Unification has forced the two major parties (CDU and SPD) to adopt the organisational model of an electoral-professional party in the East German federal states. This is likely to accelerate the more gradual gravitation of the major West German party organisations towards this model and to influence the links parties have with voter and interest groups.

PARTY AND PARTY SYSTEM CHANGE: CONCEPTUAL FRAMEWORK

The *focus* of this study is on the party system, defined as 'the *system of interactions* resulting from inter-party competition',[26] rather than properties of its component elements, that is, the individual parties. Important developments in individual parties will, however, be referred to where they have a significant impact on the patterned interactions in the system of inter-party competition as a whole. In describing changes in the party system and individual parties, V.O. Key's[27] classic distinction between 'parties-in-the-electorate', 'parties-as-organisations' and 'parties-in-government' has proved to be useful, despite some reservations in the literature.[28] Parties-in-the-electorate simplify choices for voters, inform citizens about political issues, provide general symbols of identification and loyalty and mobilise citizens to participate in politics. Parties-as-organisations recruit and train political leaders, articulate and aggregate political interests. Parties-in-government create majorities in parliament, organise the government, implement policy objectives, organise dissent and opposition, ensure responsibility for government actions, control government administration and foster stability in government.[29]

It will be argued here that the high degree of stability of the German party system – despite socio-economic change and unification – reflects the relatively high level of organisational adaptability of the main parties. At first glance, this seems to contradict the more sceptical findings in organisational ecology, emphasising the difficulties organisations generally have in adapting to rapid environmental change both for internal (for example, internal political constraints and constraints of organisational history) and external (for example, legal barriers or legitimacy constraints) reasons.[30] Yet, due to their access to state resources and their ability to shape the political agenda, parties may be better able to cope with environmental change than other organisations.[31] Another factor improving the adaptability of German parties is their decentralised nature in a federal system of government, which facilitates intra-organisational learning through the diffusion of successful practices, which have been tried at a lower level of the organisation.[32] Despite the overall stability, there have been significant changes on all three dimensions of party: electoral and organisational changes due to longer-term socio-economic change were reinforced by unification, after an initial delaying effect. As for 'party-in-government', there has been stability at the national level but significant change in terms of the development of two distinctive regional party systems, largely due to the role of the PDS as major (government) party in Eastern Germany and its lack of electoral support and organisational strength in the West.

There have been a number of theoretical interpretations accounting for such changes in the relationship between the three main dimensions of 'partyness'.[33] Panebianco[34] captures significant elements of the variation by constructing two ideal typical party organisations: the 'mass bureaucratic party', which is largely based on Duverger's[35] 'mass party', and the 'electoral-professional party' which bears similarities with some elements of Katz and Mair's[36] later concept of 'cartel party'. In its relationship to the electorate, the mass-bureaucratic party attempted to integrate relatively well-defined class and religious groups on a permanent basis. Duverger showed that party organisations created and maintained a stable sense of belonging within the socio-economic groups they sought (or claimed) to represent through strong vertical organisational ties with sections of civil society, a mass membership, a host of collateral groups or activities (for example, party cooperatives, trade unions, and so on) and the maintenance of solid and unified political sub-cultures. By 1945 the heyday of mass bureaucratic parties was over. They saw themselves increasingly challenged by what Kirchheimer[37] called 'catch-all parties'. Catch-all parties did not abandon all ties with specific social groups, but responded to socio-economic change and secularisation by opening up to a wider array of such groups. This involved a de-ideologisation process, the weakening of ties with collateral, religious and trade-union organisations, the reduced weight of members, the strengthening of the leaders' organisational power to determine party policies and strategy and the weakening of the links parties have to specific voter milieus.[38]

In his analysis of the transition from mass-bureaucratic to electoral-professional party, Panebianco emphasises, amongst other factors, the professionalisation of modern electoral-professional parties.[39] Although mass-bureaucratic parties had professional party bureaucrats too, these were mainly used to maintain close ties with the membership. In the new type of electoral-professional party, the focus of experts and technicians with special knowledge (especially in media management, marketing, survey research and the like) is more on the members of the electorate. These experts often have only loose ties with the party. The gradual shift from the ideal type of a mass-bureaucratic to the one of an electoral-professional party has, according to Panebianco, significant consequences for the party's organisation, which he summarises as follows:[40]

TABLE 1

CHARACTERISTICS OF MASS BUREAUCRATIC AND
ELECTORAL-PROFESSIONAL PARTIES

Mass bureaucratic parties	Electoral-professional parties
(a) central role of the party bureaucracy (political-administrative tasks, largely membership-focused)	central role of professionals (specialised tasks)
(b) membership party, strong vertical organisational ties, appeal to the 'electorate of belonging'	electoral party, weak vertical ties, appeal to the 'opinion electorate'
(c) pre-eminence of internal leaders, collegial leadership personalised	pre-eminence of the public representative, personalised leadership
(d) financing through membership and collateral activities (party cooperatives, trade unions etc.)	financing through interest groups and public funds
(e) stress on ideology, central role of the believers within the organisation	stress on issues and leadership, central role of careerists and representatives of interest groups within the organisation

Source: A. Panebianco, *Political Parties: Organization and Power* (Cambridge: Cambridge University Press, 1988), p.264.

According to Panebianco, one of the key variables determining the speed of transformation is the degree of institutionalisation in a party before transformation begins. 'The higher the degree of institutionalisation, the more the party can resist transformatory pressures.'[41] This is corroborated by studies of the dynamics of organisational change in party systems showing that existing parties are relatively slow to change their basic organisational structure and addresses, at least to some extent, the contradiction between our findings and the findings of organisational ecology cited above. Organisational change is more likely to be introduced by successful new parties, whereas existing parties tend to adapt more gradually to changes in their environment, if and when such changes threaten their competitive position in the electoral arena.[42] This also provides a theoretical argument to corroborate Grabow's[43] observation that the less institutionalised party organisations in the Eastern German federal states have been quicker to adopt a modern model of party organisation resembling the electoral-professional party type, while their Western German counterparts (at least the main parties) still have a mass membership and relatively strong institutions integrating these members. Therefore, the process of transformation should be expected to be slower in the Western German case.

How are these two ideal-typical distinctions – 'party-in-the-electorate', 'party-as-organisation' and 'party-in-government' on the one hand, and mass bureaucratic party and electoral-professional party on the other – related? In the traditional mass bureaucratic party, the 'party-as-organisation' linked the 'party-in-government' and the 'party-in-the-electorate'. In the electoral-professional party, by contrast, the direct link of the party elite with the electorate has been strengthened, although – given partisan dealignment (see below) – the term 'party-in-the-electorate' may be less and less appropriate. Similarly, the 'party-as-organisation' has lost in substance (for example, membership) and importance as a strategic resource for the 'party-in-government'. Instead, the latter relies increasingly on professional expert advice, often from outside the party. The reliance on grass-roots members is greatly reduced by state subsidies to political parties, including parliamentary party groups, and radical changes in the electronic media environment revolutionising election campaigns.[44] These developments explain why 'party-in-government' could remain relatively stable, although 'party-in-the-electorate' and 'party-as-organisation' declined – in Germany and many other advanced industrial societies.

POLARISATION AND BLOCKAGE?

Let us first examine the empirical evidence supporting the prediction that socio-economic change and unification are likely to lead to a fractionalisation of the party system and a transition from moderate to polarised pluralism, with severe implications for the dynamics of coalition formation, cabinet stability and government performance. According to Sartori,[45] moderate pluralism is characterised by centripetal competition, whereas competition in systems of polarised pluralism is centrifugal, that is, not only are the parties of the centre-left and centre-right competing against each other for voters, but also against significant contenders at the extremes of the political spectrum. If this is the case, compromise between centrist parties becomes more difficult to achieve. To what extent has unification, along with more long-term socio-economic change, led to dramatic changes on the 'party-in-the-electorate' dimension with serious implications for the 'party-in-government' dimension? More precisely, to what extent can we speak of a situation of polarised pluralism? Generally speaking, there is not a great deal of evidence to suggest that extremist, anti-democratic parties on the left and right have significantly increased in strength.[46] At the national level, unification has made little difference to the pattern of party representation in the Bundestag. The Western German party system has largely been reproduced in Eastern Germany (mainly through the merger of most Eastern German parties with their Western counterparts). The only major exception, the Party of Democratic Socialism (PDS), the successor of the former ruling Communist Party of the German Democratic Republic, had secured representation in the Bundestag until 2002 as a result of its regional strength in parts of Eastern Germany. Nevertheless, the party has failed to establish itself as an all-German party (see Table 4).

The amount of continuity, and the dissimilarity with any 'Weimar scenario', becomes evident when we look at the fractionalisation of the party system, especially with a longer-term perspective. The 'effective number of parties' is a measure that weights the number of parties by their share of seats in parliament:[47] It declined from almost four in the first Bundestag (1949–53), to approximately 2.5 in the fourth Bundestag (1961–65, see Table 3). This concentration process was partly a result of the CDU/CSU's electoral success and the demise of a number of smaller parties; in part it was helped by changes in the electoral law.[48] This first phase of concentration (1949–61) was followed by a second phase (1961–83) characterised by a three-party system. A third phase, characterised by a moderate increase in fractionalisation and the effective number of parties, began in 1983, well before unification, when the Green Party straddled the five per cent threshold for the first time. Between 1980 and 1994 the absolute number of parties and party groups represented in the Bundestag increased from three (1980) to five (1994, with a brief peak of seven after the accession of 144 Eastern German parliamentarians in October 1990). The 'effective number of parties' in the current (2002)

TABLE 2

LEFT–RIGHT PLACEMENT[1] OF PARTIES AND PARTY STRENGTHS (% OF SEATS)
IN THE FEDERAL REPUBLIC OF GERMANY, 1949–2002[2]

Election	KPD	PDS	GR	B'90	SPD	FDP	CDU/ CSU	Z	GB/ BHE	DP	WAV	BP	NR
1949	3.73	—	—	—	32.59	12.94	34.83	2.49	—	4.23	2.99	4.23	1.49
1953	—	—	—	—	31.01	9.86	50.10	—	5.54	3.08	—	—	—
1957	—	—	—	—	34.00	8.25	54.33	—	—	3.42	—	—	—
1961	—	—	—	—	38.08	13.43	48.50	—	—	—	—	—	—
1965	—	—	—	—	40.73	9.88	49.40	—	—	—	—	—	—
1969	—	—	—	—	45.16	6.05	48.79	—	—	—	—	—	—
1972	—	—	—	—	46.37	8.27	45.36	—	—	—	—	—	—
1976	—	—	—	—	43.15	7.86	48.99	—	—	—	—	—	—
1980	—	—	—	—	43.86	10.66	45.47	—	—	—	—	—	—
1983	—	—	5.42	—	38.76	6.83	49.00	—	—	—	—	—	—
1987	—	—	8.45	—	37.42	9.26	44.87	—	—	—	—	—	—
1990	—	2.57	—	1.21	36.10	11.93	48.19	—	—	—	—	—	—
1994	—	4.46	7.29		37.50	6.99	43.75	—	—	—	—	—	—
1998	—	5.38	7.03		44.54	6.43	36.62	—	—	—	—	—	—
2000	—	0.33	9.12		41.63	7.79	41.13	—	—	—	—	—	—

Sources: T. Saalfeld, 'Germany: Stable Parties, Chancellor Democracy, and the Art of Informal Settlement', in Wolfgang C. Müller and Kaare Strøm (eds.), *Coalition Governments in Western Europe* (Oxford: Oxford University Press, 2000), pp.41–3 and *Bundestagswahl: Ein Analyse der Wahl vom 22. September 2002* (Mannheim: Forschungsgruppe Wahlen, 2002), p.83.

Notes: 1   For explanations on the left–right placement of parties see ibid., pp.41–3.
2   Measurement at the beginning of each government's term; 1949–90: appointed members for Berlin excluded; 2002: two individual PDS members (0.33%) elected without recognised party status.

Abbreviations:
KPD: Kommunistische Partei Deutschlands; PDS: Partei des Demokratischen Sozialismus; GR: Grüne; B'90: Bündnis '90; FDP: Freie Demokratische Partei; CDU: Christlich Demokratische Union Deutschlands; CSU: Christlich-Soziale Union in Bayern; Z: Zentrum; GB/BHE: Gesamtdeutscher Block/Bund der Heimatlosen und Entrechteten; DA/FVP: Demokratische Arbeitsgemeinschaft (later renamed Freie Volkspartei); DP: Deutsche Partei; WAV: Wirtschaftliche Aufbau-Vereinigung; BP: Bayernpartei; NR: Nationale Rechte.

Bundestag is 2.80, that is, it is higher than in 1953 but well below even the least fractionalised Reichstag of the Weimar Republic.

A similar picture emerges when we look at the ideological polarisation of the party system. There is little evidence of a sudden and dramatic ideological polarisation due to the arrival of the PDS, or a move of the centre-left parties, SPD and Greens, to the left in response to a challenge from the extreme left. Figure 1 is based on the overall left–right scores calculated by the Party Manifesto Group[49] for each party represented in the Bundestag for each national election between 1949 and 1998. The data are factor scores based on quantitative content analyses of the parties' election manifestos. Figure 1 represents the range between the most left-wing party and the most right-wing party in the German Bundestag (assuming a one-dimensional ideological spectrum). The calculations were made with and without the PDS in order to ascertain the differential impact the PDS has had on the degree of ideological polarisation. The ideological range was highest for the 1957 elections and declined sharply between 1961 and 1965. From 1972 we can observe a somewhat stronger re-polarisation of the party system with a peak in 1998. The appearance of the left-wing PDS has had a significant impact. The idcological polarisation in 1998 was stronger than in any election since 1961. Nevertheless, Figure 1 demonstrates that the ideological re-polarisation of the party system started nearly two decades before unification and that the ideological range is only marginally stronger than in 1983, the first time the Green Party gained representation in the Bundestag.

Despite the re-polarisation, one should not overlook the fact that the PDS has remained a regional party whose impact is not strong enough nationally to seriously challenge the major party on the centre-left, the SPD. If the electoral strength of the parties is taken into account (as a factor used to weight the ideology scores), the impression of continuity is even stronger.

FIGURE 1

MAXIMUM RANGE OF LEFT–RIGHT POSITIONS IN (WEST) GERMAN ELECTION
MANIFESTOS, 1949–98 (WITH AND WITHOUT PDS)

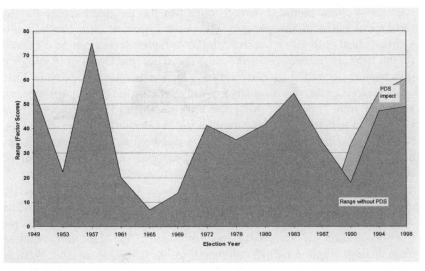

Source (raw data): Ian Budge *et al.*, *Mapping Policy Preferences* (Oxford: Oxford University Press, 2001).

FIGURE 2

MAXIMUM RANGE OF WEIGHTED LEFT–RIGHT POSITIONS IN (WEST)
GERMAN ELECTION MANIFESTOS, 1949–98

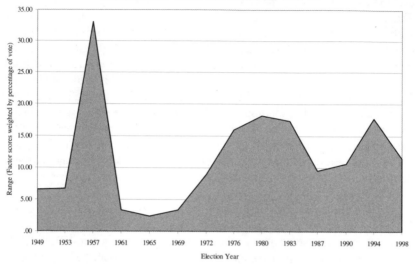

Source (raw data): Ian Budge *et al.*, *Mapping Policy Preferences* (Oxford: Oxford University
    Press, 2001)

Figure 2 shows the ideological range of the party system with the parties'
left–right scores weighted by the percentage of votes they received in the
relevant election. Figure 2 demonstrates that the weighted scores for the
ideological range of the party system have increased with the first all-
German election in 1990, but that similar or higher scores can be observed
for the 1957, 1976, 1980 and 1983 elections. Thus, indicators of ideological
polarisation derived from the parties' election manifestos provide little
evidence to suggest a dramatically growing polarisation of the party system,
a change from 'moderate' to 'polarised' pluralism. The prediction of a
blockage of parliamentary decision-making in Germany which – due to the
country's decentralised nature and large number of veto points – relies
heavily on inter-party and intra-party consensus as a precondition of
successful policy co-ordination, has not materialised.[50]

Thus, as far as the national party system at the level of the directly
elected legislative chamber is concerned, the conditions for stable, centrist
coalitions have remained favourable even after unification. The modest re-
fractionalisation of the party system since 1983 has not reached
destabilising proportions (if compared to the situation in the Weimar
Republic). It has not even reached the levels of the immediate post-war
years. As a result of these favourable party-system attributes, cabinet

FIGURE 3

PARTY CONTROLLING THE MEDIAN LEGISLATOR IN THE GERMAN BUNDESTAG, 1949/53–1998/2002

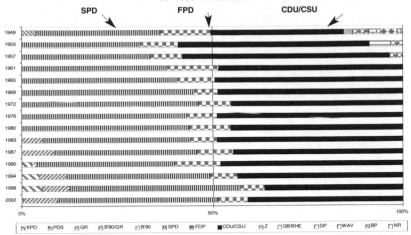

Source (raw data): Table 2

stability has remained high since the 1970s. Since unification all cabinets (under Kohl and Schröder) lasted the entire legislative term (between 1,368 and 1,426 days).

These relatively moderate changes at the parliamentary and governmental level may, however, conceal the potential for a more fundamental shift in the power structure within the parliamentary party system at the level of the Bundestag and, in particular, some East German *Landtage*. At the national level, the 1998 elections witnessed the FDP's loss of its traditional role as a pivotal party (that is, choosing who it wishes to govern with in a coalition from among the major parties). In the literature, such a pivotal party is often referred to as the party controlling the 'median legislator'. According to Laver and Schofield's summary, the median-legislator theorem 'predicts a more or less dictatorial role for the party that controls the median legislator' in the policy space.[51] Figure 3 provides information on the party controlling the overall median legislator on a single left–right dimension. The unit of observation are the parties at the beginning of a legislative term.

Figure 3 shows that the FDP had consistently held the position of a pivotal party between the 1961–65 and 1994–98 parliaments. The increasing number and strength of parties 'left' of the FDP led to a change in the 1998–2002 Bundestag, when, for the first time in the Federal Republic's history, the SPD held the position of a party controlling the median legislator. This outcome was repeated in the 2002 elections. These data indicate that the SPD has been successful, partly due to its own efforts to capture the political centre,[52] and partly as a result of changes in the party system (appearance of the PDS on the left due to unification) to become the current median party in German politics at the national level. The prospects are favourable for the SPD to defend this position in several Eastern German federal-state parliaments (*Landtage*). This means that the SPD may be able to move into a pivotal position between PDS and CDU in the Eastern German states, even if its share of the vote remains relatively modest. The fact that it was able to govern in Saxony-Anhalt as a single-party minority government between 1998 and 2002 is a case in point. Given the fact that the party space is, in reality, a multi-dimensional one,[53] the emerging bipolarity will not necessarily reduce the ability of the main parties to reach a consensus through logrolling and side payments.[54]

Another less obvious consequence of the increased electoral volatility, particularly in Eastern Germany, is that the parties' electoral environment has become more uncertain. There is agreement in the literature that the extent of party identification in West Germany had already begun to decline as early as in the 1980s.[55] The decline of party identification can be said to have accelerated through unification, as East German voters' attachments to political parties have generally been lower than in the West.[56] The main behavioural consequence has been higher volatility. Two recent examples may suffice to illustrate the extent to which volatility has increased. In the federal-state parliament elections of 21 April 2002 in Saxony-Anhalt, the SPD's share of the vote dropped by 15.9 per cent, from 35.9 per cent in the previous (1998) elections to 20.0 per cent in 2002. The CDU gained nearly the same number of percentage points (15.3 per cent), and the FDP gained 9.1 per cent. A few months before, in the federal-state elections in Berlin (21 October 2001), the SPD – battered in Saxony-Anhalt – had gained 7.3 per cent compared to its share of the vote in the previous (1999) elections, whereas the CDU had lost 17.1 per cent (a decline from 40.8 to 23.7 per cent) in a landslide. Such dramatic changes are not confined to the East of Germany as the results of the 2001 Hamburg federal state elections show.[57]

Yet there is little evidence to support the presence of a trend towards 'Weimar conditions' both at the electoral and governmental level. Table 3 presents data on aggregate volatility in the Weimar Republic and in the Federal Republic since 1949. Pedersen's index of aggregate volatility measures the average change in party vote shares between adjacent elections.[58] It is calculated as the sum of all absolute gains and losses for participating parties between two adjacent elections, divided by two.[59] The data do not provide evidence for a linear and accelerating increase in aggregate volatility. After considerable levels of aggregate volatility, especially between 1949 and 1953 and between 1957 and 1961, which were due to the post-war restructuring of the West German party system, the

TABLE 3

PARTY SYSTEM AND CABINET CHARACTERISTICS FOR THE WEIMAR REPUBLIC
(1919–32) AND THE FEDERAL REPUBLIC OF GERMANY (1949–2002)

Election	Average cabinet duration in days in the parliament following election	Aggregate volatility (Pedersen Index)	Number of parties in parliament	Share of anti-system parties	Effective number of parties in parliament (Laakso and Taagepera Index)
Weimar Republic					
1919	160	—	8	0.0	4.10
1920	205	32.1	10	0.9	6.41
1924 (May)	195	27.0	11	19.9	7.10
1924 (December)	288	9.8	11	11.9	6.21
1928	319	13.2	14	13.4	6.13
1930	390	22.1	14	31.8	7.10
1932 (July)	169	21.2	14	52.4	4.30
1932 (November)	57	6.2	13	50.7	4.79
Federal Republic					
1949	1,452	—	9	4.9	3.99
1953	479	19.3	5	0.0	2.77
1957	713	9.2	4	0.0	2.39
1961	353	14.3	3	0.0	2.51
1965	480	7.7	3	0.0	2.38
1969	1,125	6.7	3	0.0	2.24
1972	708	6.0	3	0.0	2.34
1976	1,390	4.1	3	0.0	2.31
1980	284	4.6	3	0.0	2.44
1983	1,398	8.4	4	0.0	2.51
1987	681 (1,362)[1]	6.0	4	0.0	2.80
1990	1,368	9.1	5	0.0	2.65
1994	1,412	8.9	5	0.0	2.91
1998	1,426	8.4	5	0.0	2.90
2002	—	7.2	4	0.0	2.80

Notes: The small category 'others' in Mackie and Rose's data was treated as a party for the calculation of the Pedersen Index, the Rae Index and the effective number of parties in parliament (Laakso and Taagepera), but not for the number of parties. The PDS was counted as a party in parliament although they were not recognised as a full parliamentary party according to the Bundestag's rules of procedure in 1990 and 1994. The same is true for the group of the 'National Right' in the first Bundestag.

    1   It is contentious in the German debate whether the PDS should be considered an anti-system party opposed to liberal democracy. Since the Constitutional Court has not banned it, it is not treated as such a party, whereas the 'National Right' (including members of the Socialist Reich Party [SRP]) and the Communist Party (KPD) in the first Bundestag (1949–53) are treated as anti-system parties, because they were banned in 1952 and 1956 respectively. As for the Weimar Republic, only the KPD and NSDAP were counted as anti-system parties, although the constitutionality of a number of other parties such as the DNVP was questionable.

Sources: Data for the Weimar Republic calculated from T.T. Mackie and R. Rose, *The International Almanac of Electoral History* (Basingstoke: Macmillan, 1974), p.159; cabinet duration data were kindly provided by Ekkart Zimmermann. Data for the Federal Republic of Germany calculated from P. Schindler, *Datenhandbuch zur Geschichte des Deutschen Bundestages 1949 bis 1983* (Bonn: Presse- und Informationszentrum des Deutschen Bundestages, 1983), pp.34–9; *Datenhandbuch zur Geschichte des Deutschen Bundestages 1983 bis 1991* (Baden-Baden: Nomos, 1994), pp.80–82; Kürschners Volkshandbuch, Deutscher Bundestag 13. Wahlperiode (Darmstadt: Neue Darmstädter Verlagsanstalt, 1995), p.37; Presse- und Informationsamt der Bundesregierung: *Bulletin* No. 69 (21 Oct. 1998), p.859; T. Saalfeld, 'Deutschland: Auswanderung der Politik aus der Verfassung?' in: W.C. Müller and K. Strøm (eds.), *Koalitionsregierungen in Westeuropa: Bildung, Arbeitsweise und Beendigung* (Wien: Signum, 1997), p.68. 2002 calculated from *Bundestagswahl: Eine Analyse der Wahl vom 22 September 2002* (Mannheim Forschungsgruppe Wahlen 2002), p.83.

Pedersen index drops to relatively low levels, indicating a significant amount of stability for the period between 1965 and 1983. The elections of 1983, when the Green Party first managed to overcome the five-per cent threshold of Germany's electoral law, and the period following unification indicate a doubling of aggregate volatility, if compared to the mid-1970s, especially since unification. Nevertheless, the level of aggregate volatility has remained significantly below Weimar levels or even below the levels of the early Federal Republic. At least at the federal level, aggregate volatility in recent years has been significantly lower than during the 1950s.

Evidence of increased volatility can also be found at the level of individual voters. Harald Schoen and Jürgen Falter[60] demonstrate on the basis of panel data that over 30 per cent of the West German and nearly 40 per cent of the East German respondents said they had switched between parties from 1994 to 1998. These switches were by no means limited to changes of party preference between different government parties or opposition parties. Schoen and Falter estimate that over 18 per cent of the West Germans and nearly 15 per cent of the East Germans switched between government and opposition parties (in both directions), that is, from CDU/CSU or FDP to SPD or Greens, or *vice versa*.

Even if a 'Weimar scenario' seems exaggerated, such dramatic swings in different, and often unpredictable, directions can be expected to have negative reverberations for the stability of the all-German party system at the governmental level in the longer term. They can impair the ability of the parties to fulfil their role as a central node in the policy process linking different arenas of the decision-making process. For example, growing volatility can be expected to lead to a larger degree of electoral uncertainty in the bargaining environment, which the political parties face in coalition formation. This may lead to a reduced ability, and willingness, to accept the possible (or even likely) short-term electoral costs of coalition for the benefit of stable longer-term co-operation.[61] A more uncertain electoral environment can thus be expected to have a negative impact on cabinet stability and party co-operation which has been central to the consensual policy style associated with the Federal Republic's 'Grand Coalition State'.[62] In a strategic environment characterised by a high degree of electoral uncertainty, the costs of co-operation and the incentives for coalition termination for the sake of short-term electoral gain may be considerable, and there may be fewer incentives for the parties to compromise in policy terms.[63] The bargaining environment becomes tougher and resembles more a one-shot 'Prisoners' Dilemma' than a situation characterised by a high degree of electoral certainty, repeated interaction and incentives for the parties to engage in long-term co-operation, for example through deferred reciprocal compensation.[64]

COMPLETE TRANSFER OR REGIONALLY DIFFERENTIATED TRANSFER OF THE WEST GERMAN PARTY SYSTEM TO THE EAST?

The second and third scenario outlined above focus on the extent to which unification has been, or will be in the longer term, merely a transfer of West Germany's party system to the Eastern German federal states, not only at the levels of 'party-as-organisation', but also at the levels of 'party-in-the-electorate' and 'party-in-government'. In the second scenario, predicting complete institutional transfer, 'party-as-organisation' has been one of the driving forces in structuring the supply-side of electoral competition in unified Germany. The transfer of West German party organisations to the Eastern states through mergers in the run-up to the first all-German elections of December 1990 and the organisational and electoral decline of the PDS in the early 1990s seem to have led to an almost complete institutional transfer from West to East. The lack of credibility of the PDS in the West is an additional 'demand-side' factor reinforcing this development, as, so the argument goes, is the gradual erosion of its electoral base in the East due to generational replacement and the likely improvement of the economy (see above).

The early history of party-system development in Eastern Germany prior to, and shortly after, unification seems to lend considerable support to the scenario of a complete institutional transfer due to the high organisational adaptability of the (West) German parties. With the collapse of the regime of the Socialist Unity Party (SED) in the German Democratic Republic (GDR), the SED as a party came under intense pressure. The successful palace revolt against Erich Honecker, the SED leader, and his replacement by Egon Krenz, could not reverse the dynamics of the 'peaceful revolution' in the GDR. From December 1989 onwards, the GDR regime opposition gained in momentum but also experienced a strong organisational differentiation and fragmentation.

Even before formal unification, the Federal Republic's political parties began to take an active interest in the development of the rapidly changing GDR party system. With strong support from West German parties, the conservative German Social Union (DSU) and East Germany's Social Democratic Party (SDP) were founded. Former 'block parties' associated with the SED regime began to dissociate and emancipate themselves from the GDR's ruling party. The GDR's Christian Democratic Union (CDU), the German Farmers Federation (DBD), the Liberal-Democratic Party (LDPD) and the National Democratic Party (NDPD) began to change both in terms of their party programmes and – gradually – their leadership personnel. The SED, which renamed itself first SED-PDS and later PDS (Party of Democratic Socialism), changed both in organisation and programme in order to survive its most severe crisis since its formation initially facing rapid electoral decline and organisational disintegration.[65]

After an initial phase of reticence, which was largely due to the ties the East German 'block' parties had had with the SED regime, the West German parties became increasingly pro-active and interventionist, especially when unification and the extension of party competition of the Western German parties to Eastern Germany became likely. The gradual merger of the East and West German Social Democrats (SPD) was hampered by the fact that the East German Social Democrats were a newly formed party with very little organisation on the ground. The West German CDU and FDP, by contrast, could rely on an existing organisational infrastructure, but had to manage the transition of the East German Christian Democrats and Liberals from 'block parties' implicated in the GDR regime to electorally credible democratic organisations. The Christian Democrats, therefore, initially formed an alliance with a number of oppositional civic movements with conservative, Christian or liberal ideologies (*Bürgerbewegungen*), which had gained considerable credibility in opposition to the SED regime. Some progressive civic groups formed an alliance, which developed links with the West German Greens. Only the PDS, the successor party of the former SED, remained without the support and resources of a major West German party organisation, reinforcing prediction of its imminent disintegration.[66]

The first free elections in the GDR, the elections to the People's Chamber (*Volkskammer*) in March 1990 led to a surprising victory of the CDU and the 'Alliance for Germany', the umbrella organisation providing a platform for a number of conservative civic organisations associated with the CDU. The weak performance of the Social Democrats is often explained as being a result of its leadership's equivocal attitude to unification and the fact that – as a newly-formed party – it had been organisationally at a disadvantage vis-à-vis the CDU and FDP, the two parties which could rely on the organisational resources of the CDU and LDPD block parties in the East. The civic movements arguing for a reformed Socialist model in the GDR were electorally marginalised. With a clear victory for CDU and FDP, the elections had cleared the way for unification.[67]

From August 1990, the West and East German parties began to merge formally in preparation of the first all-German election of December 1990. These mergers largely took the form of a transfer of resources, personnel and organisational know-how from West to East, supporting the scenario of a complete institutional transfer. In the case of the CDU, FDP and SPD, the merger consisted of the federal-state organisations of the East German parties joining their West German counterparts to form all-German organisations. The East German Greens (Bündnis '90) did not merge with the West German Greens until 1993. The CSU's attempt to expand from Bavaria to East Germany by supporting the DSU as its sister party in the East failed, partly due to CDU resistance. Only in the case of the PDS did the merger process work in the opposite direction. The former ruling party of the GDR attempted to set up its own organisations in the West. Nevertheless, the party has remained marginal in the West, both in electoral and organisational terms.

Yet the scenario of a complete institutional transfer of the West German party system to the East has always hinged on the fate of the PDS. The

TABLE 4

MOST RECENT ELECTION RESULTS TO THE GERMAN FEDERAL-STATE PARLIAMENTS (LANDTAGE, PERCENTAGE OF SECOND-VOTES WHERE APPROPRIATE) AND THE GENERAL ELECTION (BUNDESTAG) 1998 (PERCENTAGE OF SECOND VOTES)

	Federal State				Election			
	Year	Turnout	PDS	Greens	SPD	FDP	CDU or CSU	Others
West German federal states								
Baden-Württemberg	2001	62.6	–	7.7	33.3	8.1	44.8	6.1
Bavaria	1998	69.8	–	5.7	28.7	1.7	52.9	11.0
Bremen	1999	60.1	2.9	8.9	42.6	2.5	37.1	6.0
Hamburg	2001	71.0	0.4	8.6	36.5	5.1	26.2	23.2
Hesse	1999	66.4	–	7.2	39.4	5.1	43.4	4.9
Lower Saxony	1998	73.8	–	7.0	47.9	4.9	35.9	4.3
Northrhine-Westphalia	2000	56.7	–	7.1	42.8	9.8	37.0	3.3
Rhineland-Palatinate	2001	62.1	–	5.2	44.7	7.8	35.3	6.9
Saarland	1999	68.7	0.8	3.2	44.4	2.6	45.5	3.5
Schleswig-Holstein	2000	69.5	1.4	6.2	43.1	7.6	35.2	6.5
Berlin								
Berlin	2001	65.9	22.6	9.1	29.7	9.9	23.7	5.0
East German federal states								
Brandenburg	1999	54.3	23.3	1.9	39.3	1.9	26.5	7.0
Mecklenburg-Upper Pom.	2002	71.1	16.4	2.6	40.6	4.7	31.1	4.3
Saxony	1999	61.1	22.2	2.6	10.7	1.1	56.9	6.5
Saxony-Anhalt	2002	56.5	20.4	2.0	20.0	13.3	37.3	7.0
Thuringia	1999	59.9	21.3	1.9	18.5	1.1	51.0	6.1
General election 2002								
West German federal states	2002	80.7	1.1	9.4	38.3	7.6	40.8	2.8
East German federal states	2002	72.8	16.8	4.8	39.8	6.4	28.3	3.9
Total Bundestag elections	2002	79.1	4.0	8.6	38.5	7.4	38.5	3.0

Sources: Karl-Rudolf Korte, *Wahlen in der Bundesrepublik Deutschland* (Bonn: Bundeszentrale für politische Bildung, 3rd edn., 2000), p.76; Cornelia Weins, 'The East German Vote in the 1998 General Election', in Stephen Padgett and Thomas Saalfeld (eds.), *Bundestagswahl '98: End of an Era?* (London: Cass, 2000), p.49; Statistische Landesämter Baden-Württemberg, Hamburg, Rhineland-Palatinate, Berlin and Saxony-Anhalt. 2002: *Bundestagswahl: Eine Analyse der Wahl vom 22 September 2002* (Mannheim: Forschungsgruppe Wahlen 2002), pp.7–9, 91.

history since the mid-1990s demonstrates that early predictions of the party's imminent death had been premature. After the collapse of the SED party regime, it suffered a spectacular loss of members, especially those who had joined the party for instrumental reasons. Initially, it had also suffered significant electoral setbacks. Yet, subsequently, the party has not disintegrated. It is still the strongest membership party in the Eastern German federal states (see Table 5). Electorally, it has not only stabilised but gradually improved its position at least until 2002. Table 4 provides information about the most recent results of elections at the national and federal-state level since 1998. Despite its weak performance in the 2002 general election, there is as yet no sign of a decline of the PDS's electoral support. Data show that the party is capable of attracting approximately one-fifth of the vote in the Eastern German federal states and Berlin, although it has remained almost completely unsuccessful in its attempt to extend its electoral base significantly in the West.

These data contradict the basic assumptions of the 'complete-transfer scenario', which is based on the expectation that the PDS is a transitory phenomenon, and will gradually disappear as a serious force in German politics. The support base of the PDS is largely limited to the East but stretches beyond the materially disadvantaged and those feeling relatively deprived. In the East and Berlin, the party has also been able to attract support from young voters without attachment to the social 'milieu' underpinning SED rule until 1989.[68] These developments corroborate the scenario of a regionally differentiated rather than a complete transfer of the West German party system to the East.

In the Eastern German federal states and the federal state of Berlin, the PDS has generally sought to present itself as a left-wing alternative to, and potential coalition partner of, the SPD, accepting the constitutional rules set out in the Basic Law. Despite the electoral strength of the PDS and sporadic successes of the extreme right (for example, in Saxony-Anhalt, 1998–2002 with 12.9 per cent for the extreme right-wing German People's Party [DVU]), the Eastern German federal-state parliaments have generally not been characterised by the centrifugal tendencies of 'polarised pluralism' as described by Sartori.[69] Rather, the PDS has joined formal coalitions with the SPD (Berlin and Mecklenburg-Upper Pomerania) or tolerated SPD minority governments (Saxony-Anhalt, 1998–2002). In other words, it has pursued a strategy of respectability. Its co-operation with, and support for, the SPD has, in effect, also been a tacit support for the traditionally consensual policy style in Germany's system of relatively co-operative federalism. Due to their direct participation in two federal-state governments, the PDS is also (indirectly) represented in the Bundesrat, the Upper House of the Federal Republic's legislature representing the federal-state governments.

TABLE 5

PARTY-POLITICISATION OF THE BUNDESRAT: CONSENT LAWS REJECTED
BY THE BUNDESRAT AND PERCENTAGE OF BILLS PASSED AFTER
MEDIATIONS, 1949–98

Bundestag term	Total number of bills passed	Consent laws	Bundesrat majority for government parties in the Bundestag?	Consent laws rejected by the Bundesrat		Bills passed after referral to the Conference Committee of Bundestag and Bundesrat
	N	%		N	%	%
1949–53	559	41.8		12	(3.6)	12.8
1953–57	518	49.8	Yes (1955, 1957)	11	(2.5)	12.0
1957–61	428	55.7		4	(1.2)	11.4
1961–65	429	53.4	Yes (1962–63)	7	(2.0)	8.6
1965–69	461	49.4	Yes	10	(3.0)	7.6
1969–72	334	51.7		3	(1.0)	9.3
1972–76	516	53.2		19	(5.3)	18.6
1976–80	354	53.7		15	(5.7)	20.0
1980–83	139	52.2	Yes (1983)	6	(4.7)	14.4
1983–87	320	60.6	Yes	0	(0.0)	1.9
1987–90	369	55.2	Yes (1987–89)	1	(0.2)	3.5
1991–94	507	56.6		21	(2.6)	16.4
1994–98	565	59.2		21	(2.3)	14.7

Sources: Peter Schindler, *Datenhandbuch zur Geschichte des Deutschen Bundestages 1949 bis 1999*. Baden-Baden: Nomos 1999 and Wolfgang Renzsch, 'Bundesstaat oder Parteienstaat: Überlegungen zu Entscheidungsprozessen im Spannungsfeld von föderaler Konsensbildung und parlamentarischem Wettbewerb in Deutschland', in Everhard Holtmann and Helmot Voelzkow (eds.), *Zwischen Wettbewerbs- und Verhandlungsdemokratie: Analysen zum Regierungssystem der Bundesrepublik Deutschland* (Wiesbaden: Westdeutscher Verlag 2000), p.64; Roland Sturm, 'Vorbilder für eine Bundesratsreform? Lehren aus den Erfahrungen der Verfassungspraxis Zweiter Kammern', *Zeitschrift für Parlamentsfragen*, 33 (2002), pp.176–7.

Yet there is no evidence that the presence of the PDS in the Bundesrat has changed the patterns of conflict and co-operation in the chamber.

The role of the PDS, a relatively extreme left-wing party, as government party in the federal states and the increasingly competitive nature of Germany's federalism could have been expected to lead to more adversarial relations between federation and federal states, especially when the parties controlling the government majority in the Bundestag did not control a parallel majority in the Bundesrat. Parallel majorities in Bundestag and Bundesrat are said to favour a 'unitarisation'[70] of German federalism. This 'unitarisation' is often said to express itself in a low level of conflict between Bundestag and Bundesrat, measured, for example, by a low percentage of bills passed by the Bundesrat but rejected by the Bundesrat and a low percentage of bills referred to the Conference Committee (*Vermittlungsausschuss*) of Bundestag and Bundesrat. If and when the parties forming the federal government do not control a majority in the Bundesrat (the German equivalent to 'divided government'), there is scope for a 'federalisation' of policy-making, that is, manifest disagreement and conflict between the two chambers. This expresses itself in less federal-government control over the Bundesrat and a stronger element of bargaining between the federal government and federal-state governments in informal bodies and the Conference Committee of Bundestag and Bundesrat.

The data in Table 5 support the view that the changes of the party system resulting from unification have not dramatically increased the level of conflict in the Bundesrat, despite the fact that unification has led to a stronger degree of regional conflicts of interest, especially between the affluent Southern German federal states and the Eastern federal states. Data about the percentage of consent laws (that is, bills requiring mandatory Bundesrat consent) passed by the Bundestag but rejected by the Bundesrat has not shown any dramatic changes since unification (Table 5). Since 1990, the percentage of Bundestag consent bills rejected by the Bundesrat was higher than in the preceding two Bundestag terms (1983–90), but significantly lower than, for example between 1972 and 1983. Similarly, the percentage of bills passed after referral to the Conference Committee (*Vermittlungsausschuss*) of Bundestag and Bundesrat increased, if compared to the period 1983–90, but is approximately at the same level as in the decade before 1983. In other words, there is no evidence that unification has considerably changed the patterns of party-political and federal consensus and conflict in the Bundesrat.

EAST GERMAN PARTY ORGANISATIONS AS THE 'VANGUARDS OF CHANGE'?

At the organisational level, German parties have undergone significant changes, and these changes may be strongly influenced by unification in the longer run. Given the importance of party organisations as links not only between citizens and government but also in terms of connecting different arenas of decision-making in Germany's federal system and within the European Union, such change may have considerable implications for governance. Thomas Poguntke describes German parties as organisations characterised by far more 'horizontal and vertical fragmentation' than the very hierarchical mass-bureaucratic party model (see above) would suggest.[71] Poguntke echoes the prevailing consensus of students of party organisation in Germany when he claims that the main German parties 'are closer to a stratarchic than to an oligarchic model' and that they are, 'as a

TABLE 6

PARTY MEMBERSHIP IN GERMANY, 1975–2000
(31 DECEMBER OF THE RESPECTIVE YEAR)

Party		1975	1985	1991	1995	2000
CDU	West	590,482	718,590	641,454	585,839	560,606
	East	–	–	109,709	71,804	56,116
	Total	590,482	718,590	751,163	657,643	616,722
CSU	West	132,591	182,852	184,513	179,647	178,400
	East	–	–	–	–	–
	Total	132,591	182,852	184,513	179,647	178,400
FDP	West	74,032	66,727	68,641	58,693	51,599
	East	–	–	68,916	21,416	11,122
	Total	74,032	66,727	137,557	80,109	62,721
GRÜNE	West	–	37,024	37,533	43,418	43,938
	East	–	–	1,340	2,827	2.693
	Total	–	37,024	38,873	46,245	46,631
PDS	West	–	–	572	2,388	3,956
	East	–	–	172,007	112,470	79.349
	Total	–	–	172,579	114,858	83,475
SPD	West	998,471	916,386	892,657	790,473	706,925
	East	–	–	27,214	27,177	27,742
	Total	998,471	916,386	919,871	817,650	734,667
All main parties		1,795,576	1,884,555	2,204,556	1,896,152	1,722,616

Note: Party membership figures are reported for approximately five-year intervals from 1975 to 2000. 1991 was chosen over 1990, because 1990 data for Eastern Germany are unreliable. CDU, SPD, FDP and Greens exclude the members in Berlin from their calculation of the East German membership; the PDS include the Berlin members under the rubric 'Ost'. Despite this inconsistency, the data provide a useful picture in general.

Sources: 1975 and 1985: U. Andersen and W. Woyke, *Wahl '98. Zur Bundestagswahl 1998: Parteien und Wähler, Wahlrecht und Wahlverfahren, Politische Entwicklung* (Opladen: Leske + Budrich, 1998), p.208; 1991–1995: O.W. Gabriel and O. Niedermayer, 'Entwicklung und Sozialstruktur der Parteimitgliedschaften', in: O.W. Gabriel, O. Niedermayer and R. Stöss (eds.), *Parteiendemokratie in Deutschland* (Bonn: Bundeszentrale für politische Bildung), p.281. 2000: Bundesgeschäftsstellen of the parties (CSU: Landesgeschäftsstelle).

result of the extensive legal regulation of party politics, ... also fairly similar as regards the main structure of their hierarchy of decision making bodies'. He also maintains that the 'most conspicuous change over the past three decades has been a substantial loosening of ties between parties and society', although he warns that 'we should be cautious in attributing parties too hastily to the sphere of the state' as done in the cartel-party model.[72] There is considerable empirical evidence to support this claim, if we analyse the development of membership enrolment in the Bundestag parties and their finances.

Susan Scarrow demonstrates that party enrolments have generally fallen in Western industrial societies, and that Germany has not been an exception to this pattern.[73] Aggregate enrolment almost doubled between 1960 and 1980, but has declined since. In order to standardise the absolute figures to account for changes in the size of the electorate (for example, through unification), she provides data on the Member/Electorate Ratio. These figures show that the percentage of voters organised in political parties in Germany declined from a high point of 4.5 per cent in the 1980s to 3.2 per cent in the 1990s (1990, 1994), which is still slightly above the 2.9 per cent measured for the 1950s. In addition, the percentage of members participating actively in their local party branches also declined.[74]

A closer look at some disaggregated figures confirms that all parties represented in the Bundestag have lost a substantial share of their members between 1975 and 2000. Table 6 reveals that the enrolled membership of all Western German parties began to decline after their respective high points between the mid-1970s and mid-1980s. Initially, unification boosted the membership of most Western German parties. The FDP, for example, more than doubled its membership as a result of its merger with its Eastern German counterpart, the former Liberal Democratic Party (LDPD). Soon, however, CDU, FDP and PDS began to lose large numbers of members in Eastern Germany and continued to experience a gradual membership decline in the West. The SPD and Greens, by contrast, had never been able to build up a significant membership base in the East. They stagnated at very low levels. In terms of membership, the CDU, FDP, SPD and Greens are predominantly Western German parties, whereas the PDS has not managed to expand its membership base significantly in Western Germany and has largely remained an Eastern German party.

In addition, the internal organisation of parties has become more fragmented. The traditional, hierarchically integrated (mass) party, so the argument goes, has become increasingly unsuitable as a vehicle for party leaders to organise electoral campaigns effectively and efficiently. Wiesendahl argues that the office-seeking rationale of party leaders is in tension with the policy-oriented goals of grass-roots activists. Therefore, German parties can be interpreted as 'organised anarchies' comprising 'two incompatible organisational spheres, each with their independent rationales, resources and routines. The two spheres are prevented from clashing by loose coupling' of a 'pre-modern membership party at the ground and the modernised electoral professional service party at the top'.[75] Empirical evidence from comparative studies supports this view and shows that the West German parties increased their central staff by 8.6 per cent between 1972 and 1989, and their parliamentary staff by 525 per cent between 1969 and 1989. However, staffing levels for the organisational units at sub-national level fell.[76] These empirical observations are in line with some influential comparative theoretical texts. For example, Katz

TABLE 7

MAIN SOURCES OF INCOME OF THE GERMAN BUNDESTAG PARTIES IN 1999
(BY TERRITORIAL LEVEL)

	SPD		CDU		CSU		Greens		FDP		PDS	
	Mill. DM	%	Mill. DM	%	Mill. DM	%	Mill. DM	%	Mill. DM	%	Mill. DM	%
1. Membership contributions												
National party	25.6	16.2	12.4	11.8	7.2*	36.6	4.5	21.6	0.04	0.4	0.09	0.5
Länder organisations / Districts	66.9	42.5	21.9	20.8	–*	–*	4.7	22.6	3.9	36.5	3.4	19.5
Local branches	65.0	41.3	71.0	67.4	12.6	63.7	11.7	55.8	6.8	63.1	14.0	80.0
Total	157.5	100.0	105.3	100.0	19.8	100.0	20.9	100.0	10.8	100.0	17.5	100.0
2. Donations												
National party	1.0	3.0	5.7	8.7	5.9	38.4	0.3	3.5	2.9	15.3	1.9	26.0
Länder organisations/ Districts	2.6	7.6	10.6	16.3	–*	–*	0.8	8.1	4.0	20.6	2.2	28.7
Local branches	30.2	89.4	49.0	75.0	9.4	61.6	8.9	88.4	12.3	64.1	3.4	45.3
Total	33.7	100.0	65.3	100.0	15.3	100.0	10.1	100.0	19.3	100.0	7.5	100.0
3. State funding												
National party	61.6	65.5	51.8	67.6	18.9	100.0	13.9	82.2	11.6	87.0	12.7	87.4
Länder organisations/ Districts	32.4	34.5	24.8	32.4	–*	–*	3.0	17.8	1.7	13.0	1.8	12.6
Total	93.9	100.0	76.6	100.0	18.9	100.0	17.0	100.0	13.4	100.0	14.5	100.0

Note: The CSU has two rather than three main organisational levels

Sources: Deutscher Bundestag, *Bekanntmachung von Rechenschaftsberichten der politischen Parteien für das Kalenderjahr 1999* (1. Teil – Bundestagsparteien) (Berlin: Bundestag, 2000) Drs. 14/5050).

and Mair claim that modern 'cartel parties' increasingly become part of the state and seek to secure their existence through state funding and patronage rather than membership resources.[77] This is supported also by Panebianco's assertion regarding the emergence of electoral-professional parties.[78]

Table 7 confirms that the local branches and regional organisations on the one hand, and the national party organisations on the other, are funded in different ways. In 1999, for example, the SPD national party executive received only 16.2 per cent of the 157.5 million DM in membership dues and 3.0 per cent of the 33.7 million DM in donations made to the party. Main recipients of membership dues and donations are the regional organisations and local branches. By contrast, the national party headquarters receives nearly two-thirds of its 93.9 million DM income in state subsidies. The other main parties (with the exception of the CSU as a regional party) demonstrate similar patterns. Although the national party organisations are not completely independent of financial resources and voluntary work provided by its grass-roots organisations, there is evidence for a certain degree of independence.

Based on a careful empirical investigation of party organisations in East Germany, Grabow concludes that the organisation of the two major parties in the Eastern German federal states exhibit very strong elements of electoral-professional parties.[79] Unlike most other studies on the impact of unification on the German party system, Grabow focuses on the CDU and SPD rather than the PDS. He argues that due to local constraints, especially the lack of large, traditional membership parties, the CDU and SPD organisations in the East are far more advanced in adopting the electoral-professional party model than their Western counterparts and that, if anything, the experience in the East will eventually influence party development in the Western part of the Republic. The importance of candidates and their personalities as central electoral 'resource' is much higher in the East than in the West. Within the Eastern German parties, members of the various parliaments and government members enjoy more influence than their colleagues in the West. The differences are so strong that Grabow speaks of a 'different type of organisation' in the East, despite national institutional frameworks and party laws applying to both Eastern and Western German party organisations.[80] Despite continuously declining memberships, the Western German CDU and SPD organisations still have a mass membership, and still seek to extend their membership or stop the decline. Especially in the Eastern German SPD, all attempts to build up a comparable membership and organisational structure in the East have failed. Although there are grassroots organisations and sub-organisational structures, they are considerably weaker, and there is a stronger dominance of incumbents and candidates.

The professionalisation of electoral campaigns, that is, the primary reliance on candidates, mass media and professional consultants rather than members, has gone further in the East than in the West.[81] It is true, as von Beyme maintains, that these developments had begun much earlier in the West of the Federal Republic.[82] However, the lack of a membership base in the East and the low institutionalisation especially of the SPD meant that it was easier, indeed it was a necessity, to rely less on members and more on the organisational elements typical of a modern electoral-professional party.

CONCLUSIONS

The evidence presented here provides a mixed picture of persistence and change in the German party system since unification. The adaptability of the political parties (including the PDS) and their ability to use their agenda-setting powers enabled them to preserve their position despite considerable political and socio-economic change. Nevertheless, there has been significant change, especially with regard to the parameters of electoral competition (that is, partisan dealignment and growing volatility) and party organisation (that is, strengthening of organisational characteristics associated with the model of electoral-professional parties and loosely coupled anarchies). The changes at the governmental level have been more modest and largely confined to the Eastern German federal states including Berlin. There is little evidence for a significant ideological polarisation of party competition, and the main parties have continued to produce stable and ideologically moderate governments. The moderating pivotal position of the FDP has been eroded at the national level since 1983 and, since unification, in the Eastern German federal states. Yet it would be premature to assume that this development could not be reversed.

The four interpretations sketched above vary in their empirical accuracy. Ten years after German unification, the initial fear of a significant re-fractionalisation and re-polarisation of the German party system, of the ascendancy of significant extremist parties on the left and right of the party spectrum and of the return of 'Weimar circumstances' (the first scenario) have not come true. Some short-term electoral successes (not only, but also) in Eastern Germany notwithstanding, the extreme right has not become a significant political factor in the East, despite the socio-economic, cultural and political frictions associated with unification. The PDS, the successor organisation of the former SED, has challenged the established parties from the left, but has moderated its stance and has become an acceptable coalition partner for the SPD at the federal-state level. Nevertheless, the electoral and organisational environment within which parties operate in Eastern Germany is characterised by a higher degree of volatility and uncertainty than in the West in the two decades between 1961 and 1983.

The scenario of polarisation and blockage has therefore lost credibility since the mid-1990s. Similarly, the evidence presented in this contribution does not support the scenario of a complete institutional transfer of the West German party system to the East. The PDS has not disappeared. After a period of contraction, it has adapted itself to the new electoral environment and has developed into a significant regional party of the East. However, it has not managed to establish itself as a credible electoral alternative in the West of the Federal Republic, despite some modest gains in some urban areas (for example, the west of Berlin).

Apart from the persistence of the PDS in Eastern Germany, the East German party system seems to reflect the West German one: CDU, FDP,

Greens and SPD have established their organisations in the East. The CDU and FDP could rely on some organisational resources of former 'block parties', the Greens and SPD had to start from scratch. Superficially, therefore, one could still argue there has been a 'near-complete' transfer. Yet, the dynamics of the party system in East and West are very different. Electoral volatility is higher in the East. The electoral parameters of party competition, therefore, are more uncertain. The PDS is a significant electoral and political factor in the East, leading to an East German party system where CDU, PDS and SPD are the major parties and the SPD frequently finds itself in a pivotal role between the two other major parties.

In the West, by contrast, the competitive dynamics of the party system resemble more a two-block system, a centre-left block consisting of SPD and Greens and a centre-right block consisting of CDU/CSU and FDP. Although the FDP has lost its pivotal role in the 1998 elections, only the future will tell whether it will be able to recapture this position in the longer term.

The role of the PDS at the national level will depend on its ability to recover from the electoral disaster of the 2002 Bundestag election. It could become a part of the centre-left block; it could disappear permanently from the Bundestag as a result of the five per cent threshold of Germany's electoral law and the reduction of the size of the Bundestag in 1998 making it harder to win three direct mandates and to benefit from the 'three-mandates waiver'.[83] In sum, therefore, the interpretation of a regionally differentiated transfer of the West German party system seems to be the most accurate description of the developments in the first decade after unification.

The fourth interpretation focuses on 'party-as-organisation'. Although this dimension seems to capture properties of individual parties rather than the party system, the dynamics of inter-party competition depend to some extent on the parties' ability to mobilise resources through their organisations. Therefore, it is worth referring to changes in 'party-as-organisation' in an article that is mainly concerned with the party system. Are the East German regional party organisations, the CDU and SPD organisations in particular, models for a new type of party organisation, which Panebianco[84] has described as electoral-professional parties? The West German organisations of CDU, CSU and SPD – highly institutionalised in Panebianco's sense[85] – have slowly moved towards such a model since the 1970s, but still seek to maintain a large membership base which is often at odds with the need of party leaderships to react swiftly to a more uncertain electoral environment. The result has been an 'anarchic' and sometimes conflictive coexistence of an increasingly professionalised leadership on the one hand and the membership base on the other. There is some empirical evidence to suggest that the Eastern German party organisations of CDU and

SPD, lacking the large membership base and institutionalisation of their West German sister organisations, have gone further in creating electoral-professional organisations dominated by the parliamentary parties, party leaders and small, professional campaign units. To what extent this will accelerate a process of adaptation in the West of the Federal Republic, that is, to what extent there will be a transfer from East to West, remains to be seen.

NOTES

1. K. Strøm, 'Parties at the Core of Government', in R.J. Dalton and M.P. Wattenberg (eds.), *Parties without Partisans: Political Change in Advanced Industrial Democracies* (Oxford: Oxford University Press, 2000), p.180.
2. P.J. Katzenstein, *Policy and Politics in West Germany: The Growth of a Semisovereign State* (Philadelphia: Temple University Press, 1987), pp.35 and 44.
3. A.B. Gunlicks, 'Campaign and Party Finance in the German "Party State"', *Review of Politics*, 50/1 (1988), pp.30–48; K.-H. Naßmacher, 'Parteienfinanzierung in Deutschland', in Oscar W. Gabriel, Oskar Niedermayer and Richard Stöss (eds.), *Parteiendemokratie in Deutschland* (Opladen: Westdeutscher Verlag, 1997), pp.157–76; T. Saalfeld, 'Court and Parties: Evolution and Problems of Political Funding in Germany', in Robert Williams (ed.), *Party Finance and Political Corruption* (Basingstoke: Macmillan, 2000), pp.89–122.
4. S.M. Lipset and S. Rokkan, 'Cleavage Structures, Party Systems and Voter Alignments: an Introduction', in Seymour Martin Lipset and Stein Rokkan (eds.), *Party Systems and Voter Alignments* (New York: Free Press, 1967), p.50.
5. P. Mair, *Party System Change: Approaches and Interpretations* (Oxford: Oxford University Press, 1997), p.3.
6. Ibid., pp.10–13.
7. Dalton and Wattenberg (eds.), *Parties without Partisans*; R. Inglehart, *Modernization and Postmodernization: Cultural, Economic and Political Change in 43 Societies* (Princeton, NJ: Princeton University Press, 1997).
8. Forschungsgruppe Wahlen e.V. (Thomas Emmert, Matthias Jung and Dieter Roth), 'Das Ende einer Ära – Die Bundestagswahl vom 27. September 1998', in Hans-Dieter Klingemann and Max Kaase (eds.), *Wahlen und Wähler: Analysen aus Anlass der Bundestagswahl 1998* (Wiesbaden: Westdeutscher Verlag, 2001), p.18.
9. P. Moreau, *Die PDS: Anatomie einer postkommunistischen Partei* (Bonn: Bouvier, 1992); see also U. Backes and E. Jesse, *Politischer Extremismus in der Bundesrepublik Deutschland* (Berlin: Propyläen, 1993), p.41.
10. D. Hough, *The Fall and Rise of the PDS in Eastern Germany* (Birmingham: University of Birmingham Press, 2001), p.23.
11. S. Koch-Baumgarten, 'Postkommunisten im Spagat: Zur Funktion der PDS im Parteiensystem', *Deutschland Archiv*, 30/6 (1997), p.873.
12. G. Sartori, *Parties and Party Systems: A Framework for Analysis* (Cambridge: Cambridge University Press, 1976).
13. E. Holtmann, 'Weimarer Verhältnisse von Osten her?' in E. Holtmann and H. Sahner (eds.), *Aufhebung der Bipolarität* (Opladen: Leske und Budrich, 1995), p.83.
14. H.-J. Veen, 'Zwischen Rekonzentration und neuer Diversifizierung: Tendenzen der Parteienentwicklung fünf Jahre nach der deutschen Einheit', in Winand Gellner and Hans-Joachim Veen (eds.), *Umbruch und Wandel in westeuropäischen Parteiensystemen* (Frankfurt am Main: Lang, 1995), p.117.
15. R.-O. Schultze, 'Widersprüchliches, Ungleichzeitiges und kein Ende in Sicht: Die Bundestagswahl vom 16. Oktober 1994', *Zeitschrift für Parlamentsfragen*, 26/2 (1995), p.344.
16. H.-G. Betz and H.A. Welsh, 'The PDS in the New German Party System', *German Politics*, 4/3 (1995), p.92; see also E. Jesse, 'Die Landtagswahl in Sachsen vom 19. September 1999:

Triumphale Bestätigung der CDU', *Zeitschrift für Parlamentsfragen*, 31/1 (2000), p.76.

17. G. Neugebauer, 'Hat die PDS bundesweit im Parteiensystem eine Chance?' in M. Brie, M. Herzig and T. Koch (eds.), *Die PDS – empirische Befunde und kontroverse Analysen* (Köln: Papyrossa, 1995), p.51.
18. For a more detailed review of the evidence see Hough, *The Fall and Rise of the PDS in Eastern Germany*, pp.13–20 and 31–34.
19. Oskar Niedermayer, 'Das gesamtdeutsche Parteiensystem', in Oscar W. Gabriel, Oskar Neidermayer and Richard Stöss (eds.), *Parteindemokratie in Deutschland* (Opladen: Westdeutscher Verlag, 1997), pp.129–30.
20. Hough, *The Fall and Rise of the PDS in Eastern Germany*.
21. Koch-Baumgarten, 'Postkommunisten im Spagat', p.872.
22. Hough, *The Fall and Rise of the PDS in Eastern Germany*, p.35.
23. K. Grabow, *Abschied von der Massenpartei: Die Entwicklung der Organisationsmuster von SPD und CDU seit der deutschen Vereinigung* (Wiesbaden: Deutscher Universitäts-Verlag, 2000).
24. A. Panebianco, *Political Parties: Organization and Power* (Cambridge: Cambridge University Press, 1988).
25. M.G. Schmidt, 'Germany: The Grand Coalition State', in J.M. Colomer (ed.), *Political Institutions in Europe* (London: Routledge, 1996).
26. Sartori, *Parties and Party Systems*, p.44.
27. V.O. Key, *Politics, Parties, and Pressure Groups* (New York: Crowell, 5th edn. 1964).
28. Alan Ware, *Political Parties and Party Systems* (Oxford: Oxford University Press, 1996), pp.6–7.
29. I am drawing on the summary by R.J. Dalton and M.P. Wattenberg, 'Unthinkable Democracy: Political Change in Advanced Industrial Democracies', in Dalton and Wattenberg (eds.), *Parties without Partisans*, p.5.
30. Cf. Michael T. Hannan and John Freeman, 'The Population Ecology of Organizations', *American Journal of Sociology*, 82/5 (1977), pp.929–64.
31. Cf. Mair, *Party System Change*.
32. Cf. the case study by J. Schmid, *Die CDU: Organisationsstrukturen, Politiken und Funktionsweisen einer Partei im Föderalismus* (Opladen: Leske + Budrich, 1990).
33. K. von Beyme, *Parteien im Wandel: Von den Volksparteien zu den professionalisierten Wählerparteien* (Wiesbaden: Westdeutscher Verlag, 2000); R.S. Katz and P. Mair, 'Changing Models of Party Organization and Party Democracy: The Emergence of the Cartel Party', *Party Politics*, 1/1 (1995); T. Poguntke, *Parteiorganisation im Wandel: Gesellschaftliche Verankerung und organisatorische Anpassung im europäischen Vergleich* (Wiesbaden: Westdeutscher Verlag, 2000).
34. *Political Parties*, pp.262–9.
35. M. Duverger, *Political Parties: Their Organization and Activities in the Modern State* (New York: Wiley, 1954).
36. Katz and Mair, 'Changing Models of Party Organization and Party Democracy'.
37. O. Kirchheimer, 'The Transformation of West European Party Systems', in Joseph LaPalombara and Myron Weiner (eds.), *Political Parties and Political Development* (Princeton, NJ: Princeton University Press, 1966), pp.177–200.
38. The German 'Volkspartei' (people's party) model has been a hybrid of both mass-bureaucratic party and catch-all party. It adopted elements of the catch-all party but continued to seek to expand their mass membership like traditional mass-bureaucratic parties, cf. Grabow, *Abschied von der Massenpartei*, p.24.
39. Panebianco, *Political Parties*.
40. Ibid., p.264.
41. Ibid., p.265.
42. Poguntke, *Parteiorganisation im Wandel*.
43. Grabow, *Abschied von der Massenpartei*.
44. Ibid., pp.25–31; Katz and Mair, 'Changing Models of Party Organization and Party Democracy'.
45. Sartori, *Parties and Party Systems*.

46. T. Saalfeld, 'Germany: Stable Parties, Chancellor Democracy, and the Art of Informal Settlement', in Wolfgang C. Müller and Kaare Strøm (eds.), *Coalition Governments in Western Europe* (Oxford: Oxford University Press, 2000), pp.32–85.

47. The calculation of the effective number of parties (N) is straightforward: $N = 1/\Sigma s_i 2$, where s represents the proportion of seats if the i-th party. If we assume there are two parties, one with 45% of the seats one with 55% of the seats, $N = 1/(0.45^2 + 0.55^2) = 1/(0.20 + 0.30) = 1/0.50 = 2.0$. In this example, the effective number of parties is (almost) exactly 2. If there were three parties with 45% of the seats, 50% of the seats and 5% of the seats in a parliament, N would be 2.20. See M. Laakso and R. Taagepera, 'Effective Number of Parties: A Measure with Applications to Western Europe', *Comparative Political Studies*, 12 (1979), pp.3–27.

48. See Saalfeld, 'Germany', pp.32–5.

49. I. Budge *et al.*, *Mapping Policy Preferences: Estimates for Parties, Electors, and Governments 1945–1998* (Oxford: Oxford University Press, 2001).

50. F.W. Scharpf, *Games Real Actors Play: Actor-Centered Institutionalism in Policy Research* (Boulder, CO: Westview, 1997).

51. M. Laver and N. Schofield, *Multiparty Government: The Politics of Coalition in Europe* (Oxford: Oxford University Press, 1990), p.111.

52. B. Hombach, *The Politics of the New Centre* (Cambridge: Polity, 2000).

53. Cf. F.U. Pappi, 'The West German Party System', *West European Politics*, 7/1 (1984), pp.7–26; Inglehart, *Modernization and Postmodernization*, p.245; Grabow, *Abschied von der Massenpartei*.

54. Cf. Scharpf, *Games Real Actors Play*, pp.128–30.

55. R.J. Dalton, 'The Decline of Party Identifications', in Dalton and Wattenberg (eds.), *Parties without Partisans*, pp.19–36.

56. Forschungsgruppe Wahlen, 'Das Ende einer Ära'.

57. Thorsten Faas and Andreas Wüst, 'The Schill Factor in the Hamburg State Election 2001', *German Politics*, 11/2 (2002), pp.1–20.

58. M. Pedersen, 'The Dynamics of European Party Systems', *European Journal of Political Research*, 7 (1979), pp.1–26.

59. The aggregate volatility ('Pedersen Index') is calculated as follows: $V_t = TNC_t/2$, where Vt is the aggregate volatility at time t and TNC_t is the total net change of the votes all parties have received in the election at time t. $TNC_t = \Sigma|\Delta p_{i,t}|$ and $\Delta p_{i,t} = p_{i,t} - p_{i,t-1}$, where pi,t is the percentage of the vote (or seats) obtained by party p_i in the elections at time t, and $p_{i,t-1}$ is the percentage of the vote (or seats) obtained by party pi in the previous elections (time t-1). $0 = V_t = 100$. For example, let us assume there are two parties: Party 1 obtained 45% of the vote in the elections at time t compared to 40% of the vote in the elections at time t-1; Party 2 obtained 35% of the vote in the elections at time t compared to 50% in the elections at time t-1. Hence, $\Delta p_{1,t} = p_{1,t} - p_{1,t-1} = 5$; $\Delta p_{2,t} = p_{2,t} - p_{2,t-1} = -15$; $TNC_t = \Sigma|\Delta p_{i,t}| = \Sigma|5-15| = 5+15 = 20$; $V_t = TNC_t/2 = 20/2 = 10$.

60. H. Schoen and J.W. Falter, '"It's time for a change! – Wechselwähler bei der Bundestagswahl 1998', in Klingemann and Kaase (eds.), *Wahlen und Wähler*, pp.57-90.

61. Cf. generally C. Mershon, *The Costs of Coalition* (Stanford, CA: Stanford University Press, 2002).

62. Schmidt, 'Germany: The Grand Coalition State'.

63. Cf. A. Lupia and K. Strøm, 'Coalition Termination and the Strategic Timing of Parliamentary Elections', *American Political Science Review*, 89/3 (1995), pp.648–65; C. Mershon, 'The Costs of Coalition: A Five-Nation Comparison', in Shaun Bowler, David M. Farrell and Richard S. Katz (eds.), *Party Discipline and Parliamentary Government* (Columbus: Ohio State University Press, 1999), pp.227–68.

64. G. Sartori, *The Theory of Democracy Revisited. Part One: The Contemporary Debate* (Chatham, NJ: Chatham House, 1987), pp.214–56; Scharpf, *Games Real Actors Play*.

65. Niedermayer, 'Das Gesamtdeutsche Parteiensystem', pp.109–10.

66. Ibid., pp.110–11.

67. Ibid., p.111.

68. Hough, *The Fall and Rise of the PDS in Eastern Germany*, pp.13–20, 31–4.

69. Sartori, *The Theory of Democracy Revisited*.

70. R. Sturm, 'Vorbilder für eine Bundesratsreform? Lehren aus den Erfahrungen der Verfassungspraxis Zweiter Kammern', *Zeitschrift für Parlamentsfragen*, 33/1 (2002), p.170.
71. T. Poguntke, 'Parties in a Legalistic Culture: The Case of Germany', in Richard S. Katz and Peter Mair (eds.), *How Parties Organize: Change and Adaptation in Party Organizations in Western Democracies* (London: SAGE, 1994), p.210.
72. Poguntke, 'Parties in a Legalistic Culture', pp.211–12.
73. S.E. Scarrow, 'Parties without Members? Party Organization in a Changing Electoral Environment', in Dalton and Wattenberg (eds.), *Parties without Partisans*, p.89.
74. Ibid., pp.90 and 96.
75. E. Wiesendahl, 'Changing Party Organisations in Germany: How to Deal with Uncertainty and Organised Anarchy', in Stephen Padgett and Thomas Saalfeld (eds.), *Bundestagswahl '98: End of an Era?* (London: Cass, 2000), pp.119–20 (verbatim quote p.120).
76. D.M. Farrell and P. Webb, 'Political Parties as Campaign Organizations', in Dalton and Wattenberg (eds.), *Parties without Partisans*, p.117.
77. Katz and Mair (eds.), *How Parties Organize*.
78. Panebianco, *Political Parties*.
79. Grabow, *Abschied von der Massenpartei*.
80. Ibid., p.293.
81. Ibid., pp.295–6.
82. Ibid.
83. According to the Electoral Law, a party must achieve 5% of the national vote to be represented in the Bundestag. This rule is to be waived, if the party gains three direct (constituency) mandates in Germany's additional-member system. In the 1990 and 1994 elections, the PDS failed to overcome the 5% threshold but achieved proportional representation because it had won three direct mandates.
84. Panebianco, *Political Parties*.
85. Ibid.

The Impact of Unification on German Federalism

ARTHUR B. GUNLICKS

Paraphrasing the medieval custom regarding kings, some students of Germany today are tempted to cry, 'The Republic is dead. Long live the Republic!' Whether the Bonn Republic is really 'dead' and has been replaced by the Berlin Republic is, in fact, not all that clear. Evidence exists both for and against the thesis. With respect to German federalism, a case can certainly be made that there have been a rather large number of changes since unification in October 1990 and that many if not most of these are due at least in part to the impact of unification. Whether these constitute a new federal system or merely some adjustments – some of which are rather significant – remains to be seen. The purpose of this paper is to review briefly some of the most important changes in the German federal system and to provide an analysis of their effects.

The changes are divided into several categories. First, some of the obvious territorial changes are outlined. Second, a number of constitutional changes at both the federal and Land levels are considered. Third, the strengthened role of the Länder in European-level policy is described. Fourth, the perennial topic of fiscal federalism is discussed. Fifth, we look at the related perennial topic of boundary changes and consolidation of the Länder. Finally, the changing party system in the Länder and the growing discussion about direct democracy are analysed.

TERRITORIAL CHANGES

From the time Baden-Württemberg was created in 1952 until 1990, the Federal Republic of Germany (West Germany) was composed of eight 'territorial Länder', two city-states and West Berlin, which legally was under Allied occupation but for most practical purposes was another city-state in the Federal Republic. The German Democratic Republic created its own five Länder between December 1946 and early 1947. However, they were replaced by 15 districts, including East Berlin, in July 1952, in conformity with the highly centralised reality of the East German communist regime. Shortly after the Wall came down, it became clear that

Arthur B. Gunlicks, University of Richmond

East Germany would be united with West Germany, and that unification would be with five reconstituted Länder, not with the old GDR. The most obvious change in German federalism since unification, then, has been the accession of five new Länder, the unification of West and East Berlin, and an increase in the number of Länder in Germany from 11 to 16.[1]

The 16 Länder are as diverse in size and population as before. The five new Länder are of medium size geographically and of small-to-medium size in population. There is no new Land, therefore, that can match the 'big four' in Western Germany: North-Rhine Westphalia, Bavaria, Baden-Württemberg, and Lower Saxony. Indeed, North-Rhine Westphalia has as large a population (c. 17 million) as all of the old GDR. Because these large Länder were concerned about being outvoted by a coalition of the small-to-medium-sized Länder, they pushed through a constitutional change that gives them six rather than five votes in the Bundesrat, a second chamber which is not officially an 'upper house' of parliament but rather a unique special non-elective chamber (*Länderkammer*) representing the Land governments (cabinets). It has an absolute veto right over measures passed by the Bundestag that affect the Länder in some way, which is about 50–60 per cent of all bills passed, and a suspensive veto over the remaining bills. As a result of the increase in the number of Länder, the votes in the Bundesrat were increased to 69 from 41 (West Berlin had four votes, but they could be cast only in committees). Since constitutional changes require a two-thirds majority in the Bundestag and Bundesrat, the 24 votes of the four large Länder protect them from any attempt on the part of the smaller Länder to 'gang up' on them. Nevertheless, the five new Länder, with about 18 per cent of the population of Germany, have about 28 per cent of the votes; with Berlin they have almost 22 per cent of the population and 33 per cent of the votes. This over-representation has helped the Eastern Länder in the Bundesrat, but the old balance in West Germany between two large Länder in the North and two in the South is not matched by at least one in the East.

CONSTITUTIONAL CHANGES

The Federal Level

Constitutional changes began early in the unification process. In August 1990, the two German governments signed the Unification Treaty, which served as the domestic basis of German unification on 3 October 1990. East Germany agreed to join the Federal Republic according to Article 23 of its constitution, the Basic Law, which permitted 'other parts of Germany' to accede to the Federal Republic (as the Saarland had done in the 1950s). This accession procedure for the five new Länder was much quicker and easier than the process under Article 146 of the Basic Law, which called for a new constitution approved by a united Germany. This, of course, was a major reason for selecting Article 23, even though it led to considerable criticism by those who felt unification lacked the legitimacy it would have enjoyed under Article 146. The Unification Treaty provided for the abolition of Article 23 after accession. It was also this Treaty that initially changed the votes in the Bundesrat from five to six for the 'big four' Länder.[2]

Another provision of the Treaty 'recommends' to the Bundestag and Bundesrat that they consider various constitutional changes 'with respect to the relationship between the federation and the Länder'. As noted above, the Treaty repealed Article 23 and added one vote to each delegation of the 'big four' in the Bundesrat. It also changed the Preamble of the Basic Law by adding the five new Länder and by stating that the Basic Law now applies to all Germans, and it revised slightly Article 146, which allows the writing of a new constitution by the people in united Germany.

In March 1991 the Bundesrat formed a Commission on Constitutional Reform, and the Bundestag began debating constitutional issues in May while crafting provisions of the Unification Treaty. These debates revealed differences between the CDU/CSU-FDP governing parties and the SPD and Green opposition and revealed the view of the government that only minor changes were called for, in contrast to the intent of the opposition to engage in a more thoroughgoing review of the Basic Law. The SPD's demand for a referendum was rejected by the government parties. Finally, a Joint Constitutional Commission, composed of 32 members each from the Bundestag and Bundesrat, was formed in January 1992. It considered recommendations made by the Bundesrat and proposals by other bodies and individuals, and it held a number of public hearings. It considered 80 proposals for changing the Basic Law and looked at about half of the Basic Law's articles in the process.[3]

It was clear that federalism would be an issue in the debates on constitutional change, at least among the political elites, because there was a long-standing concern expressed by many experts and Land politicians about the decline of power or competences of the Länder vis-à-vis the federation.[4] These concerns focused on the financing of the federal system, on federal preemptions and unfunded mandates, on the growing list of 'concurrent powers' assumed by the federation, and detailed federal regulations based on the framework laws. These developments have affected especially the Land parliaments, reducing their already limited powers. In order to strengthen the Länder, the Joint Constitutional Commission recommended a number of changes that were taken up by the Bundestag in the spring and summer of 1994.

A number of changes were finally made to the Basic Law, but some of them were rather subtle and esoteric, and, overall, modest in their impact. Article 72, which deals with concurrent powers, was revised to make it more restrictive, making the federation demonstrate that taking over a concurrent power was 'essential' or 'required' and not just because it perceived a 'need' to do so. The much misunderstood phrase concerning the goal of securing 'uniform living conditions' throughout the country was also changed to achieving 'equivalent living conditions'. 'Equivalency' from Land to Land is more easily achieved than 'uniformity', especially when considering the large gap between the five new Länder and those in the West. A third paragraph was also introduced which makes it possible for a federally pre-empted concurrent power to be returned to the Länder if there is no longer a 'requirement' for federal action.

Article 75, which deals with framework legislation aimed directly at the Land legislatures for further action on the details, was also revised somewhat to prohibit the Bundestag from going into too much detail itself without demonstrating that it is 'essential' to do so. Some other rather minor changes were made in addition, including the transfer of the regulation of films (movies) from framework legislation to the Länder.[5]

Some relatively minor changes were made regarding the legislative process involving the Bundesrat, but more important was the revision of Article 24, which now grants the Länder the right to transfer, with federal approval, certain 'sovereign powers to trans-frontier institutions in neighbouring regions'. In the meantime, many such institutions have been created between border Länder and neighbouring countries or regions, for example, the 'Arge Alp' consisting of German, Swiss, Austrian and Italian Alpine regions.

Constitutions in the Länder[6]

For almost 40 years after the Basic Law went into effect, little attention was paid to Land constitutions. Amendments were made on numerous occasions, but these were almost always minor changes or technical corrections and aroused little controversy. At the end of the 1980s and the beginning of the1990s, this changed dramatically for two major reasons. A scandal in Schleswig-Holstein in 1987 involving allegations that the Prime Minister had been guilty of a serious abuse of power during an election campaign led to a thorough revision of that Land's constitution which included both far-reaching plebiscitary (direct democracy) features and provisions strengthening the parliament's control over the government (cabinet). The reforms contained in this constitution have since had a significant impact not only on the new Länder but also on several Länder in the West.

The second reason for the strong interest in Land constitutions was the re-emergence of the five new Länder and unification. The result was a third generation of Land constitutions following the first generation before the Basic Law went into effect in 1949 and the second generation which followed in the early 1950s. The Schleswig-Holstein constitution of 1990 became the inspiration for the five new Länder in the East, and their constitutions, in turn, encouraged several of the old Länder to revise their constitutions and to incorporate innovative 'modern' ideas.

The federal Basic Law, like the American Constitution, provides for a representative republic. In contrast, most of the Länder (excluding the British-occupied Hamburg, Schleswig-Holstein and Lower Saxony) provided from the beginning for some form of popular initiative and referendum. In 1990, Schleswig-Holstein incorporated the most far-reaching plebiscitary features of any 'old' constitution, and by 1997 all of the Länder had constitutional provisions for initiatives and referenda.

Direct democracy, as we shall see below, has become a vigorously discussed issue in Germany since unification. The political left failed in its efforts to introduce it into the Basic Law in 1993 and 1994, but they were successful in the new Länder and in several of the old ones. By 1990 all of the older Länder except Hamburg had provisions for some form of direct democracy at the Land level, but they were used only rarely, in part because of high signature requirements. Most of the Länder had no provisions for direct democracy at the local level; however, during the 1990s not only was direct democracy introduced in all of the Länder, but the direct election of mayors also replaced professional city managers and council-appointed ceremonial mayors in Lower Saxony and North-Rhine Westphalia, which had the old British-inspired council-manager form of government. Today, the directly elected mayor characteristic of the South German form of local government prevails throughout Germany.[7]

Another significant change brought about by unification and new constitutions in the East concerns the old, classic, basic rights and new, 'modern', social rights. The first are contained in the Basic Law, and, as a result, some of the Länder have not repeated them in their constitutions. On the other hand, the Länder are not prohibited from adding rights. The new constitutions or amendments to older constitutions have, therefore, often added rights concerning the environment and data protection, which in the meantime are also covered by the Basic Law or federal statutes. Brandenburg, however, included in its provisions on the environment certain statements that could be in conflict with federal authority, and Brandenburg and Thuringia have equality provisions regarding those who have a different 'sexual identity' or 'sexual orientation'. (In the meantime a federal law has been passed which legalises homosexual partnerships.)

Some constitutions also protect animals against inhumane treatment (now also a provision added to the Basic Law in the summer of 2002), and Brandenburg even mentions plants as worthy of respect. Art, science, research and teaching are mentioned in all of the new constitutions as objects of protection, and art and culture as well as sport are supposed to be promoted by public funds. Some of these provisions have been attacked as being in potential conflict with the Basic Law, for example, the Brandenburg constitution's restrictions on research 'that is injurious to human dignity' or 'destructive of the natural foundations of life', implying a ban on gene technology and nuclear research.

Even more controversial have been the provisions concerning social rights and state goals. Both can be found in the Basic Law and in constitutions of the old Länder, but their inclusion in the Eastern constitutions has raised new questions. Social rights include the right to employment; the right to unemployment compensation; the right to worker protection; the right to education and training; the right to public support in case of illness, old age, or emergency; the right to social security; and the right to housing. Some combination of these rights can be found in all of the new constitutions and are often expressed as 'state goals'. They are not generally enforceable in a court of law as the classical rights are, and they have been criticised for raising expectations that cannot be met and for interfering with the responsibilities of elected parliaments.

THE LÄNDER AND EUROPEAN INTEGRATION

European integration has been supported since the early 1950s by both the federal government and the Länder. Nevertheless, the Länder have often been frustrated by the loss of powers and influence they have suffered in the process of European integration. Some transfer of sovereignty must take place by definition in forming a more integrated Europe. But whereas the federal government has been a participant in negotiating such transfers and has voluntarily agreed to them, the Länder have had little to say. Transfers of Länder powers to the EU have been facilitated by Article 24 of the Basic Law, which authorises the federal government to transfer not only federal but also Land powers to the EU without Land participation.[8] In addition, certain Land powers have been pre-empted by the EU as a result of Article 235 (now Article 308) of the EEC Treaty, which serves as a kind of enabling or implied powers clause or by referring to other articles which also provide the EU with a basis for action.[9]

Over the years since the inception of the institutions of the EC/EU, the Länder have made varying attempts to gain more influence over transfers of their autonomous powers and over the policy-making process that affects their interests. These efforts had modest success at best until the ratification of the Single European Act (SEA) in 1986. At that time, the federal government was forced by the Bundesrat to consult that body before approving any decisions of the EC Council of Ministers which wholly or partially affected the exclusive legislative powers of the Länder or their essential interests. Furthermore, the federal government could deviate from this position only for compelling reasons and, upon the demand of the Bundesrat, engage as far as possible representatives of the Länder in relevant negotiations.[10]

The Maastricht Treaty, or Treaty on European Union (TEU), represents a new stage in the process of European integration. It was designed not only to adapt the EC to a new Europe following the events of 1989, but also to integrate further and bind the larger, united Germany to Europe ('a European Germany, not a German Europe'). Given the various rights of information and participation which the Länder had gained since the SEA, they were well prepared for the challenge of Maastricht.

The federal government permitted the Länder to participate in the internal preparations and intergovernmental conferences (IGC) on the Maastricht treaties. Delegates from Baden-Württemberg and North-Rhine Westphalia represented the Länder in IGC meetings on the EU, and representatives from Bavaria and Hamburg participated in similar meetings on European Economic and Monetary Union. Parallel to these conferences, the Bundesrat created a Europe Commission in which all 16 Länder and the federal government participated.[11]

In the process that followed, the Länder were able to achieve many of their goals. The principle of subsidiarity was accepted, although not all member states agree on what that means in practice. The hope of the Land prime ministers that a clear division of powers would be drawn between three levels in the EU (EU level, member state and region) was not met. The regions were given more status through the creation of the Committee of the Regions; on the other hand, like the Economic and Social Committee, it was given only consultative powers, and it has become a body more representing large cities than regions like the German Länder.[12] A third victory for the Länder was gaining the authorisation according to which subnational (in this case, Land) cabinet ministers may represent their member state in the Council of Ministers when their autonomous rights are affected.[13]

In the discussion of constitutional changes above, it was noted that the old Article 23, which had been used by the five new Länder to accede to the Federal Republic and was now obsolete, was eliminated. It was replaced by a new Article 23 focusing on Europe. Article 23 and some other changes concerning Europe, including a new paragraph for Article 24, were approved by the Bundestag and Bundesrat at the same time they ratified the

TEU in December 1992 (however, due to a challenge made before the Federal Constitutional Court, ratification did not go into effect until November 1993, after the Court approved the German ratification of the TEU).

The new Article 23 and the laws that have been passed pursuant to it replace the various agreements that were made in the past between the Länder and the federal government concerning Länder rights in the integration process.[14] The first paragraph of Article 23 suggests that the EU will preserve the principles of federalism and subsidiarity, and it binds future transfers of sovereignty to the consent of the Bundesrat. It provides for a comprehensive exchange of information concerning the EU between the federal government and the Bundestag and Bundesrat, and it gives the Bundesrat the opportunity to state its opinion before the federal government participates in the EU legislative process.

The Bundesrat is to have the right to participate in the decision-making process of the federal government. Where the federal government has exclusive power but the interests of the Länder are affected, the federal government is to take into account the opinion of the Bundesrat. Where the autonomous rights of the Länder are affected, the opinion of the Bundesrat shall prevail while keeping in mind the overall responsibility of the federal government. And where the exclusive legislative authority of the Länder is involved, the Federal Republic shall be represented in EU councils by a representative of the Länder sent by the Bundesrat. In this case, the representation shall take place with the participation and agreement of the federal government in order to preserve the interests of the federation.

This last provision can be seen as an exception to the rule that the federal government represents the country as a whole in foreign affairs; on the other hand, the Bundesrat representative must co-operate with the federal government. By 1995 representatives of the Länder nominated by the Bundesrat were participating in about 400 EU committees and other bodies.[15]

It is worth noting that the 'Law Regarding the Cooperation of the Federation and Länder in Matters Concerning the EU of March 1993' provides that a two-thirds majority in the Bundesrat can force the federal government to accept its position in case of conflict on a matter covered by Article 23, paragraph 5, of the Basic Law. This, of course, underlines the view that European policy is no longer foreign policy but a form of domestic politics.[16]

A serious problem for the Bundesrat and Länder in actually being able to take advantage of their new rights concerning the EU is the flood of information that comes from Brussels. The problem is not new, and the Bundesrat has had an 'EC Committee' since the Treaties of Rome to consider proposals for regulations from the EC Commission and proposals to the Council of Ministers sent to the Bundesrat by the federal government. This EC Committee has been very busy, which can be seen by the fact that the Bundesrat considered 6,355 proposals from the EC between 1957 and 1994. The EC Committee has recommended a Bundesrat position for most of these proposals. The numbers exceed the number of domestic bills sent to the Bundesrat by the federal government over the same period of time. The 'flood of paper' has increased since 1989, when it began to reach 70–80 documents each day. These are placed in a computer and sent to all or some of the Länder on demand. Relevant documents are also sent to Bundesrat committees. For proposals in the Council of Ministers that affect the autonomous powers of the Länder, the federal government informs the Länder of the time frame for decision-making in the Council and the Bundesrat secretariat ensures that the appropriate committees hold meetings on the proposals in time to meet the deadlines. All of this requires close co-operation between the federal government and the Bundesrat and the Bundesrat and the Länder, and it demonstrates the demands and complexity involved in Bundesrat participation in matters involving the EU.[17] Having 'chosen a consensual approach in dealings with the Federal Government' throughout the first half of the 1990s, 'there have been no great trials of strength pitting Bundesrat against Federal Government in the exercise of Article 23 powers'.[18]

A relatively new instrument in the Bundesrat is the EC Chamber, authorised in 1988, and called the 'Europe Chamber' since 1992 with the amendment of Article 52, paragraph 3a, of the Basic Law. This Chamber is to decide for the Bundesrat when there are serious time pressures or when confidential material is involved. Each Land has one member or a representative with the same voting rights as in the plenary sessions. So far this chamber has met only three times. The last meeting was in December 1999, when the Chamber majority voted to ask the federal government to oppose an EU environmental proposal that was to be considered in a few days. The federal government voted for the measure anyway 'for reasons of state'. If, however, the Länder had opposed the measure by a two-thirds majority, the federal government would probably have been bound to accept the Chamber's decision.[19]

FISCAL FEDERALISM

It was apparent in Article 7 of the Unification Treaty that financing the routine government services and activities and almost unimaginable needs for infrastructure improvements in the new Länder would be a major challenge for the unified Germany. The provisions in the Basic Law calling for uniformity of living conditions did not help, because whatever the misunderstandings concerning this requirement had been in the past, it was clear that there could be no such thing in the coming years. In the German system of fiscal equalisation, the Länder whose per capita revenues are above average make transfer payments to the Länder with below average revenues.[20] This system of transfer payments has always been controversial, and for decades it has led to tensions between the 'rich' and 'poor' Länder in the West. Although it was clear even before the Wall fell in November 1989 that the system of fiscal equalisation needed reform, a political solution did not seem to be in sight.

With unification, the situation changed dramatically. Unless a temporary separate regulation for the five new Länder could be found, the former West German fiscal equalisation system would be overwhelmed. All of the West German Länder, with the exception of the poorest, Bremen and perhaps the Saarland, would become paying Länder, and they would have to give up their supplementary federal grants. Because this scenario was unacceptable to the old Länder, provisions were made in the Unification Treaty for a special set of arrangements for the new Länder. Various temporary arrangements were made to have the Western Länder share with the federation the expense of helping the East, and by 1991 about $100 billion (at the then prevailing exchange rate) was being transferred. However, given the economic conditions in the East, the heavy burdens on the federation, and the realisation by the old Länder that admitting the new Länder to the West German system of fiscal equalisation would have devastating consequences for them, it became clear that the federal government and the Länder would have to devise a new financing system before 1995, when the new Länder were scheduled to join the equalisation system as regular members.

As a result of these pressures, the finance ministers of the 16 Länder and the federation formed a working group in 1991, which, after hard bargaining, negotiated a compromise package that came to be called the 'Solidarity Pact'. Starting in 1995, the Solidarity Pact provided for annual transfers of DM 56 billion for ten years to the East along with billions in loans for housing, infrastructure, environmental cleanup and business promotion. It also provided DM 40 billion for old debts. A 7.5 per cent 'solidarity surcharge', reduced to 5.5 per cent in 1997, was placed on income taxes throughout Germany to help finance these grants and loans. The five new Länder were included in the horizontal equalisation scheme, in compensation for which the Länder share of VAT revenues was raised from 37 to 44 per cent (changed to 49.5 per cent in 1996). While the Solidarity Pact did cost the old Länder, it was clear at the end that the federation had to bear the greatest burden of financing the new Länder.[21]

The Solidarity Pact did not satisfy everyone. In fact, dissatisfaction with the German system of fiscal federalism grew during the 1990s and carried over to the new century. Many arguments can now be heard about the need for less sharing of the important tax revenues at the federal and Land levels and more autonomy for the Länder to craft their own tax systems; for a less 'co-operative' and a more 'competitive federalism'; for less dependency of the poor Länder on the rich Länder, and so forth. Since unification, the gap between rich and poor Länder has increased significantly, and a massive transfer of funds to the East continues. The result has been to fuel the argument that the eastern Länder have become even more dependent on fiscal transfers than their 'poor' relations in the West. In contrast to the optimistic predictions at the time of unification, it now looks as though the Eastern Länder will lag behind Western Germany for a long time, probably several decades. What effect the continued dependency of the Eastern Länder will have on the German system of fiscal equalisation to secure 'equivalent' living conditions remains to be seen.

In 1998 Bavaria, Baden-Württemberg and Hesse (later joined by North-Rhine Westphalia) formally announced their intention to bring a case before the Federal Constitutional Court to ask it to require a change in the fiscal system that would leave a larger share of revenue in their treasuries and reduce the unconstitutional 'levelling' effects of the system. In November 1999, the Court decided that the system did, indeed, have to be changed in its broad principles by the end of 2002 and in its legislative details by the end of 2004. The Court ruled that German legislators and the Bundesrat must decide just what changes should be made, but it indicated that the regular equalisation payments may not exceed 95 per cent of the average revenues, in contrast to the current 99.5 per cent. Nor may the recipient Länder end up with a higher rank order in their financial capacity than the provider Länder after all transfers have taken place.[22]

In the meantime, a commission consisting of the 16 prime ministers had been formed in December 1998 by the new Chancellor, Gerhard Schröder, with the charge to come up with a recommendation for reforms in the system. One might have thought that the Court's decision in November 1999 would have forced the prime ministers to think of some creative changes, but the deliberations did not lead to a consensus in the commission. By June 2001 it looked as though the prime ministers would not be able to reach an agreement, but on June 23 Chancellor Schröder stepped in to break the Gordian knot by offering to have the federation pay the price for an agreement. The maximum payment the richer Länder now make (80 per cent of above average tax revenues) to the equalisation fund will be reduced to 72.5 per cent, and Länder that enjoy an increase in tax revenues over the previous year will be able to set aside 12.5 per cent before it is counted in the amount owed for the fiscal equalisation transfer. These changes will cost the federation DM 1.5 billion annually, and they will save the Länder between DM 200 and 400 million annually.[23]

In addition, the new Länder will continue to receive heavy subsidies under a new solidarity pact that goes into effect in January 2005 following the expiration of the ten-year pact negotiated in 1993. The federation agreed to pay two-thirds of the DM 306 billion package the East is to receive between 2005 and 2019 in instalments that are to be reduced every year after 2009. This means that the payments in the first years will be considerably higher than the current DM 20.6 billion. In 2020 special aid to the East is supposed to cease for good, but the unpopular solidarity surcharge on German taxpayers will have to continue until then.[24]

BOUNDARY REFORM OF THE 'LÄNDER'

The system of fiscal equalisation in Germany has probably produced more uniform living conditions throughout the country than in any other major European state, including unitary states such as Great Britain and France. Even the new Länder, whose per capita income is about half of the average of the old Länder, are able today to provide a level of services and infrastructure that is not significantly lower than in the Western Länder. This is the obvious strength of the system. But criticism and dissatisfaction are growing, and the demands for change are strong.

It seems apparent that the major problem in the fiscal equalisation system lies in the gap in fiscal capacity between the richer and poorer Länder. With the exception of Lower Saxony, the poorest Länder – Bremen and the Saarland in the West and Berlin and the five new Länder in the East – are the smallest in population. Hamburg is, of course, the exception among the richer Western Länder. One of the arguments against more autonomy for the Länder in their present form is that the small and poor Länder are simply in no position to take advantage of greater fiscal autonomy. If they are to continue to offer reasonably uniform or equivalent living conditions, they must have financial support from the federation and/or their richer counterparts.

Thus, there is really little prospect of granting the Länder real fiscal autonomy. This is precisely why, according to some German critics, Article 29, para.1 of the Basic Law says that the Länder 'can' be consolidated (before 1976, Article 29 read: 'The federal territory is ... to be newly constituted') in order to guarantee that they have the size and capacity to carry out their tasks effectively. Some experts who are opposed to the excessive emphasis on egalitarian levelling through increased centralisation of tax legislation and fiscal transfers argue that if the Länder were to be given more fiscal autonomy, their populations would soon notice the difference in the ability of the Land government to provide the services they want and would, as a result, be amenable to a consolidation of their Land with a richer neighbour. A federal system with 7–10 Länder would mean the creation of Länder that would be more autonomous fiscally; would have lower costs per capita for numerous services, personnel and institutions, such as ministers, parliaments and courts; and also able to provide the equivalent living conditions that the public apparently demands.[25] A 'Europe of the Regions', in which the EU Commission and Council of Ministers can devolve certain activities according to the subsidiarity principle, also requires fiscally and administratively strong Länder.[26]

The pro-consolidation case thus presents a persuasive argument which draws on discussions that reach back to the early days of the republic;[27] on the analogy of comprehensive county and municipal boundary reforms that took place in all of the territorial Länder in the late 1960s and early 1970s in the Western Länder and took place the new Länder in the 1990s;[28] on the results of a comprehensive, highly detailed expert commission report in 1973[29] on reorganising Land boundaries; and on a massive scholarly literature that has appeared over the decades.[30] But Bernhard Vogel, the former Prime Minister of Rhineland-Palatinate and the current Prime Minister of Thuringia, noted in 1990, as five newly created Länder were being added to the Federal Republic, that 'now is the time', and if action to consolidate the Länder does not take place early after unification, it will be far more difficult to act later.[31]

Unfortunately for the advocates of Land boundary reform, there are also persuasive arguments against their position as well as practical difficulties of achieving reform. Article 29, para.1, speaks not only of reorganising Land boundaries in order to guarantee that they have the size and capacity to carry out their tasks effectively; it also says that in the process due regard shall be given to regional identities, historical and cultural ties, economic expediency and the requirements of regional and Land planning. Thus, any large-scale redrawing of boundaries would inevitably be rejected by large numbers of people who have developed feelings of identity with their Land.[32] Even the people in the former East Germany, who lived in a highly centralised state that eliminated any pretence of being a federation in the early 1950s, apparently preferred creating five new Länder[33] which had at least some historical basis to continuing to live in one territory that would have been roughly equivalent in population to North-Rhine Westphalia in the West.

A related argument is that smaller Länder are 'closer to the people' and perhaps therefore more responsive to the political and cultural wishes of the population.[34] The small states, provinces and cantons in the United States,

Canada and Switzerland, respectively, are not constantly targeted as obsolete and in need of being consolidated with surrounding neighbours, so why should small Länder in Germany be considered so dysfunctional? Of course, the proponents of reform in Germany would argue, among other things, that the Länder have functions unique to German federalism, that is, implementing with their local governments most federal legislation with the responsibility of financing most of the expenditures incurred.[35]

Perhaps even more formidable in overcoming the resistance to boundary change are the provisions of the Basic Law, Article 29, paras. 2–8, calling for a complicated referendum process. This process begins with a federal law that must be approved by a majority vote in a referendum in all of the Länder whose territory is affected. If a majority in one Land does not approve, it can be overridden by a two-thirds vote in the territory that is directly affected (unless a two-thirds majority of the Land rejected the referendum). Based on the American experience with referenda on the consolidation or annexations of local government units, these provisions probably make Land boundary changes unlikely if not impossible. An obvious example already exists in the defeat in May 1966 by voters in Brandenburg of the proposal that was approved by Berliners – at least West Berliners – and all of the major political elites in the two territories to merge the City of Berlin with the surrounding Land of Brandenburg. Again, proponents of reform may argue that this referendum was affected by too many extraneous matters, such as resentment by Easterners against their former capital city and the much richer West Berlin. But others would suggest that if a fusion of these two obvious candidates cannot pass, there is little hope for other efforts. In any case, there are no current efforts to consolidate any Land territory in any part of Germany.

THE POLITICAL PARTY SYSTEM AND DIRECT DEMOCRACY

The German Party System

The German party system changed at the national level from a multi-party system in the late 1940s and 1950s to a two-and-a-half-party system of CDU/CSU (Christian Democratic Union/Christian Social Union), SPD (Social Democratic Party of Germany) and FDP (Free Democratic Party) by the end of the 1950s. In 1983 the Greens gained seats for the first time in the federal parliament, thus creating a four-party system. In 1990, the PDS (Party of Democratic Socialism [former communist party – SED]) joined the party system, benefiting from special provisions for that year's federal election that did not require five per cent of the total German vote as a condition for entering the parliament. Since that time, a five-party system has developed; however, not all five parties are capable of forming coalitions. The PDS is not acceptable to any of the other parties as a partner, and the differences between the Greens and the CDU are so deep that a coalition of these two parties is most unlikely. Given the potential effects of changes in the German economy and society, there are also some lingering questions about the long-term prospects of the FDP, Greens and PDS.

The situation is quite different at the Land level. Here, the FDP is represented in only eight of the Land parliaments, all in Western Germany except Berlin and, since March 2002, Saxony-Anhalt. The Greens are generally comfortably above the five per cent level and thus have seats in the Western Länder, except in the Saarland, but they are not represented in any of the parliaments in the new Länder. In contrast, the PDS is the third party in the new Länder and even the second strongest party in Saxony, Thuringia and Saxony-Anhalt, while it has no representation in any Land parliaments in Western Germany. The radical right parties are represented in two Land parliaments, one each in the old and new Länder (but with only one seat in Bremen).

Thus there are two party systems at the Land level: a four-party system in the old Länder, consisting of the larger CDU (CSU in Bavaria) and SPD and the smaller Bündnis 90/Greens and FDP; and a three-party system in the new Länder, consisting of the CDU, SPD and PDS. The one exception in the East since March 2002 is the addition of the FDP in Saxony-Anhalt. Given the strength of the PDS (usually 20 per cent or more) in Land elections, one can speak of three large parties in the new Länder and Berlin. As at the national level, the CDU and Greens are unlikely coalition partners in the Western Länder, and the PDS is not generally acceptable as a coalition partner for the CDU and SPD in the Eastern Länder.

This has changed recently, however, in that the SPD agreed in 1994 and 1998 to form a minority government in Saxony-Anhalt with the toleration of the PDS in parliament, and in 1998 the SPD and PDS formed a regular government coalition in Mecklenburg-West Pomerania which continued after the September 2002 election. In 2001 the CDU–SPD coalition government collapsed in Berlin, and in the summer of 2001 the SPD formed a minority government with PDS toleration. Following the new elections in Berlin in October 2001, the SPD tried but failed to form a coalition government with the Greens and the FDP, so it turned to the PDS and formed a coalition with it in January 2002. These concessions to the PDS by the SPD have aroused considerable controversy,[36] not only between SPD and CDU/CSU, but also within the SPD. But these and other coalition arrangements do demonstrate the limited influence of the national parties on Land party coalition formation as well as the view that the Land parties should have more flexibility in forming coalitions than would be acceptable at the federal level.

TABLE 1

GOVERNMENTS IN THE LÄNDER (AS OF NOVEMBER 2002)

Länder governed by the CDU or CSU alone:
  Bavaria since 1996 – Prime Minister Edmund Stoiber
  Saxony since 1990 – Prime Minister Kurt Biedenkopf (since May 2002, Georg Milbradt)
  Saarland since 1999 – Prime Minister Peter Müller
  Thuringia since 1990 – Prime Minister Bernhard Vogel
Länder governed by the SPD alone:
  Lower Saxony since 1994 – Prime Minister Sigmar Gabriel
Länder with CDU/FDP coalition governments:
  Baden-Württemberg since 1996 – Prime Minister Erwin Teufel
  Hesse since 1999 – Prime Minister Roland Koch
  Saxony-Anhalt since 2002 – Prime Minister Wolfgang Böhmer
Länder with CDU/FDP/PRO coalition government:
  Hamburg since 2001 – Mayor Ole von Beust
Länder with SPD/CDU coalition governments:
  Bremen since 1995 – Mayor Henning Scherf
  Brandenburg since 1999 – Prime Minister Manfred Stolpe (since June 2002, Matthias Platzeck)
Länder with SPD/Green coalition governments:
  North-Rhine Westphalia since 1995 – Prime Minister Wolfgang Clement (since November 2002, Peer Steinbrück)
  Schleswig-Holstein since 1996 – Prime Minister Heide Simonis
Länder with SPD/FDP coalition governments:
  Rhineland-Palatinate since 1991 – Prime Minister Kurt Beck
Länder with SPD/PDS coalition governments:
  Mecklenburg-West Pomerania since 1998 – Prime Minister Harald Ringstorff
  Berlin since 2002 – Mayor Klaus Wowereit

At the end of the 1990s it was clear that the SPD had more opportunities than the CDU to form coalition governments in the Länder. It could form a grand coalition with the CDU in both the old and new Länder, a coalition with the Greens or the FDP in the former and a coalition with the PDS in the latter, at least in Mecklenburg-West Pomerania and Saxony-Anhalt (and Berlin). The CDU, in effect, was limited to forming a grand coalition or, in the West only, a small coalition with the FDP (in Hamburg with the FDP and PRO).

The occasional, largely unpredictable, success of a party outside the respective party systems, for example, by one of the radical right parties, does not justify adding them to the two different party systems described above. Their success is too unpredictable even in those Länder in which they have shown the greatest strength. In any case the radical right parties are not acceptable coalition partners for any of the established parties, and as a result they have never held any government responsibility in any of the Länder. On the other hand, a middle class populist 'flash' party in Hamburg (STATT-Partei) did join a coalition with the SPD from

1993 to 1997. A disgruntled working class voter group (AFB) was also able to gain temporary representation in Bremen from 1995 to 1999, but it did not join a government coalition. And in September 2001 a new 'flash' party, the law and order Schill party (Partei Rechtsstaatliche Offensive – PRO) emerged with 19 per cent of the vote in Hamburg, enough to eject the SPD, which had been a governing party in that city for 44 years. After the election, the CDU and FDP, which had barely passed the five per cent barrier, joined with the Schill Party to form a new coalition government.

Direct Democracy[37]

As noted above, the Basic Law, like the American Constitution, does not provide for direct democracy. The one exception is Article 29, which deals with the rearrangement of Länder boundaries. In contrast, all Land constitutions today provide for direct democracy. The older Länder had two-step procedures: a petition for a referendum (*Volksbegehren*) and a referendum (*Volksentscheid*) The 1990 constitution of Schleswig-Holstein introduced a three-step procedure. First, it provided for a 'peoples' initiative (*Volksinitiative, Volksantrag* or *Bürgerinitiative*), a petition to place certain items on the Land parliament's agenda. Second, a petition (*Volksbegehren*) for a popular referendum on a specific bill in case the parliament fails to act on the initiative within three to six months. If the parliament does not accept the petition proposal within a period of time (for example, two months), then a referendum (*Volksentscheid*) will be held on the bill (as well as an alternative that the parliament might offer). In striking contrast to the United States, qualified majorities are required for approval of legislative referenda (a majority of those voting and at least one-fourth or one-third of the eligible voters). Another major difference from the United States is that the topics of these plebiscitary procedures may not include judges, constitutional decisions, the bureaucracy, or budgets, taxes, public employee salaries, political finance or other financial matters. Needless to say, these restrictions are controversial. The signature requirements for these petitions are also controversial, because they vary from about one per cent of the population in some Länder in the East to as high as 20 percent in some Länder in the West.

The changes in the constitution of Schleswig-Holstein not only encouraged the new Länder to follow; it also raised the interest of many political activists in the West to reconsider their constitutional arrangements and to think also about the adoption of some other aspects of direct democracy, including the direct election of mayors. In general, the 1990s were a period when there was a sharp increase in the discussion of various features of 'plebiscitary' democracy, including the direct election of the prime ministers of the Länder.

Initiatives, petitions for referenda, and referenda are hardly everyday occurrences in the Länder. Between 1946 and 1992 there were only 23 referenda, including referenda on seven Land constitutions in the American and French occupation zones in 1946–47 and in North-Rhine Westphalia in 1950. There were also three special referenda in these early years: one in Hesse on socialisation of industry; one in Rhineland-Palatinate on schools; and one in Bremen regarding co-determination. There were three referenda in Bavaria dealing with voting age in 1970; with the electoral law in 1973; and with the addition of environmental protection to the Land constitution in 1984. There were four referenda in Hesse: on the election law in 1950; on the voting age in 1970; on the direct election of mayors and country managers in 1991; and on the protection of the environment as a state goal in 1991.[38]

There have been several legislative initiatives. In Bavaria there was a petition and a referendum on schools, in 1973 a constitutional change regarding television and radio, and in 1991 a petition and referendum on waste collection. In each case the Land parliament passed a competing proposal for the final referendum which was close to the original initiative and which then succeeded. In North-Rhine Westphalia in 1978 the CDU, the Catholic Church and parents' groups stopped a school reform proposed by the SPD. The SPD government dropped the legislative bill after 30 per cent of the electorate signed a petition for a referendum.[39]

A parliamentary dissolution was attempted in Baden-Württemberg in 1971 by those opposed to the local government territorial reforms, but it failed because the 50 per cent threshold of eligible voters required for passage was not reached. In 1981 unofficial petitions for the dissolution of the West Berlin city parliament were signed by more than 18 per cent of the voters (20 per cent were required for an official, formal petition), and in response the parliament dissolved itself.[40]

In the 1990s there were referenda in three of the new Länder (1992 and 1994) and in Berlin (1995) on their constitutions. Bremen held a referendum on a partial reform of its constitution in 1994, Hesse on lowering the age for voting in 1995, and Bavaria on introducing referenda at the local level in 1995. There were also examples of the Land parliaments taking action under the threat of popular action. In North-Rhine Westphalia the SPD-controlled Land parliament agreed to a law providing for the direct election of mayors after the CDU had collected 50,000 signatures for a petition in favor of the change. In Lower Saxony the Land parliament added a statement referring to God in the preamble of its 1993 constitution after a citizens' initiative collected 120,000 signatures for a petition calling for this change. In Rhineland-Palatinate the SPD/FDP government revoked its legislation on human organ transplants after the CDU opposition took steps to initiate a petition against the law. In 1995 in Baden-Württemberg the grand coalition government dropped its intention to eliminate Whit Monday as a holiday in order to help finance the new nursing home insurance programme, after 30,000 signatures were collected on a petition.[41]

In the meantime, a referendum was held in Berlin and Brandenburg in 1996 in which the merger of the two territorial units was rejected, and referenda were held in Bavaria in February 1998 on eliminating the second chamber, the Senate, and in March 2000 on schools. In 1998, Schleswig-Holstein held a referendum on the very controversial spelling reforms (*Rechtschreibreform*) introduced by all of the Land governments, Austria and Switzerland. To the consternation of the government, the reforms were rejected, but the Land parliament repealed the referendum statute in 1999, an action that was upheld by the Federal Constitutional Court by its refusal to hear the case.

CONCLUSION

The brief overview of major changes provided above demonstrates that indeed there have been a number of significant changes in the German federal system since unification. Whether these changes qualify as sufficient to justify the thesis that German federalism has not only changed but is a qualitatively *different* system is highly questionable. Some of the changes have been brought about rather directly by unification, the most obvious example being the unification of Berlin and the emergence of five new Länder. The constitutional changes made in the first half of the 1990s at the federal level were clearly the result of unification; however, some of them were also objects of reform efforts long before unification. The new Land constitutions in the East were obviously the result of unification, but the influence of the new constitution in Schleswig-Holstein in 1990 just before unification also had a significant impact on Land constitutions in both eastern and western parts of the country. Participation by Land governments in European decision-making is a good example of changes that had been made in part even before unification but were expanded and consolidated after unification.

One can make a persuasive case that fiscal federalism has been put under great stress by unification, and that this required reforms or at least changes. Unification also revived the debate over territorial reorganisation, that is, boundary changes of the Länder. Of course it must be kept in mind that such changes have not occurred, even though some observers argue that they are virtually inevitable.[42] The German party system has obviously been affected by the addition of the PDS at the national level, but its impact has been greatest in the East, where it competes as more or less as an equal against the SPD and CDU and has even joined in a coalition government with the SPD in Mecklenburg-West Pomerania and Berlin and supported an SPD minority government in Saxony-Anhalt until April 2002. The emergence of 'flash' parties in Bremen and Hamburg and the sporadic success of the far-right Republicans appear to be related to unification only indirectly at best. On the other hand, the success of the far-right DVU (German People's Union) in the East (especially in Saxony-Anhalt in 1998) can be seen in the context of dissatisfaction, especially by young male voters, with the failure of unification to bring about significant improvements in economic conditions. Direct democracy has become a major topic of discussion and debate in Germany, and numerous changes have been made. Germany has a long way to go before it becomes the California of Europe, but initiatives and referenda at the local and Land levels are now far more common than anyone could have imagined in 1990.

In short, the German federal system, like other political systems, is highly sensitive to a variety of domestic and even European political, economic and societal pressures. Both unification and developments in European integration have led to new pressures or influenced older ones in different ways. This process will continue, and in the coming decades questions will also continue to be raised about the nature of German federalism.

NOTES

1. For a detailed analysis of the recreation of the five new Länder in Eastern Germany, see Arthur B. Gunlicks, 'Federalism and German Unification', *Politics and Society in Germany, Austria and Switzerland*, 4/2 (1992), pp.52–66.
2. Arthur B. Gunlicks, 'German Federalism After Unification: The Legal/Constitutional Response', *Publius: The Journal of Federalism*, 24/2 (Spring 1994), pp.83, 89.
3. Ibid., pp.89–90.
4. See, for example, Hartmut Klatt, 'Forty Years of German Federalism', *Publius: The Journal of Federalism*, 19/4 (Fall 1989), pp.185–202.
5. For commentaries on the changes of Articles 72 and 75, see, for example, Bruno Schmidt-Bleibtreu and Franz Klein, *Kommentar zum Grundgesetz* (8. Aufl; Neuwied: Luchterhand Verlag, 1995), and Michael Sachs (ed.), *Grundgesetz Kommentar* (München: C.H. Beck'sche Verlagsbuchhandlung, 1996).
6. This section is based on Arthur B. Gunlicks, 'State (Land) Constitutions in Germany', *Rutgers Law Journal*, 31/4 (Summer 2000), pp.971–98; idem, 'Land Constitutions in Germany', *Publius: The Journal of Federalism*, 28/4 (Fall 1998), pp.105–25; and idem, 'The New Constitutions of East Germany', *German Politics*, 5/2 (Aug. 1996), pp.262–75.
7. For forms of local government in post-war Germany, see Arthur B. Gunlicks, *Local Government in the German Federal System* (Durham: Duke University Press, 1986), pp.73–81.
8. Charlie Jeffery, 'Farewell the Third Level? The German Länder and the European Policy Process', in Charlie Jeffery (ed.), *The Regional Dimension of the European Union* (London: Frank Cass, 1997), p.57.
9. Rudolf Hrbek, 'Doppelte Politikverflectung: Deutscher Föderalismus und Europäische Integration', in Rudolf Hrbek and Uwe Thaysen (eds.), *Die Deutschen Länder und die Europäische Gemeinschaften* (Baden-Baden: Nomos Verlagsgesellschaft, 1986), p.19.

10. Heiderose Kilper and Roland Lhotta, *Föderalismus in der Bundesrepublik Deutschland: Eine Einführung* (Opladen: Leske + Budrich, 1996), pp.217–18.
11. Ibid., pp.223–4.
12. Ibid., pp.226–9.
13. Jeffery, 'Farewell to the Third Level?', p.67.
14. Ibid., pp.61–2.
15. Walter Rudolf, 'Die Bedeutung der Landesparlamente in Deutschland', in Detlef Merten (ed.), *Die Stellung der Landesparlamente aus deutscher Sicht* (Berlin: Duncker & Humblot, 1997), p.68.
16. Kilper and Lhotta, *Föderalismus*, pp.229–31, and Jeffery, 'Farewell the Third Level?', pp.56–7, 59.
17. Ibid., pp.219–21; for a detailed discussion of the activities of the EC Committee, see Georg-Berndt Oschatz and Horst Risse, 'Bundesrat und Europäische Gemeinschaften', *Die öffentliche Verwaltung*, 42/12 (June 1989), pp.510–12.
18. Jeffery, 'Farewell the Third Level?', p.72.
19. Wolfgang Fischer and Claus Dieter Koggel, 'Die Europakammer des Bundesrates', *Deutsches Verwaltungsblatt* (1 Dec. 2000), pp.1742–51.
20. For a detailed description and analysis of the German system of public finance, see Arthur B. Gunlicks, 'Financing the German Federal System: Problems and Prospects', *German Studies Review*, 23/3 (Oct. 2000), pp.533–55, and Clifford Larsen, 'States Federal, Financial, Sovereign and Social: A Critical Inquiry into an Alternative to American Financial Federalism', *The American Journal of Comparative Law*, 47 (Summer 1999), pp.429–88.
21. Gunlicks, 'Financing the German Federal System', pp.539–40, and Gunlicks, 'German Federalism After Unification', pp.84–8.
22. *Frankfurter Allgemeine Zeitung*, 12 Nov. 1999: 1 and 13 Nov. 1999, p.1; *Die Zeit*, 18 Nov. 1999, p.25; and *Das Parlament*, 26 Nov. 1999, p.9.
23. *Süddeutsche Zeitung*, 25 June 2001, pp.1–2, 24.
24. Ibid., and *Das Parlament*, 51/27 (19 June 2001), p.1.
25. For a strong argument for various reforms of German federalism, with territorial reform serving as 'the key for the protection of German federalism against deformation', see Uwe Leonardy, 'Deutscher Föderalismus jenseits 2000: Reformiert oder deformiert?' *Zeitschrift für Parlamentsfragen*, 30/1 (Feb. 1999), p.162.
26. Hartmut Klatt, 'Länder-Neugliederung: Eine staatspolitische Notwendigkeit', *Zeitschrift für Beamtenrecht*, 5 (1997), p.149.
27. Lower Saxony, North-Rhine Westphalia and Hesse were created after 1945 by the British and Americans, by consolidating several older territories, and Baden-Württemberg was created by the Germans in the early 1950s by consolidating three former territories.
28. For descriptions and analyses in English of the local government territorial reforms in the Western Länder, see Arthur B. Gunlicks, *Local Government in the German Federal System* (Durham: Duke University Press, 1986), Ch.4; idem, 'The Reorganization of Local Governments in the Federal Republic of Germany', in Arthur B. Gunlicks (ed.), *Local Government Reform and Reorganization: An International Perspective* (Port Washington: Kennikat Press, 1981), Ch.10; and idem, 'Restructuring Service Delivery Systems in West Germany', in Vincent Ostrom and Frances Bish (eds.), *Comparing Urban Service Delivery Systems* (Beverly Hills: Sage Publications, 1977), pp.173–9.
29. Bundesministerium des Innern, *Bericht der Sachverständigenkommission für die Neugliederung des Bundesgebietes*, Bonn 1973 (Bericht der Ernst-Kommission).
30. For a recent comprehensive review of the literature, developments and need for Länder consolidation, see Klatt, 'Länder-Neugliederung', pp.137–49.
31. Bernhard Vogel, 'Mehr Länder, weniger Föderalismus', *Staatswissenschaft und Staatspraxis*, 2 (1990), pp.129–31.
32. Klatt points out that feelings of identity have much to do with the times. Thus, the artificial Länder created by the Allies after 1945 seem to have become a source of identity for most of their citizens. Klatt, 'Länder-Neugliederung', p.149. Hans-Wolfgang Arndt, on the other hand, suggests that a strong identity of people with the Länder never developed after the War and that the small Länder have no right to exist indefinitely at the expense of the others. See

'Finanzverfassungsrechtlicher Reformbedarf – vom unitarischen Föderalismus zum Wettbewerbsföderalismus', *Wirtschaftsdient*, 2 (1998), pp.77, 80.

33. See, for example, Peter Badura, 'Die Finanzverfassung im wiedervereinigten Deutschland', in. Jörn Ipsen *et al.* (eds.), *Verfassungsrecht im Wandel* (Köln: Carl Heymanns Verlag, 1995), p.20.
34. Larsen, 'States Federal', p.464.
35. See Uwe Leonardy, 'Territorial Reform of the Länder: A Demand of the Basic Law', in Arthur B. Gunlicks (ed.), *German Public Policy and Federalism* (New York: Berghahn Books, 2003 forthcoming).
36. See, for example, Wolfgang Renzsch and Stefan Schieren, 'Grosse Koalition ohne Alternative?' and Winfried Steffani, 'Wer trägt die Verantwortung? Wider die wissenschaftliche und politische Verharmlosung des "Magdeburger Modells"', *Zeitschrift für Parlamentsfragen*, 29/1 (Feb. 1998), pp.187–90.
37. For a recent review in English, see Hermann Heussner, 'The Challenge of Direct Democracy', *German Public Policy and Federalism*, forthcoming.
38. Otmar Jung, 'Daten zu Volksentscheiden in Deutschland auf Landesebene (1946–1992)', *Zeitschrift für Parlamentsfragen*, 24/1 (Feb. 1993), pp.5–9.
39. Ibid., pp.9–11.
40. Ibid., p.11.
41. Otmar Jung, 'Direkte Demokratie: Forschungsstand und Forschungsaufgaben 1995', *Zeitschrift für Parlamentsfragen*, 26/4 (Nov. 1995), pp.660–61.
42. See Uwe Leonardy, 'Territorial Reform of the Länder', *German Public Policy and Federalism*, forthcoming.

Local Government and Politics in East Germany

HELLMUT WOLLMANN

This article focuses on the institutional side of the 'multi-dimensional' transformation that East Germany experienced in the wake of the collapse of the communist regime. Therefore, the study will deal with (in the terminology of a well-known distinction) polity rather than with politics and policy.

The institutional transformation of post-socialist countries has often been conceived as having been mainly shaped, particularly in its early 'foundation' period, by three sets of factors:[1]

- the constellation of actors, interests, strategies, the 'will and skill' of relevant actors;
- the institutional 'starting conditions' impinging upon the take-off of the transformation process as 'endogenous' factors, including the institutional and cognitive 'legacies' from the communist past which can amount to 'path-dependencies' that shape the further institutional trajectory;
- and external ('exogenous') factors (such as actors, political pressure, but also ideas 'from outside') impacting on the institutional development.

This conceptualisation of the institutional transformation can be related to 'neo-institutionalism',[2] the 'historical' variant of which tends to turn the analytical lens at the institutional and cognitive legacies and its structural imprints, while its 'actor-centred' variant would be inclined to analytically concentrate on actor constellations and their 'voluntaristic' discretion and situational contingency.

EAST GERMANY – A UNIQUE CASE (SONDERFALL) OF INSTITUTIONAL TRANSFORMATION?

Institutional Transformation in East Germany:
A Case of Exogenous Determination?

In analysing and discussing the institutional transformation of post-socialist countries, East Germany has been interpreted as a specific, if not unique case (*Sonderfall*).[3] This is because in East Germany the collapse of the

Hellmut Wollmann, Humboldt University-Berlin

communist regime and the system transformation coincided with the process of German unification and with the GDR's integration into the 'old' Federal Republic, thus being imbued with an integrationist logic. Hence, East Germany's transformation seemed, from the very beginning, to be propelled by a triad of exogenous factors. These include:

- 'institution transfer' by extending the institutional and legal world of the 'old' Federal Republic unto East Germany;[4]
- 'personnel transfer' in that tens of thousands of West German experts (temporarily or permanently) moved to East Germany to get involved in the transformation process; and
- huge 'financial transfers' from West German public budgets and social security funds to East Germany.

At first glance, East Germany's system change looks essentially like a singular case of exogenously driven and determined transformation in that West Germany's organisational blue-prints and operational patterns were extended to East Germany and shaped the transformation process. In its spectacular mix of demolition and reconstruction it bore many traces of what Joseph Schumpeter, alluding to the elementary forces of capitalism, has called 'creative destruction' (schöpferische Zerstörung). This institutional adaptation set in and gained momentum in spring 1990 when the democratically elected GDR parliament (Volkskammer) passed the new Municipal Charter (DDR-Kommunalverfassung) of 17 May 1990, which largely followed the local self-government model in place in the 'old' Federal Republic. In July 1990 it decided to re-establish the five Länder which the communists had abolished in the early 1950s. In doing so, it adopted two basic constitutional characteristics of the 'old' Federal Republic. It must be borne in mind, however, that the GDR parliament at the same time linked up with the constitutional and institutional fabric which East Germany, in its pre-communist and pre-Nazi history, had in common with the rest of Germany.

The most blatant act of 'institutional transfer' was effected when, on the basis of the meticulous Unification Treaty (Einigungsvertrag) which had been elaborated by the two German governments, the GDR 'acceded' (Beitritt) to the 'old' Federal Republic at midnight on 3 October 1990. In that 'logical second', the latter's entire constitutional and legal world was extended and transplanted to East Germany, while the GDR as a separate state ceased to exist. This largely exogenously driven expansion of the 'old' FRG's 'ready-made state'[5] and the unparalleled abruptness with which it occurred distinguish East Germany's transformation from those in the other post-communist countries in Central-Eastern Europe and make it a 'unique case' (Sonderfall).

The institutional transfer was accompanied, and carried along, by a massive personnel transfer from West to East, as thousands of West Germans went to East Germany, either temporarily or permanently. This influx also mirrored the 'political and administrative elite vacuum' that resulted from the removal of most of leading political and administrative functionaries of the communist regime.[6] Thus, 'transferees' from West Germany's federal Länder as well as local government levels came to play an important role in East Germany's transformation process. This, again, stood in marked contrast with the Central-East European countries in which, notwithstanding the incursion of foreign consultants and advisers, an elite import of such a scale was inconceivable.

Thirdly, another important factor in the triad of exogenous factors is the massive financial transfer to the East. Since the early 1990s, this figure has amounted to some $75 billion annually, which has had the effect of reinforcing the exogenous determination of Eastern German development and the process of unification.

'Endogenous' Adaptation and Self-Development?

A number of factors, however, qualify the picture of a strictly exogenously determined institution-building process. True, essential principles of West Germany's 'ready-made state' were extended to East Germany, particularly inasmuch as they are stipulated in the Federal Constitution or laid down in federal legislation. But beyond such areas of 'imposed' institution formation, the institutional wasteland that resulted from the political and administrative demise of the GDR created great scope for institution-building. In this situation, East German Länder parliaments and governments, and by the same token local authorities, enjoyed considerable latitude in developing institutional solutions of their own in terms of endogenous adaptation and self-development, if not innovation.[7]

Secondly, and moreover, there was really no single West German model that could have been transferred to the East. Instead, the Federal Republic's political and administrative system is, at all levels and in most sectors, characterised by a significant degree of institutional differentiation and variability, not least with regard to the organisation of Länder administration, Länder–local relations and local authorities.[8] Thus the repertoire of institutional solutions on which East Germany's 'institution-builder' could draw was diverse and varied.

Thirdly, account must be taken of the fact that East Germany's political arenas in which the decisions on institution-building were reached were predominantly made up of East Germans, that is, East Germany's new political elite that emerged from the 'peaceful revolution' and from the 'founding' elections to Länder parliaments and the local councils. On the

Länder level, the new parliaments, following the elections held in October 1990, were composed entirely of East Germans.[9] For instance, after the first elections in Brandenburg, a coalition of Social Democrats, Greens and Free Democrats was put together. This brought to Brandenburg's coalition politics the elements of bargaining and compromise, typical of the 'normalcy' of parliamentary decision-making and reflecting the swiftly developing pattern of endogenous East German policy-making. Likewise, East Germans dominated the political executive of the Länder governments particularly by occupying most of the prime ministerial and ministerial positions. It should be remembered, however, that in the administration of the Länder, the West German 'imports' did occupy influential positions, particularly in the top echelon of the state secretaries.

At the county and municipal levels, as early as in spring 1990, following the local council elections of 6 May 1990, a new political elite emerged that also consisted, to a large extent, of 'new politicians' (*'Neupolitiker'*) who had not held any political function under the communist regime.[10] The newly elected councils expelled most of the former communist power holders from county and municipal administrations and, on the basis of the new Municipal Charter of 17 May 1999, elected or appointed a largely new set of political and administrative local leaders: mayors, deputy mayors (*Beigeordnete*) and section heads (*Amtsleiter*). It should be added, though, that at the local level, leading administrative positions were also occupied by West Germany 'transferees', although to a smaller extent than in the higher echelons of Land administration.

The factors influencing institution-building in local government, then, suggest an ambivalent picture. On the one hand, West German organisational schemes and experiences clearly had an impact upon the organisational efforts of East German local governments. Of great importance in this respect were twinning partnerships with individual West German counties and municipalities as well as the organisational recommendations put forward by the Kommunale Gemeinschaftsstelle für Verwaltungsvereinfachung (KGSt). This is a municipally funded non-profit institution which has had great influence on West German local government organisation since the late 1940s. On the other hand, East German local authorities quickly developed into lively political arenas with actors and groups from different professional and political backgrounds as well as with different political and personal ambitions. Taken together, this constellation of factors has significantly impinged upon the local decision-making process in organisational matters, adding up to a strong 'endogenous' character.

DEVELOPMENT OF LOCAL DEMOCRACY AND LOCAL POLITICS

The following sections offer an analysis of the legal regulation of local democracy and consider some of the more crucial aspects of its practice.[11] We begin with a consideration of the nature of legal regulation following unification.

Legal Regulation: GDR-Municipal Charter of 17 May 1990

As was already said, the Municipal Charter of 17 May 1990 was passed by the democratically elected GDR parliament and was largely tailored to the local self-government model in place in the 'old' Federal Republic. This included the latter's traditional concept of a broad scope of local government responsibilities and functions, thus reflecting an exogenous stamp. At the same time, the new Municipal Charter made some remarkable moves to adopt strong direct democratic procedures by providing for local referendums and procedural opportunities for citizen groups to play an active (though advisory) role in the deliberations of the local councils. It was explicitly argued in the legislative discussions that these provisions were meant to retain and translate the experiences of the 'round tables' and the 'grass-root' activities of protest groups that contributed significantly to the collapse of the communist regime. Hence, the insertion of the local referendums as a procedure of local direct democracy clearly had endogenous roots. From the mid-1950s until then, Baden-Württemberg (in the south-west of the 'old' Federal Republic) was the only Land to stipulate local referendums. The GDR Municipal Charter of 17 May 1990 became a stimulus for West German Länder to follow suit. The Unification Treaty laid down that the GDR Municipal Charter remained in force in the new Länder, until the latter adopted their own individual charters.

The New Municipal Charters of the East German Länder

Once the new Länder were established and their parliaments were elected, they were swift to prepare new municipal charters of their own, making use of the legislative competence that the Länder constitutionally possess in this matter. The municipal charters, which the new Länder enacted between late 1993 and early 1994, show commonalities in their basic features, while differing in (significant) details. Falling in line with the GDR Municipal Charter of May 1990, the new charters, while still retaining the predominance of the elected councils as the pivot of representative democracy, introduce elements of local direct democracy by providing for local referendums, for the direct election of the mayor (as well as the head of county, *Landrat)*, as well as for the 'recall' of the mayor (and the *Landrat)* by local referendum

TABLE 1

DIRECT ELECTION OF MAYORS AND LANDRÄTE AND PROCEDURES OF 'RECALLING' THEM BY LOCAL REFERENDUM

Land	In force since	Direct election		Tenure		'Recall' procedure in place?		'Recall' procedures		
		Mayor	Landrat	Mayor	Local council	Mayor	Landrat	Popular initiative (min. requirement % electorate)	Council initiative (min. requirement of council votes)	Referendum vote on 'recall' initiative Min. requirement of yes-votes (% electorate)
Bad-W	1.4.56	+	–	8	5	–	–	—	—	—
Bayern	15.1.52	+	+		**5**	–	–		**2/3 majority**	**25**
Brandenburg	**5.12.93/ 20.5.98**	**+**	**–**	**8**	**5**	**+**	**–**	**25/15**	**2/3 majority**	.25
Hesse	20.1.91/20.5.92	+	+	6	5	+	+		2/3 majority	.25
Meckl-West P	**13.6.99**	**+**	**+**	**7/9**	**5**	**+**	**+**		**2/3 majority**	**33,3**
Lower S	22.8.96	+	+	5	5	+	+		¾ majority	25
NRW	17.10.94	+	+	5	5	+	+		2/3 majority	25
Rhinel-Pal	5.10.93	+	+	8	5	+	+		2/3 majority	30
Saarl	16.6.94	+	+	8	5	+	+		2/3 majority	30
Saxony	**12.6.94**	**+**	**+**	**7**	**5**	**+**	**+**	**33,3[12]**	**¾ majority**	**50**
S-Anhalt	**12.6.94**	**+**	**+**	**7**	**5**	**+**	**+**		**¾ majority**	**30**
Sch-H	23.7.96	+	+	6/8	5			25	2/3 majority	33,3
Thur	**12.6.94**	**+**	**+**	**6**	**5**	**+**	**–**		**½ majority**	**30**

Note: Data on East German Länder in **bold**.

Source: Hellmut Wollmann, 'Direkte Demokratie in den ostdeutschen Kommunen – Regelunsschub und Anwendungspraxis', in Hans-Ulrich Derlien (ed.), *Zehn Jahre Verwaltungsaufbau Ost* (Baden-Baden: Nomos, 2001), p.47.

Direct Election of Mayors (and of Landräte)

The direct election of the mayors of the municipalities, as well as of the heads of the counties (*Landräte*) was introduced by the East German Länder (with the exception of Brandenburg). Most of them installed the 'strong mayor' model in which the elected mayor is not only 'chief executive' of the local administration, but also chairs the elected local council. The exception to this rule is Brandenburg, where, in a kind of 'division of power' concept, the local councils elect a chairman of their own. In most Länder, the elective tenure of the mayors has been set to be longer than (and hence not congruent with) that of the local council.

Procedures to Recall the Mayor (and Landrat)

At the same time, in all new East German municipal charters was a stipulation that the mayors can be removed ('recalled') by local referendum from office before the elapse of their elective tenure. In three East German Länder only the elected councils can initiate the recall procedure, a restriction in line with most West German Länder, while in Brandenburg and Saxony the recall procedure can be initiated also from the citizenry. In Brandenburg the minimum requirement for such a 'citizen' initiative was originally set as low as ten per cent of the local electorate.

Local Referendums

Furthermore, local referendums, which had been already introduced in the GDR Municipal Charter of May 1990, have also been stipulated in new Länder's municipal legislation, with some differences between the Länder (see Table 2). While in all Länder local referendum procedures can be initiated by the citizens themselves (with minimum requirements between five and 20 per cent of the electorate), in some Länder they can also be commenced by the councils (with minimum requirements between two-thirds and one-half of the council members). For the adoption of a referendum it is required that, besides the simple majority of those taking part in the vote, between 25 and 30 per cent of the electorate must approve. A number of significant other procedural and substantive restrictions on local referendums have been set. While covering 'all matters of the local community', the crucial business of the local budget and the local revenues are explicitly taken out of the reach of local referendums.[12]

On the one hand, it should be noted that, particularly in view of these and other procedural and substantive restrictions, the institutionalisation of the local referendums in the East German (and, by the same token, in the West German) Länder falls far behind the pertinent legal provisions in Switzerland and in the US as the homelands of direct local democracy. On the other hand, it should be pointed out that, despite such reservations, in the

TABLE 2

LEGAL REGULATION OF LOCAL REFERENDUMS

Land	In force since?	Also for counties?	Council initiative Min. requirement (% local electorate)	Voting on referendum Min. requirement of votes in local council	Voting on referendum Min. requirement of yes-votes (% local electorate)
Bad-Württ	1.4.56	–	10 to approx. 5	2/3 majority	30
Bayern	1.10.95 / 1.4.99	+	10 to 3	2/3 majority	20/10
Brandenb	**5.12.93**	**+**	**10**	**1/2 majority**	**25**
Hesse	20.5.92	–	10	——	25
M-West P	**12.6.94**	**+**	**10 to 4.42**	**1/2 majority**	**25**
Lower S	22.8.96	+	10	——	25
North R-W	17.10.94/ 28.3.00	+	10 to approx. 3	——	20
Rhinel-P	15.10.93	+	15 to approx. 8.8	——	30
Saarland	1997	+	15 to approx. 12.4	——	25
Saxony	**12.6.94**	**+**	**15 (5)**	**2/3 majority**	**25**
Saxony-A	**12.6.94**	**+**	**15 to ca. 5**	**2/3 majority**	**30**
Schlesw-H	5.4.90	+	10	2/3 majority	25
Thuringen	**12.6.94**	**–**	**20**	**——**	**25**
GDR Municipal Charter	**17.5.90- 93/94**	**–**	**10**	**1/2 majority**	**25**

Notes: data on East German Länder in **bold**.

Source: Hellmut Wollmann, 'Direkte Demokratie in den ostdeutschen Kommunen – Regelunsschub und Anwendungspraxis', in Hans-Ulrich Derlien (ed.), *Zehn Jahre Verwaltungsaufbau Ost* (Baden-Baden: Nomos, 2001),

combined introduction of the direct election of the mayors (and *Landräte*) along with the 'recall' procedures and of local referendums, the municipal legislation in the East German (as well as in the West German) Länder has become a frontrunner among European countries.

Local Democracy in Practice: Local Council Elections

The comparative data on electoral turnout in local council elections across Länder show a striking similarity between the East German and the West German Länder. As a whole, the participation in local elections is remarkably high by international standards. While the local council elections on 5 May 1990, which were the first truly democratic local elections held in the still existing GDR, echoed the 'post-revolutionary' excitement in a high electoral turnout (with between 70 and 80 per cent), the subsequent local voting pattern of the East Germans has been quite similar to that of the West Germans (with voter turnouts of between 60 and 70 per cent). Some cases of exceptionally high voter turnouts in local council elections (such as in North Rhine-Westphalia in 1994 with some 80 per cent) can be explained by the local council elections being simultaneously held along with higher-level elections (for instance, to the Federal Parliament, as in 1994 in North Rhine-Westphalia, or to the European Parliament). The simultaneous conduct of local council and Land parliament elections has been intentionally ruled out in the Länder in order to avoid such 'amplification' and 'distortion' effects.

TABLE 3

VOTER TURN-OUT IN LOCAL COUNCIL ELECTIONS (%)

Year Land	1989	1990	1991	1992	1993	1994	1995	1996	1997	1998	1999
Brandenburg		74.6[1]			59.8[2]					77.8[3]	
Mecklenburg		72.4[1]				65.7[4]					50.5[5]
Saxony		76.0[1]				72.21[4]					53.81[5]
Saxony Anhalt		65.1[1]				66.2 [4]					49.6[5]
Thuringia		78.6[1]				72.3[4]					58.3[5]
Baden- Württemberg BW	61.4[6]					66.7[7]					52.9[8]
Bayern		75.0[9]						67.3[10]			
Hesse	78.0[11]			71.3[12]					66.0[13]		
Lower- Saxony			68.3[14]					64.5[15]			
North Rhine- Westphalia (NRW)	65.6[16]					81.7[17]					55.0[18]
Rhineland- Palatinate	77.2[19]					74.1[20]					62.9[5]

Notes: East German Länder in **bold**.

1	6.5.1990.	10	10.5.1996.
2	5.12.1993.	11	12.3.1989.
3	27.9.1998. combined with election	12	7.3.1993.
	to Federal Parl.	13	2.3.1997.
4	12.6.1994. combined with election	14	6.10.1991.
	Europ. Parl.	15	15.9.1996.
5	13.6.1999. combined with election	16	1.10.1989.
	to Europ. Parl.	17	16.10.1994. combined with election
6	22.10.1989.		to Federal Parl.
7	12.6.1994. combined with election	18	12.9.1999.
	to Europ. Parl.	19	18.6.1989. combined with election
8	24.10.1999.		to Europ. Parl.
9	12.6.1994.	20	12.6.1994.

Source: Hellmut Wollmann, 'Direkte Demokratie in den ostdeutschen Kommunen – Regelunsschub und Anwendungspraxis', in Hans-Ulrich Derlien (ed.), *Zehn Jahre Verwaltungsaufbau Ost* (Baden-Baden: Nomos, 2001), p.47.

Direct Election of Mayors

The first round of the direct election of the mayors (and *Landräte*) took place in the East German Länder at the same time as the local council elections in 1993 and 1994. In the subsequent round of direct elections of mayors that were held as 'stand-alone' elections, the electoral turnout dropped to about 40 to 45 per cent, which is about ten per cent lower than the voter turnout in local council elections.

Procedures to 'Recall' Mayors by Local Referendum

The new legal provision to 'recall' the mayors by local referendum can be initiated from amidst the citizens (*Bürgerbegehren*) in Brandenburg and Saxony, as noted above. It has been applied rather frequently in Brandenburg. Between 1993 and 1998 a striking number of recall procedures were set off by local citizens. As a matter of fact, up to ten per cent of full-time mayors were thus removed from office by local referendum. Temporarily the Länder politicians, mayors and the mass media got quite alarmed and excited by what was labelled a 'new popular sport' – 'bowling with the mayors' (*Bürgermeisterkegeln*). At last the Land parliament reacted to this upsurge by raising the minimum percentage of the electorate required to initiate a recall procedure. For this reason, or for others, the number of recall referendums has noticeably subsided since.[13]

Local Practice in Local Referendums

While in formal-legal terms the introduction of local referendums has made spectacular advances in the local government setting in both East and West German Länder since the early 1990s, in practical terms referendum initiatives as well as popular votes on referendums have occurred quite rarely. An indicator might be seen in the 'average frequency' of referendum initiatives or voted-on referendums which can be figured dividing the total number of initiatives or votes (in the respective Land) by, first, the number of municipalities and, then, by the number of years the referendum provision has been in force. This calculation provides a glimpse of how many years on average it takes within the individual municipality until a referendum vote is initiated.

According to such 'thumb rule' calculations, on the country-wide average a local referendum would be initiated in every municipality once in 126 years, while a referendum would be put to a popular vote every 204 years (see Table 4, also for the specification by Länder). So, by and large, the employment of local referendums has so far been very scarce. On the basis of these data, a distinct pattern along a West/East divide becomes visible. This divide reveals three West German Länder holding the three top ranks (Bavaria, North Rhine-Westphalia and Hesse with 'frequency indicators' for voted-on referendums of 1/18, 1/42 and 1/46 respectively), while the bottom ranks are composed of three East German Länder (Saxony-Anhalt, Thuringia and Mecklenburg-West Pomerania with 'frequency indicators' of 1/261, 1/395 and 1/543). If one considers the issues raised in the referendums, the data point at an another West/East distinction: while most of the referendums initiated and conducted in East German Länder deal with questions of territorial reform of municipalities, in the West German Länder the referendums are mostly directed at 'substantive' local issues, such as the location of social and service facilities, road-building and traffic measures and, more recently, nullifying

TABLE 4

LOCAL REFERENDUM ACTIVITIES

Land	Period	Number of munici- palities	Referendum iniatives			Voted-on referendums		
			Number	Ø¹ Frequency indicator	Rank- ing	Number²	Ø Frequency indicator	Rank- ing
BW	1956–99	1111	267	1/187	10	267 (128)	1/187 (1/373)	8
Bay	1995–98	2056	610	1/11	1	370 (361)	1/18	1
Bdbg	**1993–98**	**1489**	**90**	**1/94**	**8**	**58 (40)**	**1/142 (1/213)**	**7**
He	1993–99	426	116	1/39	3	46	1/54	3
Me-WP	**1992–96**	**1069**	**13**	**1/362**	**11**	**9 (n.d.)**	**1/543 (n.d.)**	**12**
LS	1997–99	1032	36	1/58	76	15	1/130	6
NRW	1994–99	396	138	1/15	2	48	1/42	2
Rh-P	1994–97	2305	57	1/122	9	31	1/231	9
Saar	1997–99	52	2	0/52	–	1	0/52	13
Sa	**1992–98**	**779**	**101**	**1/51**	**5**	**88 (53)**	**1/58 (1/96)**	**4**
Sa-Anh	**1990–98**	**1295**	**57**	**1/44**	**4-**	**41 (n.d.)**	**1/261 (k.A.)**	**10**
Sch-H	1990–97	1132	151	1/52	6	94 (81)	1/87 (1/95)	5
Thür	**1993–98**	**1053**	**14**	**1/395**	**12**	**15**	**1/395**	**11**
Insges. Ø	1956–99	14,806	1593	1/126		1082 (868)	1/204	

Notes: data on East German Länder in **bold**.
1 Average frequency indicator for referendum initiatives = number of referendum initiatives (in the respective Land) divided by the number of municipalities divided by the number of years the provision has been in force.
2 Average frequency indicator for voted-on referendums = number of voted-on referendums (in the respective Land) divided by the number of municipalities divided by the number of years the provision has been in force

Sources: Hellmut Wollmann, 'Direkte Demokratie in den ostdeutschen Kommunen – Regelunsschub und Anwendungspraxis', in Hans-Ulrich Derlien (ed.), *Zehn Jahre Verwaltungsaufbau Ost* (Baden-Baden: Nomos, 2001), p.36, references; Oscar W. Gabriel, 'Das Volk als Gesetzgeber: Bürgerbegehren und Bürgerentscheide', *Zeitschrift für Gesetzgebung* (1999), pp.310 ff., Table 1; Frank Rehmet, Tim Weber and Dragan Pavlovic, 'Bürgerbegehren und Bürgerentscheide in Bayern, Hessen und Schleswig-Holstein', in Theo Schiller (ed.), *Direkte Demokratie in Theorie und kommunalter Praxis* (Frankfurt/New York: Campus, 1999), pp.117–35; Mehr Demokratie e.V. 2002, Volksbegehrensbericht 2001, Bilanz und Perspektiven der direkten Demokratie in Deutschland. www.mehr-demokratie.de/ bu/nn/index.htm.

decisions taken by local councils to close down local facilities in order to cut costs. In addition, many referendums in the East German Länder were initiated by the local councils rather than by the citizenry at large.[14]

How do we explain this variance between East and West Germany? Three sets of explanations might be considered:[15]

- the 'institutional' hypothesis (that is, institutions, in the form of different institutional regulations, and so on, matter),
- 'cultural' hypothesis (that is, culturally bred attitudes, political habits, and so on, matter),
- 'organisational resource' hypothesis (for example, socio-political networks and organisational webs matter).

The 'institutional' hypothesis seems not to carry far. With the exception of Bavaria, where the procedural hurdles have been noticeably lower than in the other Länder, the procedural rules are quite similar between the Länder.

The 'cultural explanation' has to get along with, at least at first sight, contradictory survey data.[16] On the one hand, the Eastern Germans show a higher preference for 'direct democracy' as an ideal form of government than the West Germans. Surveys regularly carried out since 1990 indicate that, throughout this period, some 60 to 65 per cent of the East Germans expressed a strong preference for 'direct democracy' – about 20 per cent more than in West Germany. This predilection for 'direct democracy' as an ideal form of government would suggest that East Germans should be more eager than the West Germans to resort to local referendums (which, in their voting behaviour, they are not).

On the other hand, East Germans are less satisfied with the actual performance of the Federal Republic's democratic system. While in 1990, right after unification, the satisfaction rate among East Germans was 60 per cent, it has dropped, since 1993, to 40 per cent (compared to some 60 per cent and more in West Germany). This probably reflects the persistent subjective perception of many East Germans that the social and economic results of German unification have fallen short of their expectations. Such higher degree of political disappointment and alienation could suggest two opposite reactions. It could be conducive to a greater reliance and openness to local referendums as a means to express this dissatisfaction and to try to remedy the situation. Or it could nourish a sense of resignation on the part of the citizens in which it would be seen as futile to turn to local referendums as a remedy. But the latter interpretation would have to come to terms with the (contradictory) information that the voter turnout for council elections (and other parliamentary elections) in East Germany is quite similar to West Germany. Thus, the 'cultural' explanation denies us a straightforward answer.

The most plausible explanation appears to be the 'organisational resource' hypothesis.[17] This explanation argues that the disposition and readiness to seize participatory opportunities and to turn them into 'collective action' depends on the existence of socio-political networks and organisational webs which citizen and citizen groups may both turn to as well as fall back on when trying to initiate political activities, such as referendums. There is empirical evidence[18] that, as a reaction to the political abuse of socio-political organisations and of imposed 'voluntary participation' by the communist regime, the disposition among the East Germans to engage in 'self-organised' socio-political activities is now still significantly lesser in East Germany than in West Germany.[19]

Party Political Cleavage

An important underlying difference between East and West German political orientation is seen when we examine the formation and electoral strength of the political parties within the East. While the 'classical' political parties of the 'old' Federal Republic entered the electoral arena in East Germany as early as in March 1990 in the then GDR, the Communist Party (SED) changed to the Party of Democratic Socialism. In the elections of 1990, which immediately followed the collapse of the communist regime, the post- and ex-communist PDS plunged to between 15 and ten per cent of the votes in the local elections of May 1990,[20] and, in similar vein, to between ten and 15 per cent in the October 1990 elections to the Land parliaments.[21] Since then, however, PDS has continuously gained electoral strength and has won about 20 per cent of the votes in the meantime. PDS has established itself as a veritable 'regional party' in the East German Länder and municipalities, whereas in West Germany its electoral strength is still minimal. PDS has succeeded in becoming the junior partner in SPD-led (so called 'red–red') coalition governments in Mecklenburg-West Pomerania and most recently in Berlin. In electoral studies it has been argued that the persisting political attraction of the PDS among East German voters can be interpreted, first of all, as evidence of a continuing detachment from the Federal Republic, as well as an expression of the confidence among East German voters that the PDS makes both a more efficient and trustworthy political advocate of East German interests (and sentiments) than the established 'West German' political parties.[22]

DEVELOPMENT OF VIABLE ADMINISTRATIVE STRUCTURES OF
LOCAL GOVERNMENT

Territorial Reforms

When local self-government experienced its revival in East Germany during
the spring of 1990 following the democratic local council elections of 6
May 1990, and the enactment of the new Municipal Charter of 17 May
1990, the dramatic change in local politics and administration upsurge had
its territorial base in the two-tier local government structure that was made
up of 191 counties (as the upper level of local government – with an average
size of some 60,000 inhabitants) and of some 7,500 municipalities (as the
lower level tier, with an average of 4,500 inhabitants, half of them with less
than 500 people). This territorial structure resulted from the massive
organisational reform which the communist regime carried out in the early
1950s when, in order to 'streamline' the centralist state model, it abolished
the Länder, introduced the (*oblast*-type) regional administrative districts
and redrew the boundaries of the counties. This latter reform was
accomplished by cutting the counties down to an average size of 60,000
while increasing their number to 191. By contrast, the myriad small
municipalities were left unchanged, reflecting the minimal function they
were meant to play in the GDR's centralist state.[23]

Immediately after the formation of the new Länder in October 1990 the
new governments and parliaments took up the issue of carrying out
territorial reforms at the local government levels, as the territorial structure
'inherited' from the GDR was seen as largely inappropriate for the manifold
new tasks of local government. The reform debate was significantly pushed
('exogenously') by the West German advisers and 'transferees', many of
whom were shaped by their past experience with the territorial local
government reforms that had taken place in the West German Länder during
the late 1960s and early 1970s.[24] In the pursuit of these territorial reforms in
the 'old' Federal Republic, in part through massive amalgamation, the
number of counties and of municipalities was significantly reduced.[25]

In the East German Länder the territorial reform debate and practice
resembled a dual track approach. At the county (*Kreis*) level, the newly
formed Land governments and parliaments almost immediately decided to
carry through territorial reforms that reduced the number of counties from
190 to 87 with an average size of some 120,000 inhabitants.[26] The reform
process in the Länder was often accompanied by local conflicts, not least
about the future seats of county administration.

By contrast, at the municipal level, most Länder governments and
parliaments (except in Saxony) refrained from territorial reform, although
the small size of the majority of the municipalities (half of them with less

than 500 inhabitants) would have argued for amalgamation. The restraint of East German Land governments and parliaments stemmed ('endogenously') from their reluctance to interfere with the political and democratic arenas of the many small municipalities that had just been revived as a result of the 'peaceful revolution' and of the 'grass-root' movements of late 1989 and early 1990. While leaving the territorial format of the many municipalities as the political units of local self-government unchanged, the new Länder proceeded to establish, as an institutional interim level between the municipal and the county levels, a layer of local units (*Ämter, Verwaltungsgemeinschaften*) that were meant to act as the administrative 'muscle' of the related municipalities.[27] It is only recently that the East German Länder governments and parliaments have started to push for a reform of the municipal level. At first, amalgamation was pursued as a 'voluntary' process, later through legislative imposition.

Organisational Build-up

In experiencing the rupture and transition from the subordinated, cog-like function in the GDR's centralist state machinery, to the functionally and politically strong role under the local self-government model, the local authorities on the county and municipal levels have undergone a profound organisational restructuring at a dramatic pace between mid-1990 and late 1991. It should be recalled that East German local authorities acted without guidance and supervision 'from above' from spring 1990 well into 1991, as the GDR's central government was increasingly in a state of agony prior to its final demise on 3 October 1990. Furthermore, the governmental authority of the new Länder asserted itself only in early 1991. This (short, but consequential) period of a far-reaching local autonomy which often fostered all but excessive planning and investment decisions by local governments has, in retrospect, been ironically called the 'Wild East'.[28]

The process of rebuilding local administration was ('exogenously') shaped by the organisational blueprints and guidelines which lay at the basis of local government in the 'old' Federal Republic and which was carried over by the massive 'administrative aid' (*Verwaltungshilfe*) provided, particularly in this early formative stage, by advisers and 'transferees' from West German county and municipal governments.[29] A crucial role in this 'institution transfer' was played by KGSt, a municipally funded not-for-profit organisation which, since 1949, through its organisational recommendations and blueprints, has greatly influenced the development of local administration in the 'old' Republic. It should be noted that, well into the late 1980s, KGSt elaborated and propagated a basically hierarchical administrative model. In largely drawing on this traditional administrative model, KGSt developed and proposed recommendations on the organisational reconstruction of local government in East Germany.

While the secular process of rebuilding local government was, on the one hand, significantly shaped by 'exogenous' organisational blueprints and guidelines, it was, on the other hand, noticeably influenced ('endogenously') by the specific conditions of the local situation and actors constellation resulting in a considerable variability, as well as a high rate of institutional change and 'experimental adaptation' among local authorities.[30]

At a later stage, since the mid-1990s, the East German local authorities linked up with discussion about the 'New Steering Model' (*Neues Steuerungsmodell*) as a key concept for modernising local government which, related to the international New Public Management movement, has found increasing attention and following among local governments in the 'old' Federal Republic since the early 1990s. This has been facilitated through the sudden strategic shift of KGSt, which abandoned its former traditional model and advocated a NPM-derived New Steering Model.[31]

Personnel Structures

The all but paradigmatic rupture which has confronted local government is evidenced not least by the profound changes in the size, composition and profile of the local government personnel. This has surfaced particularly in two (contradictory) developments.

On the one hand, reflecting the very limited functions that county and municipal administration fulfilled in the GDR's centralist state, even in the administration of the counties (*Kreise*) and of the 'county cities'/'county-free cities' (*Stadtkreise, kreisfreie Städte*) the 'core administration' (*Kernverwaltung*) consisted of not more than some 450 employees. Adding to this group came employees of some 'subordinated institutions' (*nachgeordnete Einrichtungen*) of local administration which provided recreational, social and other such services, while the bulk of such services was rendered by the enterprises of the state economy sector as well as by upper levels of state administration.

Since late 1990, the number of employees of county and municipal administration exploded. This happened when personnel within the myriad of social, kindergarten, recreational, cultural service organisations, previously operating in subordination to state economy enterprises and state administration, were transferred ('re-communalised') to the counties and municipalities. In the cases of counties and 'county-cities', the number of local government employees skyrocketed within weeks from 450 to up to 4,000–5,000.[32] Hence, the local governments experienced an influx of personnel who had hitherto been engaged in the delivery of social, cultural, recreational services within different organisational contexts. It should be

TABLE 5

PERSONNEL OF MUNIPALITIES

Year change	In East German Länder			In West German Länder		
	Total number	Per 1,000 inhabitants	Part-time (%)	Total number	Per 1,000 inhabitants	Part-time (%)
1991	661,505	41.6	13.38	1,334,351	20.8	23.79
1992	654,738	41.6	11.66	1,360,457	21.0	24.52
1993	539,055	34.5	14.95	1,345,051	20.5	24.88
1994	476,077	30.7	25.71	1,330,365	20.2	25.14
1996	407,015	26.4	24.62	1,264,474	19.0	26.76
1999	336,030	22.1	34.12	1,201,291	17.9	30.04
change 91–92 (%)	−1.02			1,96		
change 92–93 (%)	−17.67			−1,13		
change 93–94 (%)	−11.68			−1,09		
change 94–96 (%)	−14.51			−4,95		
change 96–99 (%)	−17.44			−5,00		
change 91–99 (%)	−49.20			−9,97		

Source: Hellmut Wollmann, 'Verwaltung in der Deutschen Vereinigung', in Klaus König (ed.), *Deutsche Verwaltung an der Schwelle des 21. Jahrhunderts* (Baden-Baden: Nomos, 2002), p.48 (data compilation by Sabine Lorenz-Kuhlmann).

noted that, due to this personnel avalanche in the wake of 're-communalisation', the personnel staffs of East German municipalities grew to twice the (per capita) size of West German municipalities (see Table 5, line for 1991).

Beset by the mounting personnel expenditures and by other budgetary pressures, the local authorities, on the one hand, faced the necessity to massively reduce their suddenly and overly expanded personnel staffs, particularly in the spheres of the 'inherited' social, recreational and various service organisations. On the other hand, in the pursuit of this policy, the East German local authorities confronted the corresponding personnel data on the West German local governments which revealed a gross 'overstaffing' of the East German local authorities and served as an 'exogenous' measuring-rod and lever to reduce personnel. Since the early 1990s, the number of East German local government employees has, in fact, been drastically reduced and has, by the end of the 1990s, come close to the per capita figures of the local government level in West Germany (see Table 5). Needless to say, this operation of almost halving the number of local government employees (from some 660,000 in 1990 to some 340,000 in 1999) has required enormous political efforts by local politicians (and has entailed great individual suffering).

On the other hand, the East German local governments faced the need and challenge to recruit and develop personnel staffs that were qualified to cope with the manifold new tasks of local government. Different approaches to tackle the blatant 'qualification gap' can be discerned.

First, in the years immediately following unification, the 'administrative aid' (*Verwaltungshilfe*) which was provided to East German local authorities by West German 'twinning' municipalities and counties (*Partnerstädte, Partnerkreise*) was crucial in getting the new organisational structures effectively operating, as well as in training East German local government employees. As already mentioned, in this early period thousands of West German 'administrative aides' (*Verwaltungshelfer*) moved back and forth. In addition, a good many remained permanently in East Germany, often nicknamed '*Wossis*' ('*Ossis*' standing for East Germans – *Ost-Deutsche* – and 'W' derived from West German).

New East German personnel were also recruited for administrative leadership and rank-and-file positions. Most of these recruits were 'administrative novices' . That is, they had not worked in state administration proper prior to 1990, but came from enterprises of the GDR's (moribund) state economy sector, or from the education and science realm, or similar. Many of the East German 'administrative novices' were engineers and natural scientists. This has made for a conspicuous difference in the educational background and career pattern between East German and West German local government employees. The former show an engineer and natural science profile, while among the latter, in the higher as well as middle echelons, a legal or at least a semi-legal vocational training prevails.[33]

Second, in order to bring about a rapid adjustment of the East German personnel to the new institutional and legal world following unification, a huge campaign of vocational training was launched in late 1990 which was heavily funded by the federal and the West German Länder governments in order to offer 'crash courses' to tens of thousands of East German local government employees.[34]

Third, the more pressure was placed upon the East German local authorities to cut down their personnel staff, the less time was left to involve their personnel in such vocational training courses. As a result, 'learning by doing' and 'training on the job' became the most important mechanisms for East German employees to learn the new institutional and legal world and to cope with the towering problems at hand.

PERFORMANCE OF THE NEW ORGANISATIONAL AND PERSONNEL STRUCTURES OF LOCAL ADMINISTRATION

As noted in the introduction, the research on the institutional transformation in East Germany (as well as in other former socialist countries in Central-Eastern Europe) has so far focused on institution-building, which is treated as an 'dependent variable' in the process of state development. This draws our attention to those factors which can and do cause institution-building. However, analysis of the *performance* of the newly established organisational (and personnel) structures in East Germany has so far been largely ignored. This approach requires that we conceptualise performance as the dependent variable, and entails assessing whether and how the new institutions might 'explain' performance. Thus, the 'classic' question: 'do institutions matter?'

This 'missing link' in transformation research was recently addressed in a research project in which the *performance* of the new organisational and personnel structures was studied by singling out the operation of local administration in a certain policy field and by assessing its quality. The policy field selected was the issuance of building permits and the application of the pertinent legal provisions by the local authorities. This policy area was selected because the legislation of the federal and the Länder levels on the issuance of building permits can be seen as a particularly instructive example of the all but 'paradigmatic' rupture and transformation in the legal setting confronting the East German local actors and practitioners. In order to set criteria for assessing the performance of the East German administrative units and actors, an 'intra-national' ('German–German') comparison was pursued by including both East and West German local administrative units in the sample of 'cases'. Without going into the methodology of the 'case studies' in detail at this point, it should be mentioned that in-depth interviews were conducted, *inter alia*, with judges of East German administrative courts who were West German 'transferees' and who, in building up the administrative courts in East Germany from scratch, have observed and judicially reviewed the application of law by East German administrative units and actors from the very beginning.[35] The findings of the project reveal an almost ideal-type sequential pattern.[36]

First, in the early 1990s, immediately following unification and the transfer of the legal administration, the personnel that worked in the newly set up local government units in charge of issuing building permits exhibited a conspicuously negligent and 'unknowing' attitude towards applying the law. Many of the relevant legal provisions tended not to be applied and were allowed to 'trickle away' (*versickern*). The disposition of the personnel to disregard the law was probably fostered, apart from the complexity of the newly imported law, by the legacy of the communist regime, which had been imbued with legal disdain, if not 'legal nihilism' under the imprint of partisanship (*Parteilichkeit*) and the commands of the Communist Party. The inclination to evade the imperatives of the *Rechtsstaat* (rule of law) was also facilitated by the fact that, in this early phase, the administrative courts which are called upon to watch over the compliance with the law were still being put in place by mainly administrative judges 'transferred' from West Germany.

Second, a subsequent period can be discerned, around the mid-1990s, in which the personnel began to over-react somewhat to the previous 'negligent' application of the law by becoming hesitant to make decisions at all or, if reaching a decision, by applying the law in an overly rigid and punctilious manner. It seems that the ever stricter judicial review by the newly fully functioning administrative courts, and the new oversight by state authorities, made for an environment which induced excessive caution and apprehension among local employees.

Finally, the third conclusion to be drawn from the results of the study shows that recently the practice of law application appears to have come quite close to the 'normal' law application in the corresponding administrative units in West German counties and municipalities. This 'normalcy' which has over the years developed in West Germany law is characterised by a 'hybrid' pattern in that the principle of strict law application is blurred by, and blended with, the disposition of the law-applying agencies to make 'strategic use' of the legal provisions to pursue and achieve public goals which, strictly speaking, lie beyond the rationale of law application. In such 'informal' negotiating with would-be investors, for instance, the administrative unit controlling the issuance of permits would reach an agreement with the investor seeking a building permit. However, the agreement would require the investor to pay for public facilities beyond the private investment. Hence, a 'grey zone' has developed in law application which has been labelled 'pragmatic or useful illegality'.[37] This phenomenon is regarded by many as both an ingenious and a virtually unavoidable expedient designed to mitigate the rigidities of the (often over-regulated) *Rechtsstaat*. In effect, the process provides a broader scope of flexibility for the 'informal *Rechtsstaat*',[38] and of the 'negotiating state'.[39] In the development of West Germany´s institutional and legal world, this 'tight-rope walk' of public administration between the formalities of the rigorous *Rechtsstaat* and the informalities and 'grey zones' of the 'negotiating' *Rechtsstaat* has been checked by the judiciary. Within this context, the law-applying administrative practitioners need the double qualification of a competent knowledge of the legal provisions involved, including the interpretation of the provisions by the courts, on the one hand,

and the skill and 'craft' to use the provisions strategically, on the other hand.

The comparative empirical findings on the issuance of building permits in East and West Germany suggest that East German local practitioners have been remarkably fast in acquiring this double skill in the application and use of the law. A main reason for this lies in the very peculiarity of the East German variant of system transformation. The rapid transfer has forced the East German local actors to learn and adopt the new legal order rapidly. At the same time, the readiness to make strategic use of the legal provisions has been facilitated by the fact that many of the East German local employees, as noted above, came from a technical and natural science background and training which helped them to bring a pragmatic view to legal provisions.[40] Furthermore, traces of the communist era, in which law had an expedient tinge, may have re-surfaced.

The conclusion which holds that the performance of East Germany's institutional world and public administration has caught up remarkably fast with the 'normalcy' of West Germany has been corroborated by other observers. For instance, this was the case with respect to the revenue offices in East Germany which have come to operate and perform almost the same as their West German counterparts.[41]

COMPARATIVE PERSPECTIVE

Finally the attempt will be made to put East Germany's institutional transformation in a comparative perspective with other former socialist countries. For our purposes, we focus particularly on Poland and Hungary.[42]

Looking first at the 'foundation' period following the collapse of the communist regimes, among the former socialist countries East Germany underwent the most dramatic institutional revamping, as the former GDR's central government structure was dissolved altogether, the five Länder that had been dissolved in 1952 by the communist regime were re-instituted and local self-government was re-introduced. In the founding period, East Germany's institution-building was largely driven by being embedded in the process of German unification and, hence, by the GDR being integrated in the 'old' Federal Republic. This aspect of 'exogenous' determination most conspicuously surfaced in the Unification Treaty, which regulated in detail the nature of the GDR's 'accession' (*Beitritt*) on 3 October 1990. At precisely midnight on that date the GDR ceased to exist as a state and legal system and the 'old' Republic's entire institutional and legal system was extended to the East. The 'exogenous' levers of this incorporation were amplified by massive 'personnel' and 'financial transfers'. Yet one should bear in mind that important decisions on institutional-building were also shaped by endogenous factors springing from, and ingrained in, the East German context. Hardly had the new Länder governments been established when, still in the foundation period, they embarked upon a far-reaching territorial reform of the counties. In doing so they were strongly influenced ('exogenously') by the size of the West German counties. By contrast, the East German Länder (except for Saxony) decided not to push for a territorial reform of the municipalities as well, notwithstanding the multitude of small municipalities functionally prompting such reform. In the decision not to amalgamate the small localities, the East German Länder were led ('endogenously') by the wish not to impair the newly revived local political arenas.

In Hungary, too, the entire institutional system was largely remoulded into what was the most decentralist institutional design among all Central-East European (and even West European) countries. As has been observed, 'there is nothing half-hearted about ... the reforms of local government in Hungary. The local government legislation is extremely liberal by any international standards'.[43] A new regional level was introduced, reminiscent of the French *departement* and *prefect*, yet with very scarce supervising powers, thus underscoring the decentralist logic of the new intergovernmental setting. Although in the debate on constitutional and institutional reforms explicit reference was made to ('exogenous') models and experiences in Western Europe, the decentralist reform design was essentially shaped 'endogenously' by a constitutional consensus which, as a result of *Hungary's* characteristic 'negotiated transition',[44] was borne by the opposition forces as well as by the reformist communists.

In contrast with Eastern Germany and Hungary, Poland emerged from the founding period with an organisational set-up which, particularly by retaining the 49 regions and the single-tier local government level, left largely unchanged the intergovernmental scheme that had been put in place by the communist regime in the mid-1970s. Thus, Poland exhibits a remarkable degree of communist-era-related path dependency. In its ambivalence between the continuing prevalence of centralist structures and the re-emergence of local government, Poland's institutional arrangement following system change can be traced to the 'dilatory compromise' which was reached between the communists and *Solidarnosc* – the communists standing for the centralist intent and *Solidarnosc* for the local level, with both expecting to win in the end. The underlying dilatory compromise logic surfaced in an intergovernmental set-up which was fraught with institutional inconsistencies and 'unfinished business'.[45]

In the later part of the 1990s, the 'consolidation period', East Germany's intergovernmental setting showed a high degree of institutional continuity and stability. It seemed that the pivotal issues of institution-building in the intergovernmental setting were already decided upon during the unification process on the national level as well as in the very early foundation period. In terms of institution-building at the Länder and sub-Länder level, only comparatively minor institutional adjustments have been made or are under way, including, for instance, attempts by Länder governments to carry out territorial reforms of the municipal level which, for 'endogenous' political reasons, had not been tackled in the foundation period. It should be borne in mind that, due to Germany's federal system, it falls to the constitutional powers of the Länder to decide on institutional matters such as the territorial reform of the local government level which often makes for significant vertical and horizontal variance in institutional regulation.

In Hungary, soon after 1990, mounting criticism was voiced regarding the overly de-centralist thrust of the foundation constitution. Following the national elections of 1994, the new leftist coalition, which commanded a two-thirds majority in the parliament, proceeded to revise the constitution by abolishing the regions and by strengthening the county level, where a state office was also installed. Although the institutional adaptation and the 'reform of the reform' was chiefly premised on 'endogenous' considerations, it was also fostered exogenously, as these institutional moves were regarded by the Hungarian government as an important credential in its bid to become a member of the EU. Thus, decisions on institution-building were increasingly influenced by the EU as an exogenous player.

In Poland, too, the institutional set-up which emerged from the foundation period and its underlying dilatory compromises was seen by many to be fraught with inconsistencies and 'unfinished business'. In the intergovernmental dimension, the controversy related particularly to the territorial and functional reform of the regions and to re-introducing the counties as the upper level of a two-tier local government system. Because of protracted party competition and conflicts over the issues, a constitutional and institutional compromise leading to agreement was not achieved until 1998 when, under the newly elected centre-right government, the long postponed institutional reform was finally pushed through.[46] The number of regions has been reduced from 49 to 16 and the (historical) counties have been re-introduced. There is evidence that in the case of Poland, too, the prospect of the country being among the first round of EU accession was a driving force behind the reforms and their final completion – with the EU, thus, making its appearance as an increasingly influential 'exogenous' actor.

NOTES

1. See, e.g., Hellmut Wollmann, 'Institution Building and Decentralization in Formerly Socialist Countries: The Cases of Poland, Hungary and East Germany', *Government and Policy*, 15 (1997), pp.463–80.
2. Guy B. Peters, 'Political Institutions, Old and New', in Robert E. Goodin and Hans-Dieter Klingemann (eds.), *A New Handbook of Political Science* (Oxford: Oxford University Press, 1996), pp.205–20.
3. Helmut Wiesenthal, 'Die Transformation Ostdeutschlands. Ein (nicht ausschließlich) privilegierter Sonderfall der Bewältigung von Transformationsproblemen', in Hellmut Wollmann, Helmut Wiesenthal and Frank Bönker (eds.), *Transformation sozialistischer Gesellschaften: Am Ende des Anfangs, Leviathan-Sonderheft* (Opladen: Westdeutscher Verlag, 1995), pp.134–62.
4. Gerhard Lehmbruch, 'Institutionentransfer. Zur politischen Logik der Verwaltungsintegration in Deutschland', in Wolfgang Seibel, Arthur Benz and Heinrich Mäding (eds.), *Verwaltungsreform und Verwaltungspolitik im Prozeß der deutschen Einigung* (Baden-Baden: Nomos, 1993), pp.42–66.
5. Richard Rose Wolfgang Zapf and Wolfgang Seifert, *Germans in Comparative Perspective*, Studies in Public Policy No.218 (Glasgow: Centre for the Study of Public Policy, 1993). .
6. Hans-Ulrich Derlien, 'German Unification and Bureaucratic Transformation', *International Political Science Review*, 14 (1993), pp.319–34; Hans-Ulrich Derlien, 'Elitenzirkulation zwischen Implosion und Integration', in Hellmut Wollmann *et al.* (eds.), *Transformation der politisch-administrativen Strukturen in Ostdeutschland* (Opladen: Leske + Budrich, 1997), pp.329–416.
7. Hellmut Wollmann, 'The Transformation of Local Government in West Germany: Between Imposed and Innovative Institutionalization', in Arthur Benz and Klaus H. Goetz (eds.), *A New German Public Sector* (Aldershot: Ashgate, 1996), pp.137–63.
8. Klaus H. Goetz, 'Rebuilding Public Administration in the New German Länder: Transfer and Differentiation', *West European Politics*, 16 (1993), pp.447–69.
9. Derlien, 'German Unification and Bureaucratic Transformation'.
10. For details: Hellmut Wollmann, 'Institutionenbildung in Ostdeutschland: Neubau, Umbau und "schöferische Zerstörung"', in Max Kaase *et al.* (eds.), *Politisches System* (Opladen: Leske + Budrich, 1996), pp.47–153.
11. See Hellmut Wollmann, 'Direkte Demokratie in den ostdeutschen Kommunen – Regelunsschub und Anwendungspraxis', in Hans-Ulrich Derlien (ed.), *Zehn Jahre Verwaltungsaufbau Ost* (Baden-Baden: Nomos, 2001), pp.27–63 for a more detailed analysis.
12. See ibid.
13. Hellmut Wollmann, 'Local Government Modernization in Germany: Between Incrementalism and Reform Waves', *Public Administration*, 78/4 (2000), p.929.
14. For details, Wollmann, 'Direkte Demokratie in den ostdeutschen Kommunen', pp.38ff.
15. For a more extended argument see ibid., pp.40ff.
16. See Detlef Pollack, 'Das geteilte Bewusstsein', in Roland Czada and Hellmut Wollmann (eds.), *Von der Bonner zur Berliner Republik, Leviathan-Sonderband* (Opladen: Westdeutscher Verlag, 1999), pp.281ff.; Markus Klein, 'Was bleibt von der friedlichen Revolution? Plebiszitäre Orientierungen im vereinten Deutschland', in Heiner Meulemann (ed.), *Werte und nationale Identität im vereinten Deutschland* (Opladen: Leske + Budrich, 1998), pp.155ff.; Wollmann, 'Direkte Demokratie in den ostdeutschen Kommunen', pp.40ff.
17. Everhard Holtmann, '"Das Volk" als örtlich aktivierte Bürgerschaft. Zur Praxis kommunaler Sachplebiszite', *Archiv für Kommunalwissenschaften*, 2 (1999), pp.187ff.
18. Susann Burchardt, 'Problemlagen, Unzufriedenheit und Mobilisierung. Unterschiede in den Proteststrukturen in Ost- und Westdeutschland 1990–1994' (Diss. FB Politik- und Sozialwissenschaften, FU Berlin verv. Ms., 1999), pp.65ff.
19. Wollmann, 'Direkte Demokratie in den ostdeutschen Kommunen', p.40.
20. See table in Wollmann, 'Institutionenbildung in Ostdeutschland', p.110.

21. See table in ibid., p.77.
22. Alexander Thumfart, *Die politische Integration Ostdeutschlands* (Frankfurt/M: Suhrkamp, 2002), p.267.
23. Hellmut Wollmann, 'Transformation der ostdeutschen Kommunalstrukturen. Rezeption, Eigenentwicklung, Innovation', in Hellmut Wollmann *et al.* (eds.), *Transformation der politisch-administrativen Strukturen in Ostdeutschland* (Opladen: Leske + Budrich, 1997), pp.282ff.
24. Eberhard Laux, 'Erfahrungen und Perspektiven der kommunalen Gebiets- und Funktionalreform', in Hellmut Wollmann and Roland Roth (eds.), *Kommunalpolitik* (Opladen: Leske + Budrich, 1999), p.175.
25. While the number of the counties was cut from 425 to 237 – averaging some 150,000 inhabitants – the number of municipalities was reduced from a total of some 24,000 to about 8,400 in what, at least in some of the 'old' Länder, such as North Rhine-Westphalia, fell in line with what has been called the 'North European' pattern of local government territorial reform (see Alan Norton, *International Handbook of Local and Regional Government. A Comparative Analysis of Advanced Democracies* (Aldershot: Edward Elgar, 1994); Hellmut Wollmann, 'Local Government Systems: From Historic Divergence towards Convergence? Great Britain, France and Germany as Comparative Cases in Point', *Government and Policy*, 18 (2000), p.48.
26. See Wollmann, 'Transformation der ostdeutschen Kommunalstrukturen', p.291 table 1 for details.
27. See ibid., p.289.
28. See ibid., pp.237ff.
29. See ibid., pp.272ff.
30. See ibid., p.277.
31. This recent development cannot be further pursued in this article, for details see e.g. Christoph Reichard, *Umdenken im Rathaus* (Berlin: Sigma, 1994); Wollmann, 'Local Government Modernization in Germany'; Kai Wegrich *et al.*, *Kommunale Verwaltungspolitik in Ostdeutschland* (Basel etc.: Birkhäuser, 1997), pp.192ff.
32. See Wollmann, 'Institutionenbildung in Ostdeutschland', pp.128ff.
33. Among the 'section heads' (*Amtsleiter*) of the larger cities (from 25,000 to 250,000 inhabitants) in East Germany, two-thirds had their vocational training in engineering, natural science, medicine etc. and only 20% in the legal or quasi-legal field, whereas, conversely, two-thirds of their West German counterparts had a legal or quasi-legal vocational background and only 20% a technical etc. one (see Wollmann, 'Institutionenbildung in Ostdeutschland', p.125, table 10).
34. See Wollmann, 'Institutionenbildung in Ostdeutschland', pp.130 ff.
35. The project was conducted in 1997–1999 at Humboldt-Universität, funded by the German Science Council (Deutsche Forschungsgemeinschaft), directed by the author of this article, carried out by Sabine Lorenz-Kuhlmann and Kai Wegrich as research staff. For a detailed project report and results see Sabine Lorenz, Kai Wegrich and Hellmut Wollmann, *Kommunale Rechtsanwendung im Umbruch und Wandel. Implementation des Städtebaurechts in ostdeutschen Kommunen* (Opladen: Leske + Budrich, 2000).
36. Ibid.
37. See Frido Wagener, 'Der öffentliche Dienst im Staat der Gegenwart', *Veröffentlichungen der Vereinigung der Deutschen Staatsrechtslehrer*, 37 (1979), p.224: 'pragmatische Illegalität'; and Niklas Luhmann, *Funktionen und Folgen formaler Organisationen* (Berlin: Duncker & Humblot, 3rd edn., 1976), p.304: 'brauchbare Illegalität'.
38. Eberhard Bohne, *Der informale Rechtsstaat* (Berlin: Duncker & Humblot, 1981).
39. Fritz W. Scharpf, 'Versuch über Demokratie im verhandelnden Staat', in Roland Czada and Manfred G. Schmidt (eds.), *Verhandlungsdemokratie, Interessenvermittlung, Regierbarkeit* (Opladen: Westdeutscher Verlag, 1993), pp.25ff.
40. See Wollmann, 'Institutionenbildung in Ostdeutschland', pp.148ff.
41. Peter Eisold, 'In Thüringen mal wieder reingeschaut', *Deutsche Steuerzeitung*, 9/94 (1994), pp.268–70.
42. Hellmut Wollmann and Tomila Lankina, 'Institution Building and Decentralization in Poland

and Hungary', in Harald Baldersheim, Michal Illner and Hellmut Wollmann (eds.), *Local Democracy in Post-Socialist Countries* (Opladen: Leske + Budrich, 2002, forthcoming); Wollmann, 'Institution Building and Decentralization in Formerly Socialist Countries', p.477; Hellmut Wollmann, 'Variationen institutioneller Transformation in sozialistischen Ländern: Die (Wieder-)Einführung der kommunalen Selbstverwaltung in Ostdeutschland, Ungarn, Polen und Rußland', in Wollmann *et al.* (eds.), *Transformation sozialistischer Gesellschaften*, pp.554–96.

43. Kenneth J. Davey, 'Local Government in Hungary', in Andrew Coulson (ed.), *Local Government in Eastern Europe* (Aldershot: Elgar, 1999) pp.57–75.

44. Judy Batt, *East Central Europe from Reform to Transformation* (London: Frances Pinter, 1991).

45. Ibid.

46. Wollmann and Lankina, 'Institution Building and Decentralization in Poland and Hungary'.

Economic Consequences of German Unification

MICHAEL MÜNTER and ROLAND STURM

Two alternative scenarios for the economic future of East Germany were discussed when Germany united in 1990. The optimists foresaw a second economic miracle, the pessimists feared that the East might become Germany's 'Mezzogiorno', an area in permanent need of subsidies from the West without any significant economic growth potential of its own. After a decade, economists concluded that 'economic unification turned out to be much more difficult than political unification'.[1] Most Germans would agree to this statement by Hans-Werner Sinn, head of the IFO-economic research institute in Munich. Economic unification preceded political integration. However, the remarkable pace of developments in the political sphere was matched by a similar pace of economic change for only a relatively short period of time. Wolfgang Thierse, President of the German Bundestag, echoed Sinn's remark when he observed: 'An honest review of the facts leads inevitably to the conclusion that the economic and social condition of East Germany is on the brink [of disaster].'[2]

When analysing the process of economic unification, one should not forget, however, that it is difficult to imagine two economies converging which were more different than those of the Federal Republic of Germany (FRG) and the German Democratic Republic (GDR). After 40 years of political and cultural divergence, Germans in East and West found themselves in two separate economic worlds: the FRG had established a social market economy based on private property, economic competition, and the freedom of movement for people, goods, services and capital. The GDR, in contrast, had established a centrally planned and controlled economy with almost no private property, no economic competition, and fixed prices for most goods.

On a theoretical level, one could have argued that economic unification therefore had to be a long-term project. However, political realities forced decision-makers to opt for fast-track solutions. When the Berlin Wall fell on 9 November 1989, the possibility of rapid unification was still not on everybody's mind. The leaders of the allied powers of the Second World War, who still had a formal responsibility for Germany's sovereignty, were,

Michael Münter and Roland Sturm, University of Erlangen-Nuremberg with the exception of the American President George Bush, reluctant to move into that direction.[3] In early 1990, the domestic situation in East Germany and later on the policies of the former allied powers towards unification changed. In East Germany, those who favoured reform, but not radical dismantling, of the GDR were soon outnumbered by those who preferred unification without any delay. This was reflected by a change of the most popular slogan at the demonstrations in Leipzig, Dresden and Berlin from 'we are the people!' (*'Wir sind das Volk!'*) to 'we are *one* people!' (*'Wir sind* ein *Volk!'*).

Economic pressures also forced decision-makers to move faster. For example, in November and December 1989 more than 170,000 East Germans migrated to the West.[4] The West German government, inspired by the leadership of Chancellor Helmut Kohl and Foreign Minister Hans-Dietrich Genscher, argued that they had to act quickly, to bring good money to the East in order to prevent the East Germans from moving towards good, that is, Western, money.[5] On 7 February, Kohl offered the East German government, led by Prime Minister Hans Modrow, negotiations for a monetary union. In March, Kohl proposed an economic, monetary and social union of the two parts of Germany. This economic agenda fitted well into Kohl's electoral strategy. The CDU/CSU-led coalition government tried to influence public opinion in the GDR by luring them with the prospect of economic prosperity in the hope that this would be a vote winner for the parliamentary elections to be held in the GDR (*Volkskammerwahlen*) on 18 March 1990. Even more important, however, would be the first all-German election in December.[6]

The legal framework for economic unification was laid in the Monetary Union treaty (GEMSU), negotiated between the West and East German governments and signed in Bonn on 18 May 1990. It came into effect on 1 July 1990. Its main features were the introduction of economic union – a social market economy (*Soziale Marktwirtschaft*) in the GDR – and of monetary union. The DM became the national currency in the GDR and the responsibility for monetary policy was transferred to the (West German) Bundesbank. To introduce monetary union exchange rates for the GDR currency vis-à-vis the DM were set at 1:1 for all current payments, especially salaries, pensions and rents. The same rate was chosen for money held in bank accounts, with variations according to individual age. The rate was set at 2:1 for all other payments as well as debts. The third feature of GEMSU was the introduction of social union. This meant the extension of the West German system of social security to the East.

In sum, the hope was that now the instruments were in place to allow the East German economy to catch up. The federal government was willing to mobilise funds for a transition period in order to reduce social hardships such as unemployment. Still, adequate fiscal policies, employment policies and policies dealing with the problem of a divergence of living standards in East and West Germany had to be developed to achieve the goal of economic unification.

FISCAL POLICIES

Central to the process of unification have been the effects of fiscal policies together with those of labour market policies. Over the years, the federal government several times had to change its assumptions regarding the size of the fiscal challenge, and its fiscal strategies. 'Our policy is: there will be no tax increases for financing German unification.'[7] This was the apodictic pre-unification statement by the German Minister of Finance, Theo Waigel. He had to renounce this statement, however, shortly after the 1990 general election because the financial situation in the East had deteriorated to unexpected levels. The Christian Democratic/Liberal government decided to raise the fuel tax, introduced a 'solidarity tax' and increased the insurance tax.[8]

A pattern of fiscal policy evolved which mainly reacted to short-term budgetary pressures. For a considerable time it was based on the assumption that unification could be paid for with petty cash. And the government systematically tried to avoid opposition to its expenditures by reducing the visibility of tax increases. These were spread out over a wide range of different kinds of taxes and contributions, and a major part of expenditure needs was deficit-financed. As Eberhard Kantzenbach put it: 'From the beginning, it was obviously a priority of the government to steer the process of unification without any noticeable financial burden for West Germans at least in the short run. The main reason may have been tactical considerations concerning the general election.'[9]

Financial Transfers

Financial transfers from the West to the East were not controversial in German politics. They were seen as necessary for the transformation of the East German economy and essential to help individuals to cope with the social consequences of unification. It has to be noted, however, that social expenditures for the health system, as well as pensions and unemployment, are not tax-financed. They are covered by the social insurance systems which are sustained by contributions of employers and employees. The method by which social insurance systems are financed required contributions to be raised, or, alternatively, these systems had to be subsidised by transfers from the federal budget. The increase of the contributions to the social security systems had a negative effect on the cost of labour and made new employment for companies less attractive.

The size of financial transfers was also, and remains, a major problem. One cause of this problem is the fact that the West German government of Chancellor Kohl overstated the opportunities and underestimated the costs of unification.[10] The Chancellor and his advisors expected a self-sustaining growth in the East after five years at the most. Kohl's famous vision of 'blooming landscapes within a few years' gave expression to this expectation. 'For such a brief transition period it seemed justified to finance the take-off period of the East German economy by public deficits.'[11] Funding for the first five years of German unification was achieved through a compromise between the federal government and the Länder. In 1990 they established the German Unity Fund (*Fonds 'Deutsche Einheit'*). It mobilised DM115 billion and was expected to make a major contribution to the reconstruction of the East German economy. We know today that this was a relatively small amount with little effect. The East remains far from achieving the goal of self-sustaining growth. From the perspective of hindsight, the political effect of the German Unity Fund was above all to underscore the contribution of the West German Länder to the financing of German unification and to highlight the limits of such funding.

In quantitative terms, between 1991 and 1999 a tremendous effort was made to finance German unification. In net figures, West Germany transferred more than DM1,200 billion over those nine years, an annual average of DM137.1 billion (Table 1).

However, as Table 2 indicates, there remains a major problem: at least half of the amount of money spent was not invested in economic activities, but went into consumption.[12] In 1999, 51.4 per cent of financial transfers (about DM74 billion) went to sustain social services, most of these funds going into old-age pensions and unemployment benefits. These transfers,

TABLE 1

FINANCIAL TRANSFERS FROM THE WEST TO THE EAST, 1991–99
(IN BILLION DM)

Transfers	1991	1992	1993	1994	1995	1996	1997	1998	1999	Total
Gross	142.9	172.6	192.0	194.0	188.1	186.0	183.0	181.2	194.6	1634.4
Income[a]	33.0	39.1	41.4	45.2	46.8	48.2	47.8	48.6	50.6	400.7
Net	109.9	133.5	150.6	148.8	141.3	137.8	135.2	132.6	144.0	1233.7
% GDP[b]	4.2	4.8	5.4	5.2	4.7	4.5	4.4	4.1	4.4	–

Notes: a East German tax income; b West German GDP, Berlin excluded.

Source: OECD, *OECD Wirtschaftsberichte 2000–2001, Deutschland* (Paris: OECD, 2001), p.136.

TABLE 2

PRIORITIES OF TRANSFER PAYMENTS (%)

	1991	1993	1995	1997	1999
Industrial infrastructure	12.4	8.6	13.0	13.2	12.6
Subsidies to companies	2.5	7.6	8.0	6.3	5.8
Social expenditures	45.4	54.4	49.5	49.7	51.4
Other	39.7	29.4	29.5	30.8	30.2

Source: OECD, OECD Wirtschaftsberichte, p.136.

though they were necessary to secure social standards in the East, have by their very nature been largely ineffective in overcoming the structural weaknesses of the East German economy.

There seems little hope of reducing the huge financial transfers from the West to the East in the future. As Rüdiger Pohl, head of the Institut für Wirtschaftsforschung in Halle, put it: 'East Germany will remain dependent on large amounts of financial assistance from West Germany for years to come.'[13] This may lead to a problem of legitimacy and social cohesion. It is not clear for how long West Germans will accept burden-sharing – leaving aside the question of whether or not a reduction of transfers is politically and economically meaningful and/or practicable.[14] However, there does not seem to be any reasonable alternative to the transfers; as Pohl has also pointed out: 'Underdevelopment in the East will create costs that in the end the West will have to bear.'[15]

Taxation

The 'tax issue' was another theme much discussed during the process of the unification. The governing coalition of CDU/CSU and FDP, committed to a policy of tax cuts to stimulate individual and business investments,[16] decided early on that unification should not be financed by tax increases.[17] However, that commitment eroded when the costs of unification rose rapidly to unexpected levels. Central to this development were a sharp increase in the need for financial transfers and the much lower than planned earnings of the Treuhandanstalt responsible for the privatisation of the East German economy.[18] In the autumn of 1990, only weeks before the all-German election held in December, leading politicians in the CDU no longer ruled out tax hikes.[19] In February 1991, it was obvious that taxes had to be raised (Table 3).[20]

In the 1990s there was a lively debate on the fairness of this kind of tax policy. It was argued that tax changes focused on indirect taxation. In other words, mass incomes were primarily used to pay for transfers to the East. The government defended this strategy despite charges by critics that the system was unjust. Government strategy was to try to avoid an increase in the corporate tax burden in the hope that their financial success might provide a stimulus for new investments, particularly into the East.

Fiscal Balance

Prior to 1990, Germany's public debt was relatively low, compared to the other G7 nations. From 1985 to 1989, it amounted to roughly 43 per cent of the FRG's GDP. The comparable public debt figures for France were approximately 46 per cent, 53 per cent in the United States, and 70 per cent in Canada and Japan. Only the United Kingdom managed to reduce its debt burden significantly from 53 per cent of GDP in 1985 to 37 per cent in 1989.[21] Germany's relative position completely changed after unification. The level of the FRG's public debt rose steadily and to over 60 per cent of GDP, an unprecedented level (Table 4).

In 2000, the federal share of the national debt was 64 per cent, while that of the Länder and local government was 28 per cent and eight per cent,

TABLE 3

NEW AND INCREASED TAXATION IN GERMANY 1991–95,
THE MOST IMPORTANT CASES

1991	– solidarity tax (7.5%), new tax; to end 30 June 1992
	– tax increases (fuel tax, taxes on energy, and insurance tax)
1992	– tax increase (tax on tobacco)
1993	– tax increases (value added tax, insurance tax)
1994	– tax increase (fuel tax)
1995	– reintroduction of solidarity tax (7.5%, unlimited)
	– tax increase (insurance tax)

Sources: Peter Lehmann, *Deutschland-Chronik 1945 bis 2000* (Bonn: Bundeszentrale für politische Bildung, rev. edn., 2000), pp.513–24; Roland Sturm, 'Die Wende im Stolperschritt – eine finanzpolitische Bilanz', in Göttrik Wewer (ed.), *Bilanz der Ära Kohl, Christlich-liberale Politik in Deutschland 1982–1998* (Opladen: Leske + Budrich, 1998), pp.193–5; Ulrich Heilemann and Hermann Rappen, 'Zehn Jahre Deutsche Einheit - Bestandsaufnahme und Perspektiven', RWI-Papiere, No. 67 (Essen: Rheinisch-Westfälisches Institut für Wirtschaftsforschung, 2000), pp.33–66.

TABLE 4

GERMANY'S PUBLIC DEBT (IN BILLION DM)

	1980	1985	1989	1990	1992	1994	1996	1998	2000
Total	468.6	760.2	928.8	1,053.5	1,342.5	1,659.6	2,126.3	2,280.1	2,369.4
% GDP	31.7	41.7	41.8	n.d.	43.1	49.4	59.8	60.9	60.5

Notes: 1980 to 1989 only West Germany.

Source: Jahresgutachten 2001/02 des Sachverständigenrates zur Begutachtung der gesamt-wirtschaftlichen Entwicklung, Bundestags-Drucksache 14/7569, 21 Nov. 2001, p.415.

respectively.[22] Today, the federal debt includes all of the 'special funds' (*Nebenhaushalte*) created in the process of unification for special needs, such as servicing GDR debts, covering the costs of GDR housing estates, or the costs incurred by the introduction of the DM.[23]

It is difficult to measure the exact degree of national debt that can be directly attributed to the needs of unification. However, Heilemann and Rappen[24] estimate that approximately half of German net public borrowing during the last decade was a direct result of unification. There is no doubt, however, that other 'unresolved social and economic problems, such as the size of the public sector, the growing share of the population who are old-age pensioners or the financial crisis of the health system, also contributed to the budgetary imbalance.'[25]

The growth of the public debt has created a set of long-term problems. One such long-term problem is the need to service interest rates, which has the effect of restricting the policy options of any government – Social Democrat (SPD) or Christian Democrat (CDU). The German budgetary plan for 2002 sets aside €42.3 billion for the servicing of the public debt. This is almost a fifth (exactly 17.07 per cent) of all budgetary expenditures.

A second long-term problem is that public debt remains a burden for future generations. To regain budgetary and thus financial latitude, every future government will have to commit itself to a policy of debt reduction. Because the tax burden is already at a high level, this will require reducing expenditures. Generally speaking, however, '[t]he social and economic consequences of deficit control policies which led [from the mid-1990s] to social unrest also reduced the legitimacy of such policies in the eyes of citizens [… and] put into question positive assumptions recently made with regard to this model [the German social market economy] in the general debate on the future of capitalism'.[26]

A special feature of the debt problem is the annual deficit. Following unification, the annual deficit rose and approached the three per cent of GDP permitted by the Maastricht Treaty's Growth and Stability Pact. Indeed, in 1993, 1996 and 1997, the deficit exceeded the amount the budget set aside for investments.[27] In strict legal terms, measured by the budgetary limits set by Article 115 of the Basic Law, this meant that the Kohl government operated budgets which were technically unconstitutional. The SPD parliamentary party initiated a legal challenge to the constitutionality of this practice (with particular reference to the 1996 budget) at the German Constitutional Court. This case has yet to be resolved. Apart from such legal considerations, the character of budgeting has remained unchanged to the present day. Germany is still far from achieving a balanced annual budget. Policies designed to control the federal deficit must be legitimised, at least in part, within the context of the needs of the economic development of East Germany.

LABOUR MARKET POLICIES

Since the mid-1970s, unemployment has been the most severe economic problem in Germany. Indeed, it remains the most important issue in the public mind during general elections. Unemployment rates and levels, however, are not the same in East and West Germany. It is not surprising that after unification unemployment rates have been lower in West than in East Germany. Moreover, unemployment rates between the two parts of Germany have diverged sharply (see Table 5). The annual unemployment rates have often risen faster in the East than in the West. Furthermore, the unemployment figures are sometimes misleading in this respect as they camouflage the substantial number of East Germans who have migrated to the West, work in the West and live in the East, or are on early retirement. State subsidised employment in public work programmes and companies (*Arbeitsbeschaffungsmaßnahmen*), as well as various training programmes, have also helped to paint a more favourable and inaccurate picture of the unemployment situation in the East.

What is the reason for the unemployment problem in East Germany? In 1989/90, German politicians had to cope with a sobering economic situation in the East. The planned economy of the German Democratic Republic was in a catastrophic state.[28] Its most important structural problems were a massive distortion of market prices, especially for food, 'artificial full employment',[29] that is, intense overstaffing at most workplaces, and low productivity. During the process of economic transition from a planned to a free market economy, these structural problems came to a head overnight,

TABLE 5

UNEMPLOYMENT IN GERMANY, ANNUAL AVARAGE ('000/%)

	1990	1991	1992	1993	1994	1995
Germany	n.d./n.d.	2,602/n.d.	2,979/7.8	3,419/8.9	3,698/9.6	3,612/9.4
West	1,883/6.4	1,689/5.7	1,808/5.9	2,270/7.3	2,556/8.2	2,565/8.3
East	537 (Oct.)/ 6.1 (Oct.)	n.d./10.4	1,170/14.6	1,149/15.1	1,142/15.2	1,047/14.0

	1996	1997	1998	1999	2000	2001	2002[a]
Germany	3,965/10.4	4,384/11.4	4,279/11.1	4,099/10.5	3,889/9.6	3,852/9.4	4,296/10.4
West	2,796/9.1	3,022/9.8	2,904/9.4	2,756/8.8	2,529/7.8	2,478/7.4	2,789/8.3
East	1,169/15.7	1,363/18.1	1,375/18.2	1,344/17.6	1,359/17.4	1,374/17.5	1,507/19.2

Notes: a. figure for February 2002.

Sources: Deutsche Bundesbank, Monatsbericht 43/4 (1991), p.74; Deutsche Bundesbank, Monatsbericht 46/12 (1994), p.79, 84; Deutsche Bundesbank, Monatsbericht 47/12 (1995), p.65; Deutsche Bundesbank, Monatsbericht 50/12 (1998), p.65; Deutsche Bundesbank, Monatsbericht 54/3 (2002), p.64.

though they were known before 1989. One of the consequences of the transition process was a breakdown of most of the GDR economy. Contrary to the view which blamed the West for 'de-industrialising East Germany',[30] it was the socialist regime of the GDR that had created the dire economic situation in which East Germany found itself in 1989. Though it cannot be denied that the privatisation agency *Treuhandanstalt* – which was central to the transition process – failed in its task to create the preconditions for a thriving market economy in East Germany, it is not the only institution to blame for East Germany's economic problems.[31] Forty years of socialism turned out to be an economic legacy for the West of Germany too.

A closer look at the labour market in the East illustrates its structural deficits. As mentioned above, one of the most striking problems of the East German economy was massive overstaffing, especially in industry. In light of this, the consequence of a great number of redundancies after unification was not surprising. The sheer figures are nevertheless astonishing: 9.2 million people were employed in 1989, but only 6.5 million in May 2001, a decrease of 29.3 per cent.[32] This decrease in employment levels was brought about by several interrelated factors.

The first was the introduction of the DM at an exchange rate of 1:1 (for wages). This dealt a heavy blow to the labour market. Given the average pre-unification unofficial exchange rate for the GDR-Mark of DM0.23, this implied a revaluation of nominal wages by more than 400 per cent.[33] This wage increase could not be compensated for by the companies through corresponding increases in the prices for their products. Goods produced in East Germany could no longer be sold at competitive prices. Thus, they lost their markets and industrial production broke down.[34]

The newly established labour relations which took effect in East Germany in 1990 were a second factor accounting for the critical decline in employment within the East. As Sinn put it: 'This was the cardinal error of unification: West German employers and employees negotiated eastern wages ... This was a calculated strategy to save western sites.'[35] Shortly before the GEMSU Treaty was signed, unions and employer associations had decided to implement Western patterns of wage negotiations in the East, especially the system of collective bargaining.[36] In 1990, Western trade unions and employers agreed on double-digit wage rises in the East to extend over the first few years of unification. Unions, on the one hand, faced pressure from its rank-and-file for wages equal to those in the West. On the other hand, union organisations had to support wage increases irrespective of productivity gains, or see the role of unions as a powerful and relevant social force in East Germany eroded through the decline of new membership and the loss of credibility in the eyes of existing members. Wage policies, therefore, transformed East Germany into a land with wages which were too high relative to prevailing productivity levels, and where goods were produced that no one in the West wanted, and which Central and East Europeans could not afford to buy.

Despite these wage policies, one lasting consequence of the inefficiencies of the West German model of collective bargaining for East Germany is the declining number of members of trade unions and employer associations. Union membership was reduced by almost half between 1993 and 1998.[37] Moreover, the process of collective bargaining itself has come under fire, with only 34 per cent of all companies and 63 per cent of all employees (in 1998) covered by a collective wage agreement.[38] The numbers for the West were significantly higher (53 per cent of enterprises, 76 per cent of employees).[39]

As alluded above, a third factor accounting for the sharp fall in East German employment after 1989/90 was the collapse of Central and East European markets for East German goods. Before 1989, the GDR economy was fully integrated in the Council for Mutual Economic Assistance (Comecon). It exported more than 61 per cent to the Comecon and imported around 56 per cent from there.[40] After monetary union, the prices of East German products went through the roof. Not only did they reflect the increased labour costs, they were now also expressed in a stable international currency. One has to remember that previously it was the case that most transfers of goods between the Comecon states were not paid in international tradable currencies, but by the exchange of goods at administered prices. Therefore, for the former customers of East Germany, the new price system meant that they could no longer afford to buy East German products.

A special feature of unemployment became the social and economic plight of women within Eastern Germany. In the GDR, the percentage of working women was much higher than that of West Germany, reaching more than 90 per cent in 1989.[41] This changed dramatically after unification.[42] The growth of inequality of employment opportunities reached its peak in 1994, when unemployed women outnumbered unemployed men, 741,000 (65 per cent) to 401,000 (35 per cent). By 2000, 705,000 women were unemployed, compared to 655,000 men.[43]

There are two main reasons why female employment decreased so sharply. On the one hand, many women in the GDR were employed at workplaces that were among the first to be liquidated, such as in light industry. On the other hand, the socialist state encouraged women to work by providing a large number of kindergartens and day nurseries and other financial benefits. Much of the infrastructure vanished during the process of economic transformation following unification. Kindergartens and day-care nurseries in the GDR were often run (with the help of state subsidies) by collective combines and factories. These were dissolved after unification.

The East German labour market is part of a broader German labour market, which itself is suffering. There has been no fundamental change of the employment situation in Germany as a whole since 1992, and this has been especially the case in the East.[44] Whereas the southern Länder in the West – Bavaria, Baden-Württemberg and Hesse – have experienced relatively low rates of unemployment, no eastern Land has an unemployment rate of less than 15 per cent. Thuringia records lowest unemployment levels, with 15.4 per cent, while Saxony-Anhalt, at 19 per cent, is the highest of the five Eastern Länder.[45]

The fact is, there is not much hope for improvement in the employment situation in the the near future. The most astonishing fact in this context is that the process of economic equalisation between East and West came to a halt years ago. Since 1997, GDP growth rates have been higher in the West than in the East. Thus, the economic gap between the two halves of Germany has not been closing, but widening. In 2000, the GDP per capita in East Germany fell to 60.4 per cent of Western levels, the worst ratio since 1995.[46] East Germany needs higher growth rates for at least one and a half decades to reach Western levels, but that scenario is not likely, at least not for the time being.[47]

PERCEPTIONS OF IMBALANCE IN LIVING STANDARDS

Individual living standards do not depend merely on access to material goods. Nonetheless, we turn our attention to material measures of living standards as these are strongly connected to the consequences of German unification. The most visible improvements in the East over the last decade have been material gains.[48] East Germans have made great progress with respect to consumption levels. After ten years, Eastern Germans have reached – and in some parts surpassed – a standard of living which West German citizens had worked more than 40 years to achieve (Table 6).

Taking into account the new availability of consumer goods, one might be tempted to assume that East Germans are satisfied with their material situation, for they are so much better off than they were a decade ago. This is not the predominant perception East Germans have, however.[49] Various attempts have been made to explain this paradoxical fact.

Arnold Vaatz (a member of the East German civil rights movement and former minister in Saxony) has argued, for instance, that there is a high degree of envy in the East. 'Many would prefer to live in hunger and poverty if their neighbour is also poor, than to live in wealth with someone who is even wealthier next to them.'[50] A second explanation holds that the East Germans compare their standards of living above all to those of West

TABLE 6

PERCENTAGE OF HOUSEHOLDS WITH DURABLE CONSUMER GOODS
(FOUR-PERSON HOUSEHOLD, MEDIUM INCOME)

	East 1991	East 1998	West 1998
car	93.8	98.0	96.0
telephone	17.6	96.5	99.5
colour TV	94.9	98.6	97.3
video recorder	39.9	80.9	86.9
personal computer	14.7	48.8	54.3
refrigerator	96.0	72.8	75.6
dishwasher	1.1	43.6	78.5
microwave oven	4.8	53.8	67.4

Source: Institut der deutschen Wirtschaft, *Deutschland in Zahlen, Ausgabe 2001* (Köln: Deutscher Instituts-Verlag, 2001), p.66.

Germans and not to those in Poland, the Czech Republic or Hungary. These countries were in a similar situation of economic and political transformation at the end of the 1980s, but did not have a 'special partner' in the West. These former socialist countries relied for the most part on their own limited resources to finance the transition process. As a consequence, their citizenry suffered lower living standards relative to what East Germans have become accustomed.[51] Undoubtedly, East Germany enjoyed a 'privileged position' in the East European transformation process.[52]

In this context, Detlev Pollack has argued that it is psychologically problematic for East Germans to be proud of their achievements. It is true that they are materially better off than their Central and East European neighbours. However, Eastern Germans also know that the positive changes they observe in their country were only to a limited extent a fruit of their own efforts and to a much greater extent the result of a dependency relationship with their fellow Western countrymen.[53]

Last but not least, various political mistakes of West German politicians have contributed to the growing dissatisfaction recorded among many East Germans. In a highly instructive essay, Wiesenthal showed that in many other countries which underwent a similar process of economic and political transformation, governments have chosen a strategy that imposed great hardships at the beginning of this process – at a time when their people were most likely to accept them.[54] The West German government, by contrast, chose to avoid the hard truth. Thus, East Germans were not fully apprised of the likely consequences they were to suffer as a result of economic recovery following unification. In the tradition of the social welfare state, from the very beginning of the unification process, the FRG government offered a wide range of advantages for the new citizens which manifested the belief that the state was the ultimate primary and dependable financial fall-back during difficult times. This reinforced a view among Eastern Germans, implanted by the socialisation process in the GDR, which saw the state as a paternalistic partner in society.

Indeed, opinion polls still reflect a significant difference in the respective East and West perceptions of the role of the state.[55] On a similar note, one also detects a divergence between the two parts of Germany concerning conflicting political values such as 'individual freedom' and 'social equality'. East Germans show a sharp preference to social equality over individual freedom, whereas West Germans, on the whole, prefer the opposite.[56]

CONCLUSION AND OUTLOOK

More than a decade after the historical date of 3 October 1990, an assessment of the economic consequences of German unification has to remain ambivalent. On the one hand, there have been major economic improvements in the eastern part of Germany, most of all with regard to income levels and productivity. Living standards have undoubtedly improved and some social groups, especially old-age pensioners, are at least as well off or even better off than their West German counterparts.[57] In the meantime, some economic growth centres have developed in the East, for example, the areas of Leipzig, Dresden or Jena.[58] It is still open to debate whether they have the potential to initiate economic growth in wider parts of East Germany.

On the other hand, huge economic problems remain that will haunt politicians for years to come. Economic growth rates have been lower in the East than in the West since 1997, and there is still mass unemployment in nearly all regions of East Germany. Only one labour market district (*Arbeitsamtsbezirk*) has an unemployment rate of less than ten per cent (Sonneberg/Thuringia, 9.9 per cent).[59] There is also a marked absence of entrepreneurs and small and medium-sized firms (*Mittelstand*), which have traditionally served as the backbone of West Germany's economy.

In addition to these far-reaching structural problems which divide Germany economically, there are major psychological obstacles which still uphold the famous 'wall in the heads' within the German population. Many East Germans feel like 'second-class citizens' (*Bürger zweiter Klasse*) because they see themselves as both being worse off materially and not fully accepted socially in the united Germany.[60] Ideas about the state and the individual in East and West Germany do not converge. For many East Germans, the way out of the economic crisis seems to be unacceptable if values of social justice are violated, whereas in West Germany there is a greater readiness to adhere to the lessons of economic liberalism.

For Germany as a whole, the economic balance sheet of unification registers a strong liability with respect to growth of public debt. Indebtedness rose dramatically during the transformation process. Despite early optimism, it became clear that financial transfers were far less efficient than expected. Money went primarily into consumption. Resources directed at private investments could often not be absorbed.

The unfinished economic agenda of German unification remains a threat to social cohesion. The German model of a social market economy has come under severe pressure not only from beyond Germany's borders as a result of a lack of economic competitiveness, but also from within Germany's borders as a result of both the dependency East Germany has developed for financial transfers from the West, as well as a persistent general feeling throughout East Germany of crisis and insecurity.

NOTES

1. Hans-Werner Sinn, 'Germany´s Economic Unification, An Assessment after Ten Years', CESifo Working Paper No. 247 (München: ifo-Institut, 2000), p.2.
2. Wolfgang Thierse, *Fünf Thesen zur Vorbereitung eines Aktionsprogramms für Ostdeutschland*, 21 Dec. 2000, p.1.
3. See, e.g., Werner Weidenfeld, Peter M. Wagner and Elke Bruck, *Außenpolitik für die deutsche Einheit, Die Entscheidungsjahre 1989/90* (Stuttgart: Deutsche Verlags-Anstalt, 1998); Ulrich Albrecht, 'Die internationale Regelung der Wiedervereinigung, Von einer "no-win"-Situation zum raschen Erfolg', *Aus Politik und Zeitgeschichte*, B 40 (1996), pp.3–11.
4. Walter Heering, 'Acht Jahre deutsche Währungsunion, Ein Beitrag wider die Legendenbildung im Vereinigungsprozeß', *Aus Politik und Zeitgeschichte*, B 24 (1998), pp.20–34; Nikolaus Werz, 'Abwanderung aus den neuen Bundesländern', *Aus Politik und Zeitgeschichte*, B 39–40 (2001), pp.23–31.
5. Klaus-Dieter Schmidt and Birgit Sander, 'Wages, Productivity and Employment in Eastern Germany', in A. Ghanie Ghaussy and Wolf Schäfer (eds.), *The Economics of German Unification* (London/New York: Routledge, 1993), pp.60–72; see also Theo Waigel, 'Zeitgespräch zur deutschen Einheit', *Politische Studien*, 51/5 (special edition Dec. 2000), pp.5–9.
6. See Fritz Vilmar and Wolfgang Dümcke, 'Kritische Zwischenbilanz der Vereinigungspolitik, Eine unerledigte Aufgabe der Politikwissenschaft', *Aus Politik und Zeitgeschichte*, B 40 (1996), pp.35-45; Roland Sturm, *Politische Wirtschaftslehre* (Opladen: Leske + Budrich, 1995), p.132; Peter März, 'Kanzlerschaft im Wiedervereinigungsprozeß – Leitbilder, Strategien, Management, Historisierungen', in Konrad Löw (ed.), *Zehn Jahre deutsche Einheit* (Berlin: Duncker & Humblot, 2001), pp.39–80; a more cautious interpretation can be found in Karl-Rudolf Korte, *Die Chance genutzt? Die Politik zur Einheit Deutschlands* (Frankfurt/New York: Campus, 1994), pp.163–6.
7. Theo Waigel, '"Auf jeden kommen Opfer zu"', *Der Spiegel*, 44/47 (1990), p.139.
8. '"Bis jetzt turnt jeder allein"', *Der Spiegel*, 45/8 (1991), pp.18–20; Roland Sturm, 'Die Wende im Stolperschritt – eine finanzpolitische Bilanz', in Göttrik Wewer (ed.), *Bilanz der Ära Kohl, Christlich-liberale Politik in Deutschland 1982–1998* (Opladen: Leske + Budrich, 1998), pp.183–200.
9. Eberhard Kantzenbach, *Wirtschaftspolitische Probleme der deutschen Wiedervereinigung* (Hamburg/Göttingen: Vandenhoeck & Ruprecht, 1993), pp.16–17.
10. Sturm, 'Die Wende im Stolperschritt', pp.187–9.
11. Roland Sturm and Markus M Müller, *Public Deficits: A Comparative Study of their*

Economic and Political Consequences in Britain, Canada, Germany and the United States (London/New York: Longman, 1999), p.76.

12. Herbert Giersch and Hans-Werner Sinn, 'Zusammenwachsen heißt zusammen wachsen', *Frankfurter Allgemeine Zeitung*, 29 Sept. 2000, p.15; Kantzenbach, *Wirtschaftspolitische Probleme*, p.18.

13. Rüdiger Pohl, 'Die unvollendete Transformation, Ostdeutschlands Wirtschaft zehn Jahre nach der Einführung der D-Mark', *Wirtschaft im Wandel*, 6/8 (2000), p.236.

14. Joachim Ragnitz, 'Zur Kontroverse um die Transferleistungen für die neuen Bundesländer', *Wirtschaft im Wandel*, 2/5 (1996), pp.3–7; Joachim Ragnitz and Christian Dreger, 'Kürzung von Transferleistungen für die ostdeutschen Bundesländer: Nur kurzfristig kontraktive Effekte', *Wirtschaft im Wandel*, 6/7 (2000), pp.195–9.

15. Pohl, 'Die unvollendete Transformation', p.236.

16. Sturm, 'Die Wende im Stolperschritt'.

17. See, e.g., 'Einheit ohne Steuer-Opfer', *Der Spiegel*, 44/14 (1990), pp.134–5; Waigel, '"Auf jeden kommen Opfer zu"'.

18. '"Wir sind nicht die Zahlmeister"', *Der Spiegel*, 44/31 (1990), pp.64–6.

19. 'Steuern: Die Union wackelt', *Der Spiegel*, 44/39 (1990), pp.138–9.

20. '"Eine ehrliche Aktion"', *Der Spiegel*, 45/9 (1991), pp.18–20.

21. Deutsche Bundesbank, 'Entwicklung der Staatsverschuldung seit Mitte der achtziger Jahre', *Monatsbericht*, 43/8 (1991), pp.32–42.

22. Jahresgutachten 2001/02 des Sachverständigenrates zur Begutachtung der gesamtwirtschaftlichen Entwicklung, *Bundestags-Drucksache*, 14/7569, 21 Nov. 2001, p.415.

23. Deutsche Bundesbank, 'Die Bedeutung von Nebenhaushalten im Zuge der deutschen Vereinigung', *Monatsbericht*, 45/5 (1993), pp.43–57.

24. Ulrich Heilemann and Hermann Rappen, 'Zehn Jahre Deutsche Einheit – Bestandsaufnahme und Perspektiven', RWI-Paper No.67 (Essen: Rheinisch-Westfälisches Institut für Wirtschaftsforschung, 2000), p.10.

25. Sturm and Müller, *Public Deficits*, p.78.

26. Ibid., p.80.

27. Sturm, 'Die Wende im Stolperschritt', p.186.

28. Günter Kusch et al. (eds.), *Schlußbilanz – DDR, Fazit einer verfehlten Wirtschafts- und Sozialpolitik* (Berlin: Duncker & Humblot, 1991); Eberhard Kuhrt et al. (eds.), *Die wirtschaftliche und ökologische Situation der DDR in den 80er Jahren* (Opladen: Leske + Budrich, 1996).

29. Thomas Lange and J.R. Shackleton, 'The Labour Market in Post-Unification Eastern Germany', in Thomas Lange and J.R. Shackleton (eds.), *The Political Economy of German Unification* (New York/London: Berghahn, 1998), p.89.

30. Vilmar and Dümcke, 'Kritische Zwischenbilanz der Vereinigungspolitik', p.40.

31. Helmut Wiesenthal, 'Die neuen Bundesländer als Sonderfall der Transformation in den Ländern Ostmitteleuropas', *Aus Politik und Zeitgeschichte*, B 40 (1996), pp.48–9.

32. Institut für Arbeitsmarkt- und Berufsforschung, 'Aktuelle Daten vom Arbeitsmarkt in Ostdeutschland', *IAB-Werkstattbericht*, 15 Jan. 2002, p.2.

33. Hans-Werner Sinn, *Kaltstart, Volkswirtschaftliche Aspekte der deutschen Vereinigung* (Tübingen: Mohr-Siebeck, 2nd rev. edn. 1992), pp.64–5.

34. Heilemann and Rappen, *Zehn Jahre Deutsche Einheit*, p.14.

35. Hans-Werner Sinn, '"Dann bricht das Chaos aus"', *Der Spiegel*, 50/25 (1996), p.114–15.

36. See Wolfgang Schroeder, 'Industrielle Beziehungen in Ostdeutschland: Zwischen Transformation und Standortdebatte', *Aus Politik und Zeitgeschichte*, B 40 (1996), pp.25–34; Wolfgang Schroeder, 'Deutsche Einheit und industrielle Beziehungen, Anmerkungen zur Tarifpolitik in Ostdeutschland', *Deutchland Archiv*, 34/1 (2000), pp.101–10.

37. Statistisches Bundesamt (ed.), *Datenreport 1999, Zahlen und Fakten über die Bundesrepublik Deutschland* (Bonn: Bundeszentrale für politische Bildung, 2000), p.535.

38. Bert Rürup and Werner Sesselmeier, 'Wirtschafts- und Arbeitswelt', in Karl-Rudolf Korte and Werner Weidenfeld (eds.), *Deutschland-TrendBuch, Fakten und Orientierungen* (Opladen: Leske + Budrich, 2001), p.284; even lower figures can be found in Institut der

deutschen Wirtschaft, *Deutschland in Zahlen, Ausgabe 2001* (Köln: Deutscher Instituts-Verlag, 2001), p.108.

39. Rürup and Sesselmeier, 'Wirtschafts- und Arbeitswelt', p.284.
40. See Korte, *Die Chance genutzt?*, p.37.
41. Gisela Helwig, 'Frauen', in Werner Weidenfeld and Karl-Rudolf Korte (eds.), *Handbuch zur deutschen Einheit 1949–1989–1999* (Bonn: Bundeszentrale für politische Bildung, enlarged edn. 1999), p.386.
42. Lange and Shackleton, 'The Labour Market in Post-Unification Eastern Germany', p.99; see also Rainer Geißler, 'Nachholende Modernisierung mit Widersprüchen, Eine Vereinigungsbilanz aus modernisierungstheoretischer Perspektive', *Aus Politik und Zeitgeschichte*, B 40 (1996), pp.22–38.
43. Figures in Jahresgutachten 2001/02 des Sachverständigenrates zur Begutachtung der gesamtwirtschaftlichen Entwicklung, p.388.
44. See Institut für Arbeitsmarkt- und Berufsforschung, 'Aktuelle Daten vom Arbeitsmarkt in Ostdeutschland', p.4.
45. Ibid., p.9.
46. See Christian Tenbrock, 'Oasen in Neufünfland', *Die Zeit*, 16 Aug. 2001, p.19.
47. See Heilemann and Rappen, *Zehn Jahre Deutsche Einheit*, p.13.
48. See e.g. Detlef Pollack, 'Wirtschaftlicher, sozialer und mentaler Wandel in Ostdeutschland, Eine Bilanz nach zehn Jahren', *Aus Politik und Zeitgeschichte*, B 40 (2000), pp.13–21; Roland Habich, 'Lebensbedingungen', in Weidenfeld and Korte (eds.), *Handbuch zur deutschen Einheit 1949–1989–1999*, pp.523–38.
49. See e.g. Roland Sturm, 'Nicht in einer Generation zu erreichen, Die Angleichung der Lebensverhältnisse', in Ralf Altenhof and Eckhard Jesse (eds.), *Das wiedervereinigte Deutschland, Zwischenbilanz und Perspektiven* (Düsseldorf: Droste, 1995), pp.193–6; idem, 'Die Hälfte des Weges', *Der Spiegel*, 54/40 (2000), p.33; see also Pollack, 'Wirtschaftlicher, sozialer und mentaler Wandel in Ostdeutschland'.
50. Arnold Vaatz, 'Mißverständnisse wie im Märchen', *Süddeutsche Zeitung*, 24/25 July 1999, p.10.
51. Jan Szomburg, 'Ostdeutschland – Polen, Zwei Transformationsansätze – zwei Entwicklungswege', in Institut für Wirtschaftsforschung Halle (ed.), *Zehn Jahre Deutsche Einheit, Bilanz und Perspektiven* (Halle: Institut für Wirtschaftsforschung, 2001), pp.74–94.
52. Richard Rose and Christian Haerpfer, 'The Impact of the Ready-made State: Die privilegierte Position Ostdeutschlands in der postkommunistischen Transformation', in Helmut Wiesenthal (ed.), *Einheit als Privileg, Vergleichende Perspektiven auf die Transformation Ostdeutschlands* (Frankfurt/New York: Campus, 1996), pp.105–40.
53. Pollack, 'Wirtschaftlicher, sozialer und mentaler Wandel in Ostdeutschland', p.21.
54. Wiesenthal, 'Die neuen Bundesländer als Sonderfall der Transformation', p.53.
55. Marc Brost et al., 'Mut, Schweiß und Tränen', *Die Zeit*, 16 Aug. 2001, pp.15–16.
56. Thomas Gensicke, 'Auf dem Weg der Integration, Die neuen Bundesbürger nach der Einheit', *Deutschland Archiv*, 34/3 (2001), pp.398–410.
57. Pohl, 'Die unvollendete Transformation', pp.229–33.
58. Roland Sturm, 'Wirtschaftsförderung und Industriepolitik in Ostdeutschland – eine Zwischenbilanz nach 10 Jahren', in Konrad Löw (ed.), *Zehn Jahre deutsche Einheit* (Berlin: Duncker & Humblot, 2001), pp.147–63.
59. Institut für Arbeitsmarkt- und Berufsforschung, 'Aktuelle Daten vom Arbeitsmarkt in Ostdeutschland', p.17.
60. See e.g. Dieter Walz and Wolfram Brunner, 'Das Sein bestimmt das Bewußtsein, Oder: Warum sich die Ostdeutschen als Bürger 2. Klasse fühlen', *Aus Politik und Zeitgeschichte*, B 51 (1997), pp.13–19; Gensicke, 'Auf dem Weg der Integration'.

A Change of Course?
German Foreign and Security Policy
After Unification

FRANZ-JOSEF MEIERS

The most popular question and answer game since German unification has been: what should be Germany's role in the post-Cold War world? This is not to say that the Bonn Republic did not play any role on the world stage or did not dare to define its national interests. It is rather a recognition that Germany's foreign and security policy was guided by the notion that the world expected nothing more from it than to keep a low profile and to remain peaceful. Unified Germany by virtue of its size and central location, its growing influence in key international institutions, its economic strength and demographic size, could be expected to exert considerable influence over developments in the new Europe.

German foreign and security policy since unification presents a puzzle. No other country was as profoundly affected by the end of the Cold War as Germany. The country in the middle of Europe regained its national unity and full national sovereignty. The post-war partition of Germany and the special rights of the four victorious states in regard to Germany as a whole and Berlin are a thing of the past. With the sea-change in international relations since the early 1990s the central feature of European politics for almost 50 years was quickly unravelling. Germany is no longer in the shadow of a massive presence of Soviet conventional forces capable of launching a *blitzkrieg* attack in Central Europe. Germany's national integrity is for the foreseeable future no longer existentially threatened. Once a divided country at the fault-lines of the East–West military confrontation, unified Germany is now encircled by allies and friends. In short, in the post-Cold War era unified Germany enjoys both a much easier external environment, considerably greater freedom of action, and heightened stature in the international system.

While the end of the Cold War and reunification marked a decisive shift in the structural constraints facing the Federal Republic of Germany (FRG), the context of Germany's foreign and security policy did not alter. Contrary to the predictions of the neo-realist school of international relations that

Franz-Josef Meiers, University of Bonn

Germany would undergo a pronounced change characterised by much greater autonomy and unilateralism, even to the extent that the German government would acquire nuclear weapons,[1] Germany's foreign and security policy has been marked by a high degree of continuity. Germany remains committed to, and embedded in, a dense web of multinational institutions, namely NATO and the EU. European integration, the transatlantic link, and the commitment to multilateral co-operation continue to be the guiding principles of the foreign and security policy of united Germany.

What explains this policy continuity across the 1990 divide? Why did the more powerful Germany not embrace a more assertive and autonomous foreign and security policy, as the neo-realists expected? The *leitmotiv* of continuity raises, however, doubts about the practicability of such a state strategy. How successful can the insistence of continuity be in view of the double new preconditions of united Germany in a fundamentally changed Europe? Will the weight of the new realities not confront united Germany with new problems which the Bonn Republic did not have to worry about? This study explains the complex pattern of continuity and change in Germany's foreign and security policy that has emerged since unification.

The first argument is that continuity of Germany's foreign and security policy after unification is the result of the socialising effects of international institutions and collective identities of the Germans shaped by history and collective memory. Germany learnt lessons from the past. Enlightened national interest lies in the country's continued embeddedness in the Euro-Atlantic institutional structures by which it can achieve its central political goals, namely security and prosperity. As Anderson and Goodman put it: 'A disastrous prewar history coupled with forty successful years in an interlocking network of international institutions led Germany away from traditional nineteenth-century conceptions of state sovereignty.'[2] The institutional forces have transformed a relationship 'between Germany *and* Europe to one of Germany in Europe'.[3] By drawing the right lessons from history, 'the Federal Republic's lack of "giant" status represented a deliberate choice'.[4] Germany's 'reflexive' commitment to international institutions is reinforced by the enduring culture of restraint. This includes a pronounced preference within German society as a whole for institutionalised co-operation and multilateral action, a deep scepticism about the appropriateness and usefulness of military force, and a strong aversion to assuming a leadership role in international security affairs.[5]

The second argument is that while the thrust of Germany's foreign and security policy did not change, its role within the Euro-Atlantic institutions is changing. German unification has a liberating effect on the potential for German diplomacy. The 'gentle giant' will use its resources to articulate more forcefully its own ideas and concepts about the future shape of a wider Europe and to assume an 'agenda-setting role', to move the international institutions in the direction preferred by Germany. Germany's new situation was summarised well by Bulmer and Paterson: 'integration is no longer a means whereby Germany seeks to compensate for its semi-sovereignty. Now, ... integration has a much greater potential to be used to enhance German international power.'[6]

Germany's regained national sovereignty and resultant greater international status translate into a larger share of new international responsibilities not faced by the old Federal Republic of Germany. Unlike during the Cold War, the united Germany no longer exists in a geopolitical cocoon sheltered from the broader security issues dealt with by its major allies. The double change of a unified Germany in a fundamentally altered post-Cold War Europe means that German decision-makers have to define the country's international role and responsibilities in different terms from those of the past. As Garton Ash aptly put it, while 'the state's external dependencies have been decisively reduced, the external demands on it have significantly increased'.[7] As the country grew larger in geographic, demographic and economic terms, the Berlin Republic is no longer the front-line consumer of security but becomes a potential co-producer of security in a wider Europe. In particular, Germany's security policy was confronted with the delicate task of redefining defence beyond the traditional mission of the Bundeswehr to complement the country's commitment to multilateral security institutions.

The continuity and change of Germany's foreign and security policy after unification will be illustrated by five issue areas which were and are of strategic importance to Germany: Germany and the deepening of the European integration process; Germany and the European Security and Defence Identity (ESDI); Germany and the 'new NATO'; Germany and the participation in out-of-area missions; and Germany and the reform of the armed forces.

GERMANY AND THE DEEPENING OF THE EUROPEAN INTEGRATION PROCESS

The events surrounding and following unification gave rise to deep suspicion amongst Germany's neighbour countries, notably France and Great Britain, which viewed the emergence of a giant at their door-steps with a population of more than 80 million and a powerful economy with great concern. The British Prime Minister Margaret Thatcher feared that Germany would become 'the Japan of Europe, but worse than Japan'. The lust for power would give the German 'juggernaut' in peace 'what Hitler couldn't get in war'. With her deep concern about German ambitions she tried to forge a Franco-British axis in winter and spring 1989–90 'to curb German power'.[8] The French *couchmare* was a return of an unfettered Germany to Bismarck's sea-saw politics (*Schaukelpolitik*) moving towards an autonomous policy between the West and the East that would make Germany again the loose canon on the deck of the ship called Europe. Instead of containing the expansion of the political, geographic and symbolic boundaries of German power through a European security system in which France and Great Britain would play the leading role as suggested by Thatcher, the French government decided to use a different strategy to achieve the same goal: to constrain the emerging German Gulliver into an ever deeper web of institutional checks and balances ultimately controlled and directed by France.[9] With the joint Kohl–Mitterand letter of 19 April 1990 to the Irish EC Presidency in which both proposed the convening of an IGC on Political Union, the French strategy of addressing the geopolitical implications of German unification by reinforcing Franco-German co-operation and by deepening the European integration process ultimately prevailed.

The German government, aware of the reservations amongst its Western neighbours, gladly accepted the French approach. Chancellor Kohl personified the decision of the German government to knit the country even more tightly into an interwoven Europe. The pre-eminent German objective was to allay the concern of its European neighbours about an emerging 'Fourth Reich' and to prevent a revival of the balance-of-power system the British Prime Minister seemed to have in mind. Such a system would have led to the revival of suspicion of German power and motives, and counter-alliances to German power, resulting in the encirclement of Germany. Chancellor Kohl saw an overriding need to maintain a close partnership with Germany's Western neighbours, notably France, which he described as the 'cornerstone' of German policy and as being of 'existential interest'.[10] Consequently, unified Germany pursued a clear course of maintaining and deepening the European integration process. Together with the French partner, Germany was the driving force to formulate, ratify and implement the 1992 Maastricht Treaty, including the provisions for Common Foreign and Security Policy (CFSP) and European Monetary Union (EMU). Finally, Germany's unequivocal commitment to the European integration process was anchored in the constitution when Article 23 of the Basic Law was amended to include commitments to development of the European Union and 'the realisation of a united Europe'.

By changing its relative weight and status, unification has increased Germany's ability to impose its ideas, concepts and priorities on its European partners. Foreign Minister Hans-Dietrich Genscher often cited

Thomas Mann's famous phrase that a European Germany is preferable to a German Europe. However, as Germany's resources grew, so did its ability to 'Germanise Europe'.[11] Since unification Germany has been more assertive, using its increased power to push for its preferred policy outcomes.

Unification reinforced Germany's 'reflexive' commitment to EMU. This commitment, however, had its price. During the negotiations leading to the Maastricht accord on EMU, Germany secured its economic and political objectives, namely tight convergence criteria to ensure lasting monetary stability and an independent European Central Bank based on the German Bundesbank. The capability of the German government to mould EMU according to its economic priorities and institutional setting rested on the 'structural power of its economy and currency and its role as the anchor of the ERM, to get its way in negotiations'.[12]

The second mark of a new German assertiveness was the push by the German government for early recognition of Slovenia and Croatia by the EU in late 1991. Germany was able to force its views on the Community because of its influence and weight in spite of the warnings, in particular by the French government, about the escalatory effects this policy might have on the Balkan conflict. As Nuttall concluded: 'It thus exploited the rule of consensus which, far from preserving national sovereignty, exposed EPC to domination by the strongest or most determined partner.'[13]

The Lamers/Schäuble paper published on 1 September 1994 by the CDU/CSU parliamentarian group in the Bundestag laid out the German vision of the future shape of Europe. It argued strongly for a federalist Europe with a European Commission becoming a European government, the strengthening of the functions of the EU parliament and a fast-track for greater integration by a core of member states. The paper not only questioned the French intergovernmental approach in which the national states are the driving force, it also challenged French leadership as being the *primus inter pares* in the EC. A policy of European federalism fed the French fear that it would undermine the independence of the French unitary state and lead to further German predominance in institutions aimed at containing it.[14] Six years later, Foreign Minister Joschka Fischer strongly argued in his famous Humboldt speech for a strengthening of the European institutions. He proposed, *inter alia*, that the President of the European Commission should be elected by the European Parliament or by the people of the EU member countries. His vision of a European 'federation',[15] his ideas about a future Europe, were instantly criticised by the French government because they questioned the preferred French approach of strengthening the ability of the nation states to push the European Integration process forward.[16]

During the Intergovernmental Conference (IGC) on the Amsterdam Treaty, Germany maintained its position of having qualified majority votes as a general rule in EU non-constitutional decision-making. Towards the end of the negotiations, Chancellor Kohl struck a bargain with Eurosceptic Länder, notably the conservative Bavaria, whereby they dropped public opposition to the European single currency in return for a rejection of majority voting in the third pillar. The Länder argued that an introduction of qualified majority voting could overrule German objections in a critical area of the home and justice policy. This could confront the German Länder with an influx of asylum seekers using other EU countries as transit to Germany where they would receive higher benefits than in other EU countries.

One of the most dependable features of the European integration process has been Germany's willingness to pay the tab for making a deeper integration happen. Nowhere have the signs of greater assertiveness been more evident than specific foreign policy decisions, particularly those that require further financial contribution by the German tax-payer. At the EU semi-annual summit meeting in Cardiff in June 1998, Chancellor Kohl insisted on a big cut in Germany's extensive payments to the EU budget. Finance Minister Theo Waigel had demanded a reduction in Germany's contribution from ECU12.5 billion in 1996 or 0.65 per cent of Gross Domestic Product to about ECU7 billion or 0.4 per cent of GDP. The new stance was a clear sign that Germans across the political spectrum were no longer prepared to pay nearly two-thirds of the Union's net budget contribution at a time when the German government provided more than DM100 billion a year in subsidies to Eastern Germany which, at the same time, forced the federal government to introduce painful cuts in the federal budget to stay in line with the convergence criteria of the EMU.[17] That the German Europe policy would become more 'British'[18] – that is, take a more hard-nosed approach to German interests in Europe – was shown again by Chancellor Schröder's repeated calls for a reduction in Germany's contribution to the EU budget. During the German EU Presidency the Schröder government proposed a partial renationalisation of the Common Agricultural Policy (CAP) designed to reduce Germany's net contribution to the EU budget of about $13 billion. The proposal met stiff resistance from France, which considers the agricultural policy as one of the core areas of the *acquis communautaire*.

The last example of growing German assertiveness was the claim made by Chancellor Schröder at the Nice summit in December 2000 to allot Germany one more vote in the Council of Ministers than the other big EU member countries. Schröder's proposal questioned the central principle of France's Europe policy: the *egalité* amongst the EU member states. The reaction of French President Chirac was predictable: the German proposal was completely unacceptable. The insistence of the German government that the greater demographic size of Germany should be reflected in a greater share of votes given to Germany in the Council of Ministers was another ominous sign of Germany's growing ambition to assert its political leadership role within the European Union.

GERMANY AND THE EUROPEAN SECURITY AND DEFENCE IDENTITY (ESDI)

Along with France, Germany has been the driving force behind the development of a European Security and Defence Identity (ESDI). The Franco-German proposals had a decisive impact on the course of negotiations and their final outcome as reflected in the sections of the Maastricht Treaty dealing with a Common Foreign and Security Policy.[19] In their joint letter of 19 April 1990 to the Irish EC Presidency, Chancellor Kohl and President Mitterand pleaded for the acceleration of 'the political construction of the Europe of the Twelve' and proposed convening a second IGC on Political Union to be held in parallel to the IGC on EMU. They defined the main objectives of the IGC as 'to strengthen the democratic legitimation of the union, render its institutions more efficient, ensure unity and coherence of the Union's economic, monetary and political action', and to 'define and implement a common foreign and security policy'. In their second letter of 11 October 1990 to the Italian EC Presidency, they proposed that the CFSP should extend to all areas, including defence. 'The Political Union should include a true common security policy which would in turn lead to a common defence.'

In their third letter of 16 October 1991 to the Dutch EU Presidency they proposed making the WEU the defence component of the Political Union. In addition, they made concrete proposals for strengthening the operational role of the WEU. These included the establishment of a WEU planning and co-ordination staff, regular meetings of the military chiefs of staff, and the creation of military units that would be assigned to the WEU. At the end of their letter, Kohl and Mitterand supported the establishment of a European Corps based on the Franco-German brigade. At the Franco-German summit in La Rochelle on 21–22 May 1992, Kohl and Mitterand announced the details of the Eurocorps. The corps was to serve three major functions: (1) the defence of the territory of NATO and WEU allies; (2) peace-keeping and peace-enforcement missions; and (3) humanitarian assistance. These three missions had been adopted by WEU foreign ministers at their meeting near Bonn on 19 June 1992 as the principal tasks of the WEU.

The Franco-German proposal shaped to a great extent the provisions for a CFSP within the Maastricht Treaty. The treaty established the CFSP on the basis that 'all questions related to the security of the Union, including the framing of a common defence policy, which might lead to a common defence'. It also assigned to the WEU the role 'to elaborate and implement decisions and actions of the Union which have defence implications'. The WEU was defined as 'the defence component of the European Union' and measures were to be worked out to develop a close working relationship between the EU and the WEU. It also endorsed most of the proposals for strengthening the WEU's operational role as suggested in the third Kohl–Mitterand letter.

The same pattern of close Franco-German co-operation was evident in the IGC negotiations leading to the Amsterdam Treaty in 1997. The German and French foreign ministries put forward three related sets of proposals. They advocated the establishment of a permanent planning and analysis unit within the secretariat of the European Council, which would play a central role in preparing and implementing the Council's decisions with respect to CFSP, and the creation of a position of secretary general, who might direct the work of the new unit and represent the EU on CFSP issues. They also emphasised the need to further loosen the consensus principle to make the process of taking and implementing decisions in the area of foreign and security policy more efficient. Only decisions with direct military consequences or matters touching upon vital interests of member countries, such as defence policy or troop deployments, would be exempt from this provision. Finally, they advanced the idea for integrating the WEU into the EU in the medium term through a step-by-step process.

The development of an ESDI confronted German decision-makers with two serious issues: the relationship between NATO and EU/WEU in European security affairs and the strengthening of the operational capabilities of the European partners. The Eurocorps became the most important source of friction between the United States and the European allies. The Bush administration feared that development of a security and defence identity outside the Alliance framework together with the formation of the Eurocorps would jeopardise the primacy of NATO as the central European security organisation, lead to the marginalisation of the United States in European security affairs and undermine transatlantic cohesion by establishing a European caucus within the Alliance.[20] The Eurocorps controversy was finally resolved by the 'SACEUR Agreement', signed by SACEUR and the French and German Chiefs of Staff in January 1993. The agreement gave operational command of the Eurocorps as either main defence or rapid reaction forces of the Alliance while the French government reserved the right to decide under what circumstances French forces would be put under Nato's operational command.[21]

The vehement US opposition to the emerging ESDI, in particular the building up of the Eurocorps, confronted Germany with a situation the old Federal Republic had successfully avoided for more than four decades: being squeezed between its commitment to both a strong Alliance and a strengthened European Community. Even though Paris and Bonn broadly agreed on the outlines of a European Security and Defence Identity, they differed on how far it might develop vis-à-vis the Alliance. The root of the German and French differences is their divergent assessments of the appropriate role for the United States in European security affairs.

Germany supported the objective of an increased security role for the EC but was anxious to maintain its even-handed *sowohl als auch* policy vis-à-vis the two central pillars of Germany's foreign and security policy: the Atlantic Alliance and the European Union. The German government was eager to prevent potentially adverse effects on relations with the United States and NATO. For Chancellor Kohl, NATO and its integrated military command structure continued to be an indispensable element of security and stability on the Continent. For the German government, strengthening the European defence pillar was a complementary effort to reinforce a co-equal transatlantic partnership in no way designed to challenge the indispensable US presence in Europe. With the establishment of the Eurocorps, Bonn was trying to bring France closer to NATO, while France was trying to move Germany closer to the French view of a 'European Europe' – that is, an autonomous Europe removed from under American tutelage. Hence, the French emphasis on the WEU and converting it to a branch of the EC. Germany, on the other hand, wanted the WEU to become the European security pillar of the Atlantic Alliance and to serve as a bridge between the EU and NATO.

The differences between Germany and France again became apparent when the French government insisted on manning Nato's regional command post in Naples with a European general as an expression of a more Europeanised command structure within the Alliance. Defence Minister Volker Rühe warned that, with its unyielding position on the politically sensitive question of the Naples command, France would risk isolating itself in a new Alliance. Under these circumstances, Paris could not count on any support from the German side.[22] As long as the Europeans could not match US military capabilities in the Mediterranean, it was argued by General Klaus Naumann, chairman of Nato's Military Committee, the position should be reserved to a US admiral.[23] The critical remarks by Rühe and Naumann, however, reinforced the impression of the French that their interests were once again being dropped by the German government because of US pressure.[24]

The different emphasis France and Germany placed on the strengthening of a European defence pillar confronted German decision-makers with a fundamental policy conflict: that the traditional *sowohl als auch* policy, which required that Germany make no decision in favour of either Washington or Paris, would become increasingly difficult to sustain. The more forcefully France insists on a European security pillar to establish a European Europe, the more difficult it becomes for the German government to reconcile its pledge to an emerging ESDI with the country's commitment to the transatlantic partnership.

In contrast to the energetic leadership role in the IGC negotiations leading to the Maastricht and Amsterdam Treaties, the German government took a very low profile in the third phase of the ESDI which began with the Franco-British summit in St Malo in early December 1998. The rather timid reaction of the German government to Franco-British initiatives to improve military capabilities and to restructure the armed forces to the operational requirements of the most likely tasks was reflected in its position on the establishment of convergence criteria for an emerging European defence policy. In view of the rather dismal performance of European forces in the NATO-led operation Allied Force, both London and Paris began to urge the European partners to agree upon defence convergence criteria to make the European security and defence policy a reality.[25]

The German government was concerned that the implementation of these convergence criteria would have far-reaching consequences for the structure of the German defence budget and for the structure of the Bundeswehr as well. These criteria would force the German government to make decisions which corresponded to neither its budgetary priorities nor its political conception about the future structure of the Bundeswehr. A rise in defence spending to two per cent of gross domestic product, considered necessary in order to meet agreed military commitments, collided with the Schröder government's austerity policy to reach a balanced budget by 2006.[26] The dilemma of the German defence budget is highlighted when one considers that just to reach the average defence spending level of 1.69 per cent of the European allies in 1998 – France, Great Britain, Turkey and Greece not even included – the German defence budget would have had to rise by DM5 billion.[27]

Secondly, the adherence to a conscript-based force structure confronted German decision-makers with an emerging force structure gap between the Bundeswehr and Germany's European allies. The decision of the French government in February 1996 to transform the French armed forces into a professional army by 2002 highlighted the conceptual and structural differences between German armed forces and those of its European allies. London and Paris were well aware of the shortcomings of the Bundeswehr and began to demand that the German government take proper steps to provide the necessary structures, capabilities and equipment. British Prime Minister Tony Blair complained that 'too few allies are transforming their armed forces to cope with the security problems of the 1990s and the 21st century ... we Europeans need to restructure our defence capabilities, so that we can project force, can deploy our troops, ships and planes beyond their home bases and sustain them there, equipped to deal with whatever level of conflict they may face'.[28]

GERMANY AND THE 'NEW NATO'

Since 1990, German leaders across the political spectrum have continued to express strong support for the Atlantic Alliance and for close security ties with the United States, including a US military presence in Europe. NATO has been described as the 'backbone', 'foundation' and 'cornerstone' of German security. Likewise, the alliance has been characterised as the 'security anchor' for all of Europe and the 'bedrock' of Europe's security architecture. As Chancellor Kohl argued, the security partnership with the United States is of 'existential importance to Germany'.[29]

One of the prerequisites for the enduring pre-eminence of the Alliance was continued NATO membership of a reunified Germany. The German government, strongly supported by the Bush administration, was aware that the future stability of Europe depended to a large extent on how the unification process was handled. For Chancellor Kohl,[30] a neutral status in exchange for Soviet support for reunification was unacceptable because it contained the seeds of an unpredictable and unstable Europe. A neutral Germany might sooner or later be tempted to develop an independent security and defence policy. Without the German contribution, the Alliance would be deprived of one of its principal functions, that of embedding Germany in a Western security structure, and would have made the military presence of the United States in Europe difficult. President Bush also warned that 'if Germany were permitted to leave the Alliance, the old "Pandora's Box" of competition and rivalry would be reopened'.[31]

Reassurances that united Germany would not seek to develop military capabilities commensurate with its greater economic power and enhanced political status as well as a package of financial and economic incentives helped to convince the Soviet leadership to give up its opposition to German membership in NATO. During the Two Plus Four Negotiations which settled the external questions related to German unification, the German government agreed to reduce the peace-time strength of its armed forces from 370,000 men to 340,000, continued to honour its legal commitment not to produce and own nuclear, biological and chemical weapons, and accepted deep reductions in its conventional armament under the stipulations of the CFE Treaty of 1990.

Another German imperative was the transformation of the Alliance into a more politically oriented all-European security forum which was primarily aimed at convincing the Soviet Union that NATO was evolving into a non-threatening military alliance. German officials insisted that the Alliance would have to revise its existing military strategy of flexible response and accept a broader definition of functions stretching from the classical mission of collective defence to the new tasks of dialogue and cooperation with the former adversaries in Eastern Europe. These efforts were adopted by NATO leaders at their July 1990 summit in London. The Alliance proposed that the member states of the Warsaw Pact adopt a joint declaration in which they confirmed that they would no longer view each other as adversaries. The former adversaries were invited to establish 'regular diplomatic liaison with NATO' and to intensify their military contacts with the Alliance. In addition, NATO announced it would reduce its reliance on nuclear weapons, which would become 'truly weapons of last resort'. In the context of the Alliance's 'Strategic Concept' adopted by NATO leaders at the Rome summit in November 1991, the German government agreed both to continue hosting allied forces on German territory and to participate in six multinational corps. In addition, some national capacities for planning, command and control were established, but only to enable the Bundeswehr to take part in multilateral military operations.

German leaders also strongly supported the strengthening of the European pillar within the Alliance. These efforts were not designed to supplant Nato's primary role in European security affairs and to undermine the cohesion of the Alliance command structure. As Chancellor Kohl insisted: 'Where a common European foreign and security policy is concerned, it is for us not a question of either/or but one as well as the other. The Western European Union can serve both to strengthen the European pillar of the Alliance and to develop a security policy dimension within the Community.'[32]

German officials have argued that the strengthening of the European security pillar would help preserve NATO and to secure continued US involvement in European security affairs. The ability of the Europeans to assume more responsibility for peace and security in and for Europe would reduce the burdens shouldered by the United States in the past. It would strengthen the European pillar of NATO and thus the Alliance itself. Defence Minister Volker Rühe has described Europe's development into an equal partner of the United States as a 'prerequisite' for lasting US engagement in European security affairs.[33] In this context, the German government has consistently opposed the duplication of existing NATO military structures. Instead, Germany has preferred a modification of Nato's planning, command and decision-making structures in ways that would allow the European allies to conduct military operations independently of the United States, should it decide not to participate, while drawing upon common NATO assets.

For German decision-makers, the Combined Joint Task Force (CJTF) concept agreed upon at the NATO ministerial council meeting in Berlin in June 1996 ideally promoted the two central principles of the country's foreign and security policy: (1) the development of 'separable but not separate' defence capabilities, that is, the assured access of European allies to NATO assets and capabilities for European-only military operations which should relieve the United States from burdens in Europe, and (2) establishment of a true transatlantic partnership. Defence Minister Rühe summed up the German rationale as follows: 'With existing structural elements new possibilities of engagement have to be created.'[34]

The acceptance of a new transatlantic partnership based on a fair distribution of responsibilities amongst the North American and European allies confronted German decision-makers with two challenges: (1) Germany's contribution to the broader mission tasks and (2) restructuring the armed forces to the changing security requirements of crisis prevention and conflict management.

GERMANY AND THE BROADER MISSION TASKS

During the Cold War, military security issues revolved around the visible existential Soviet military threat. With the end of the Cold War, the new Federal Republic of Germany was confronted with a new security challenge: whether and how to participate in multilateral military operations outside Nato's treaty area.

Since 1990, Germany has faced a series of international crises and conflicts that have demanded a response by German decision-makers. The second Gulf War, the wars of secession in the Federal Republic of Yugoslavia and other conflicts around the world, have confronted the German government with demands of the United Nations and its allies to contribute to a wide array of international peacekeeping or peacemaking operations outside the NATO treaty area. Germany was suddenly forced to reconsider the restrictions imposed on the use of the Bundeswehr beyond the area covered by NATO.

German political leaders did respond to the changing expectations of its allies and partners. On 30 January 1991, Chancellor Kohl announced to the Bundestag: 'There is for us Germans no niche in world politics, and there can be no flight from responsibility. We intend to make a contribution to a world of peace, freedom and justice.' Speaking at the final departure of Allied troops from Berlin in September 1994, he said: 'We will not stand on the sidelines where peace and freedom in the world are at stake. We Germans are aware of our responsibility and will fulfil it alongside our partners.'[35]

The White Book of 1994 contained the most comprehensive official statement of German Security Policy in the post-Cold War era. It stated that conditions to secure peace and stability in Europe had fundamentally changed. 'The danger of large-scale aggression threatening our existence has been banished. Germany's territorial integrity and that of its allies will not face an existential threat for the foreseeable future.' The risk of a major war in Europe has been replaced by a 'multitude of risk factors of different nature with widely varying regional manifestations'. As the necessities of a stationary linear defence declined with the vanishing of a existential military threat, the focus is shifting to new challenges and risks which originate outside Nato's defence parameters. The ruling of the Federal Constitutional Court in Karlsruhe (July 1994) removed any constitutional objections to the participation of Bundeswehr troops above and beyond the defence of Germany and the NATO area.

Finally, Chancellor Gerhard Schröder defined the terror attacks against the United States on 11 September 2001 as a turning point in German foreign and security policy. In a speech to the Bundestag a month after the attacks, he emphasised that Germany has to demonstrate its readiness to accept greater responsibility as a result of its fully regained sovereignty and the end of the Cold War. 'We Germans, more than anyone now have a duty fully to meet our responsibility.' He pushed home the message that the country's role as a 'secondary player' has 'irrevocably passed'. The speech, building on the 1999 decision to send German forces into combat for the first time since World War II, represented a significant broadening on Germany's international role. For Schröder, 'that includes, I say this quite unambiguously, participation in military operations to defend freedom and human rights and to create stability and security'. For many analysts, this speech amounts to a sea-change in Germany's foreign and security policy and signals a desire to play a bigger role in the world, albeit within the NATO and EU framework. 'Welcome to the new Berlin Republic, a united Germany which is shedding the provincialism of the old capital in Bonn and is cutting loose from its post-war pacifist tradition.'[36]

Several developments confirmed the expectation that the government is prepared to assume a wider German role in international security affairs:

- German forces eventually became an equal partner in follow-up peace missions on the Balkans (SFOR) without any quantitative and qualitative restrictions imposed on them as in the previous IFOR mission.
- In spring 1999, German armed forces crossed the Rubicon: for the first time since World War II the German Air Force participated with 14 ECR and Recce Tornados in the 78-day-long NATO air campaign Allied Force against the former Federal Republic of Yugoslavia to halt the murder and forceful expulsion of the Kosovar population. After the successful conclusion of the campaign more than 4,000 German troops participated in the NATO-run peacekeeping operation Kosovo Force (KFOR).
- In autumn 2001, Germany assumed the role of lead nation in the NATO-run peacekeeping operation 'Amber Fox' to protect 54 EU and 124 OSCE observers in Macedonia. The Bundeswehr provided 600 of the 1,000 NATO troops.
- As a manifestation of its 'unstinting support' of the United States after the terror attacks, the federal government committed up to 3,900 troops from all three services for the US-led operation 'Enduring Freedom' to rout the Taliban regime and destroy the Al Qaeda terror network in Afghanistan. The Schröder government also committed up to 1,200 German troops to the International Security Assistance Force (ISAF), which should provide a secure environment for the political and economic reconstruction of the war-torn Afghanistan.

In short, German participation in out-of-area missions since the mid-1990s is no longer a question of whether, but when, where and how. German governments see the German participation in out-of-area operations on an equal footing with its allies and partners as evidence that the country has accepted its new role and responsibilities for peace and security in and outside of Europe. This repositioning within the international community of nations has served German interests well, Chancellor Schröder concluded.[37]

GERMANY AND THE REFORM OF ARMED FORCES

The final segment of this study analyses the efforts of the German government to provide the military component that is vital to both a successful 'new NATO' and a European defence identity. At the centre is the reform of the Bundeswehr to adapt it to the changing operational requirements of the post-Cold War security environment. Namely, the restructuring of armed forces into rapidly deployable intervention forces which can be used for the most likely security threats outside Nato's defence parameters.

From its predecessor, the Schröder government inherited a Bundeswehr which, according to Defence Minister Rudolf Scharping, is neither 'completely Alliance ready' nor good enough to play a proper part in the new European force. Defence Minister Rudolf Scharping painted a gloomy picture of the state of the Bundeswehr:[38]

- The German armed forces, still organised more for Cold War threats than for the challenges of the twenty-first century, lack the elementary capabilities for an efficient and appropriate contribution to collective defence and the new task of crisis management.
- The Bundeswehr faces the danger of losing technological contact and hence its interoperability with major allies and partners.
- The size, composition and equipment of the crisis reaction forces do not meet the rapidly growing international demands.
- The chronically underfinanced defence budget led to an investment gap of at least DM 15 billion; further unspecified demands imposed on the budget are the requirements resulting from Nato's Defence Capability Initiative (DCI) and the emerging European Security and Defence Policy.

Germany's allies called for a well trained and equipped projection force ready for crisis management tasks in the Balkans and elsewhere. The US Secretary of Defence complained that Germany failed to restructure its military and to let the defence budget plummet to 1.5 per cent of gross national product (GNP).[39] With a bloated force structure and steadily declining defence budget, the Bundeswehr risks developing into a hollow force ill-suited for the wider mission and ill-prepared to preserve its interoperability with major NATO allies. The gaps in structure and equipment were of such magnitude to render the need for a fundamental restructuring of the German armed forces inescapable. As the former General Inspector of the Armed Forces General Hans Peter von Kirchbach concluded at a commander's meeting in Hamburg in November 1999: 'A continuation or a mere adaptation of the present structure will only cure the symptoms. A fundamental change of the Bundeswehr's structure is inevitable.'[40] The message coming from the political and military leadership was clear: No more business as usual. Nothing more than a radical reform would be sufficient to transform the Bundeswehr into a force for the twenty-first century.

Scharping defines reform as a comprehensive approach to bring the force structure, size, the acquisition of modern equipment and the defence budget again into a 'lasting balance'. The three 'cornerstones' of his reform efforts are:

- The Bundeswehr in its structure, size and composition has to be turned into a fully Alliance-ready and Europe-capable force which can carry out both collective defence and peace support missions.
- The three services have to be equipped with technologically up-to-date armaments, particularly in those areas urgently needed for the broader mission.
- A dynamic finance framework has to be created which allows the implementation of the reform measures.[41]

On 14 June 2000, The German cabinet approved a plan by Defence Minister Scharping to bring the Bundeswehr into the era of crisis prevention and crisis management. The highlights of the plan[42] are:

- The force strength will be cut from 338,000 troops to 285,000 troops, with 200,000 professionals (unchanged), 83,000 conscripts (previously 135,000), and 2,000 reservists (previously 3,000).
- The overall peacetime strength of the Bundeswehr will be around 360,000, including 80,000–90,000 civilian employees (previously 140,000); with augmentation forces of around 250,000 troops, the wartime strength comes to 500,000 military personnel.
- The strength of the standing forces will be 255,000 troops plus 22,000 military posts for training and qualification and 5,000 active-duty training spaces; the size of the readiness forces will be substantially increased from 66,000 to 150,000 troops, of which 80,000 are available and ready after a very short period of preparation; the readiness forces will be supplemented by 105,000 soldiers assigned to the basic military organisation providing national territorial tasks, basic logistic, medical support, military intelligence and central military training.
- The 255,000 standing forces are structured to sustain either an operation involving up to 50,000 troops for up to a year, or two medium-sized operations involving up to 10,000 troops each for several years as well as a number of minor operations at the same time.
- The number of conscripts will drop by 40 per cent from 135,000 to 80,000; their time of service will be shortened from ten to nine months. The performance of military service will be rendered flexible. By 2002, conscripts can choose between one term (nine months) or stages (six months plus two six-week periods of active-duty training over the following years).
- The shift from a peace to an employment force being able to cover the whole mission from mechanised operations, peacekeeping and special operations under the conditions of 'joint' and 'combined' is reflected in

the new structure of the army. The declared goal of the new structure is the enhancement of readiness forces and the capability for rapid reaction in operations outside Germany. The classic divisions with 18,000 troops are replaced by five modular structured divisions with only two brigades and a force total of 10,000 troops each. The most innovative elements are the formation of the Special Operations Division (DSO) with the Command Special Forces (KSK) and two airborne brigades (7,400 troops), the Air Mobile Division (DLO) composed of an air mechanised brigade with three regiments and an army air transport brigade with three regiments (9,800 troops), and the Army Troops Command (HTrKdo) that would dispose of independent battlefield support and logistic units (22,500 troops).

- The command structure will be tightened and adapted to the requirements of combined multinational operations. A new Joint Operations Command (*Einsatzführungskommando*) will be set up at Potsdam-Geltow which will give the Bundeswehr for the first time in its history the capability of planning, preparing and conducting land, naval or air operations on its own. The command will render the Bundeswehr compatible with multinational and integrated command structures of the Alliance and at the same time will enable it to provide operational headquarters to the EU for Petersberg tasks. Joint contributions in the areas of command, support, military intelligence, medical service, logistics, training and national territorial tasks will be concentrated in the newly set up Joint Support Command (*Streitkräftebasis*), which will be treated as an independent organisational area with its own Chief of Staff (*Inspekteur*).

In sum, the German government responded both to the criticism expressed by Western allies about the half-hearted reform efforts of the Bundeswehr in the mid-1990s and the deficiencies within the structure and equipment of the Bundeswehr which became apparent in the late 1990s as a result of the participation of German forces in NATO-run peace operations in the Balkans. The major thrust of the ongoing reform is to transform the Bundeswehr from a training into an employment army which can master, in concert with its allies and partners, the most likely mission – conflict prevention and crisis management – without compromising its constitutive task of territorial and alliance defence. The reform efforts confirm the basic security orientation of the country to assure its continued Alliance readiness and Europe capability in a fundamentally changed security environment.

CONTINUITY AND CHANGE

The findings of Germany's foreign and security policy since unification can be summed up as follows. First, the unification process and its aftermath confirmed and reinforced the foreign and security policy orientation of the old Federal Republic of Germany. The continued commitment to multinational institutions, especially the European Union and the Atlantic Alliance, turned out to be the major precondition for German unification. The metaphor constantly employed by the German government was that of an anchor to reassure its neighbours that the country in the centre of Europe will continue its institutional commitments and remain a predictable and reliable partner in the pursuit of a peaceful and secure European state order.

Second, Germany's overall approach to security is still multilateral in character. Institutionalised co-operation with other countries has continued to offer Germany greater benefits at less cost than would have a more autonomous and unilateral policy. German foreign and security policy since unification provides clear evidence of the systemic and profound effects of international institutions on Germany's foreign and security policy after unification. As in the past, Germany's reliance on a web of international institutions to achieve its national goals is 'so complete as to cause these institutions to become embedded in the very definition of state interests and strategies'. In other words: Germany's institutional commitments 'have become ingrained, even assumed'. Only if the very essence of these institutions were to change would Germany reconsider its commitments, as Anderson and Goodman concluded.[43]

Third, Germany uses its previous institutional ties to exert considerable influence within these institutional structures to remake Europe to its own image as the United States so successfully did after 1945. Germany has always pursued self-interested policies in the context of Europe, but that impulse will strengthen as the greater assertiveness in its Europe policy since unification clearly shows.

Fourth, the guiding and constraining effects of a dense network of Euro-Atlantic institutions have been complemented and reinforced by Germany's distinct post-war national security culture. The enduring culture of restraint means that Germany has consciously forsaken the role of a traditional great power and developed a strong aversion to assuming a leadership role in international military affairs which William Paterson succinctly termed as 'leadership avoidance reflex'.[44]

Fifth, Germany's foreign and security policy follows the old pattern of the Federal Republic: it is prepared to assume a high profile in foreign and security affairs as the deepening of the European integration process, the transformation of NATO into a more politically oriented organisation or the strengthening of the European security pillar show, even if this high visibility conflicts with preferred policies of its major allies and partners, namely the United States and France. However, it prefers a low profile when confronted with policy issues which have a military dimension like participation in combat operations, the transformation of armed forces into professional armies or the application of convergence criteria to the common European security and defence policy. Here, Germany prefers the role of a follower rather than agenda-setter.

Sixth, the reluctant exercise of military power means that 'Germany is caught between the Scylla of collective memory which will not permit it to exercise power in a normal manner and the Charybdis of contemporary exigencies, which demand German acceptance of its responsibilities in Europe and maybe even the world'.[45] To overcome this 'unenviable predicament', Germany is pursuing a policy of incremental adaptation of its security policy as the use of force in out-of-area missions and the reform of the Bundeswehr since the mid-1990s indicate.

In sum, the new 'German Question' can be defined as finding a constructive role for the 'villain' country of the last century's two world wars. Germany faces the double task of assuring its neighbours that it is not tempted to take advantage of its position and power to establish a hegemonic role in Europe and that it does accept its new international responsibilities. The country's reputation as reliable and predictable partner depends on its indispensable contribution to the 'new NATO' and the EU with a nascent security and defence policy.

NOTES

1. See, for example, John J. Mearsheimer, *The Tragedy of Great Power Politics* (New York and London: W.W. Norton & Company, 2001), pp.393–5.
2. Jeffrey J. Anderson and John B. Goodman, 'Mars or Minerva? A United Germany, in a Post-Cold War Europe', in Robert O. Keohane, Joseph S. Nye and Stanley Hoffmann (eds.), *After the Cold War. International Institutions and State Strategies in Europe, 1989–1991* (Cambridge, MA: Harvard University Press, 1993), p.62.
3. Peter J. Katzenstein, 'United Germany in an Integrating Europe', in Peter J. Katzenstein (ed.), *Tamed Power. Germany in Europe* (Ithaca, NY: Cornell University Press, 1997), p.19.
4. William E. Paterson, 'Gulliver Unbound. The Changing Context of Foreign Policy', in G. Smith *et al.* (eds.), *Developments in German Politics* (London: Macmillan, 1992), p.139.
5. See John S. Duffield, *World Power Forsaken. Political Culture, International Institutions, and German Security Policy After Unification* (Stanford, CA: Stanford University Press, 1998); Thomas U. Berger, *National Security in Germany and Japan* (Baltimore and London: The Johns Hopkins University Press, 1998); and Thomas Banchoff, *The German Problem Transformed: Institutions, Politics and Foreign Policy 1945–1995* (Ann Arbor: University of Michigan Press, 1999).
6. Simon Bulmer and William E. Paterson, 'Germany in the European Union: Gentle Giant or Emergent Leader?', *International Affairs*, 72/1 (1996), p.17. See also Jeffrey Anderson, *German Unification and the Union of Europe* (Cambridge and New York: Cambidge University Press, 1999); Simon J. Bulmer, 'Shaping the Rules? The Constitutive Politics of the European Union and German Power', in Katzenstein (ed.), *Tamed Power*, pp.49–79; and

Jeffrey J. Anderson, 'Hard Interests, Soft Power, and Germany's Changing Role in Europe', in Katzenstein (ed.), *Tamed Power*, pp.80–107.

7. Timothy Garton Ash, 'Germany's Choice', *Foreign Affairs* (1994), pp.72–3.
8. Margaret Thatcher, *The Downing Street Years* (New York: Harper Collins, 1993), pp.798–9 and 760.
9. Stanley Hoffmann, 'French Dilemmas and Strategies', in Keohane *et al.* (eds.), *After the Cold War*.
10. Helmut Kohl, 'Grundsätze der Politik der ersten gesamtdeutschen Bundesregierung', *Bulletin*, 118 (5 Oct. 1990), p.1246; Helmut Kohl, 'Die Sicherheitsinteressen Deutschlands', *Bulletin*, 13 (10 Feb. 1993), p.103; and Helmut Kohl, 'Aufbruch in die Zukunft: Deutschland gemeinsam erneuern', *Bulletin*, 108 (24 Nov. 1994), p.990.
11. Anne-Marie Le Gloannec, 'The Implication of German Unification for Western Europe', in Paul B. Stares (ed.), *The New Germany and the New Europe* (Washington, DC: The Brookings Institution, 1992), p.273.
12. Kenneth Dyson, *Elusive Union: The Process of Economic and Monetary Union in Europe* (Harrow, UK: Longman, 1994), p.149.
13. S. Nuttall, 'The EC and Yugoslavia – Deus ex machinas or Machina sine Deo?', in *The European Union 1993: Annual Review of Activities* (Oxford: Blackwell, 1994).
14. Hoffmann, 'French Dilemmas and Strategies', pp.132, 136.
15. Joschka Fischer, 'From Confederacy to Federation – Thoughts on the Finality of European Integration', speech at the Humboldt University in Berlin, 12 May 2000, available under www.auswaertiges-amt.de.
16. French Foreign Minister Hubert Védrine went so far as to compare Fischer with the famous whistle-blower of Hamelin, who attracted the attention of the rats by playing his flute.
17. Lionel Barber, 'Germany first', *Financial Times*, 3 June 1998; Tom Buerkle, 'EU Fears Kohl Wants Contribution Cut', *International Herald Tribune*, 15 June 1998; and William Drozdiak, 'Kohl Play Nationalist Card in Shift on Europe', *International Herald Tribune*, 20/21 June 1998.
18. The term 'British' has been introduced by Hans-Friedrich von Ploetz, State Secretary within the Foreign Office. See Peter Hort, 'Die deutsche Europapolitik wird "britischer". Bonn stellt das Integrationsmodell in Frage und orientiert sich mehr und mehr an Kosten und Nutzen', *Frankfurter Allgemeine Zeitung*, 30 Oct. 1997.
19. See Finn Laursen and Sohie Vanhoonacker (eds.), *The Ratification of the Maastricht Treaty: Issues, Debates and Future Implications* (Maastricht and Dordrecht: EIPA and Martinus Nijhoff Publishers, 1994).
20. See Sophie Vanhoonacker, *The Bush Administration (1989–1993) and the Development of a European Security Identity* (Aldershot: Ashgate, 2001), pp.116–20.
21. Daniel Vernet, 'Nouveau pas de Paris vers l'Otan', *Le Monde*, 12 March 1993.
22. See his interview 'Die Ökonomie ist der Hebel', *Der Spiegel*, 42, 13 Oct. 1997, p.57.
23. 'Stagnation in Frankreichs NATO-Kurs', *Neue Zürcher Zeitung*, 3 Oct. 1997.
24. Daniel Vernet, 'Nuages franco-allemands', *Le Monde*, 3 Oct. 1997.
25. For the discussion see in particular Francois Heisbourg, 'L'Europe de la défense dans l'Alliance atlantique', *Politique Étrangère*, 2 (1999), ss.219–32.
26. Scharping argues that the Alliance and the EU had agreed to this spending ceiling. *Frankfurter Allgemeine Zeitung*, 3 April 2000.
27. Bestandsaufnahme, p.21. See also his speech at the Führungsakademie in Hamburg in September 1999.
28. Speech by Prime Minister Tony Blair at the NATO 50th Anniversary Conference, Royal United Service Institute, London, 8 March 1999.
29. Helmut Kohl, 'Die Sicherheitsinteressen Deutschlands', *Bulletin*, 13 (10 Feb. 1993), p.103.
30. See Helmut Kohl, *Ich wollte Deutschlands Einheit, dargestellt von Kai Diekmann and Ralf Georg Reuth* (Berlin: Ullstein Buchverlage, 1996); Hanns J. Küsters and Daniel Hoffmann (eds.), *Dokumente zur Deutschlandpolitik. Deutsche Einheit. Sonderedition aus den Akten des Bundeskanzleramtes 1989/90* (München: R. Oldenbourg Verlag, 1998).
31. George Bush and Brent Scowcroft, *A World Transformed* (New York: Alfred A. Knopf, 1998), p.242. See also Philip Zelikow and Condoleeza Rice, *Germany Unified and Europe*

Transformed,. A Study in Statecraft (Cambridge, MA: Harvard University Press, 5th edn., 1998).
32. quoted in Duffield, *World Power Forsaken*, p.138.
33. Volker Rühe, 'Europäische Einigung und transatlantische Partnerschaft', *Bulletin*, 86 (14 Oct. 1994), p.983.
34. Volker Rühe, 'Strukturreform der NATO. Atlantische, europäische und strategische Dimension', *Internationale Politik*, 51/4 (April 1996), p.45.
35. Helmut Kohl, 'Es darf keine Flucht aus der Verantwortung geben', *Frankfurter Allgemeine Zeitung*, 31 Jan. 1991; and *Europa Archiv*, 49/19 (10 Oct. 1994), pp.562–4.
36. Haig Simonian, 'Berlin Flexes its Muscles', *Financial Times*, 13/14 Oct. 2001.
37. 'Military's Role Called Essential', *Frankfurter Allgemeine Zeitung*, 12 June 2002.
38. See *Bestandsaufnahme. Die Bundeswehr an der Schwelle zum 21. Jahrhundert*, Bonn, May 1999; and Rudolf Scharping, 'Grundlinien deutscher Sicherheitspolitik'.
39. See his remarks to Bundeswehr commanders on 1 Dec. 1999 in Hamburg. www.usia.gov/admin/006/eur411.htm.
40. 'Die Bundeswehr – Armee im Einsatz. Standortbestimmung und Perspektiven' speech at the commander's meeting in Hamburg on 29 Nov. 1999, www.bundeswehr.de/kdrtagung/reden/rede-gi.htm.
41. See in particular his speech at the Führungsakademie in Hamburg on 9 Sept. 1999.
42. See Federal Minister of Defence, *The Bundeswehr – Advancing Steadily into the 21st Century. Cornerstones of a Fundamental Renewal* (Berlin, June 2000), § 53–8; and Scharping's speech to the Bundestag on 12 Oct. 2000, www.bundeswehr.de/news/reden/reden_minister/12102000.htm.
43. Anderson and Goodman, 'Mars or Minerva?', p.60.
44. William E. Paterson, 'Muß Europa Angst vor Deutschland haben', in Rudolf Hrbek (ed.), *Der Vertrag von Maastricht* (Baden-Baden: Nomos Verlagsgesellschaft, 1993).
45. Andrei S. Markovits and Simon Reich, *The German Predicament. Memory and Power in the New Europe* (Ithaca and London: Cornell University Press, 1997), p.7.

The Power of Institutions and Norms in Shaping National Answers to Globalisation: German Economic Policy After Unification

STEFAN A. SCHIRM

The globalisation of the world economy has been one of the most important factors influencing national economic policies in the last decades. Since the 1970s the deregulation of financial markets, liberalisation in world trade, technological innovation and the industrialisation success of some developing countries led to unprecedented growth and competition. The accelerating integration of national economies into the world market is changing the circumstances for private economic actors as well as for governmental policy-making. Globalisation defined as the increasing share of cross-border activities in total economic production increasingly blurs the distinction between 'internal' and 'external' economic processes.

The central result of this development is stronger global competition. This is foremost a pressure on private economic actors which have to compete increasingly on the world market. But it also forces states to compete with each other as locations for mobile capital, investment, technology and production. States that ignore the expectations of mobile resources are in principle 'punished' to a higher degree by withdrawal or withholding of economic resources, while states that offer profitable conditions benefit more from mobile resources than in the decades before globalisation. Therefore, globalisation changes the costs and benefits of economic policy options, stimulating world market-oriented reforms of national economic policies. Thus, globalisation leads to a general tendency of economic policies to converge around a liberal, world market-oriented paradigm.[1]

Indeed, such a policy convergence can be observed for the OECD countries since the 1980s. In Europe, the neo-Keynesian consensus of the post-war decades eroded and countries such as France, Germany and the United Kingdom embarked on a new course following the principles of monetary stability and world market competitiveness. Within this general trend, remarkable differences remain not only between Europe and the

Stefan A. Schirm, University of Stuttgart

United States, but also among European countries.[2] Three groups can be distinguished *grosso modo*. First, Thatcherism brought the United Kingdom close to the USA in what can be considered the Anglo-American way of deregulated, free-market policies. Second, a number of small European countries such as the Netherlands and Denmark successfully reformed their consensus-driven, corporatist economic policies and adjusted them to the requirements of globalisation. Third, France and Germany seem to be 'stuck in the middle', having started some reforms without changing their corporatist, state-led economic models fundamentally. France did change its course after the failed 'socialist experiment' at the beginning of the 1980s, pursuing a stability-oriented policy including some liberalisation since then. But no structural reform occurred.

Germany finds itself in a similar situation since Helmut Kohl's *Wende* after 1982 did enforce modest liberalisation, alleviation for industry and privatisation, but did not achieve the liberal economic shake-up that was promised. Economic policy after unification in 1990 turned back in several instances to neo-Keynesian formulae and continued to rely heavily on corporatist structures. The Schröder government's reform impetus remained patchy and seems to have substituted Kohl's guideline of *Aussitzen* with Schröder's *Politik der ruhigen Hand*. As a consequence, Germany today faces the *Standortdebatte* (debate on locational advantages) with some of the same arguments that contributed to the demise of the social-liberal coalition in 1982.

The differences in the economic policy courses of industrialised countries in Europe indicate national policy autonomy vis-à-vis the pressures of globalisation. Reforms do happen, but to varying degrees and in different forms. Thus, within the overall trend towards convergence, there remains considerable space for divergence. This leads to the central question of this article: why do economic policies diverge from the pressures of globalisation? In trying to explain this move from convergence towards liberal policies, we focus on German economic policy in the 1990s. Therefore, this paper does not compare variation between several countries, but analyses deviation from the liberalising pressures of globalisation in Germany. My argument is that national adjustment to the pressures of globalisation is shaped not only by the constraints of increasing global competition, but also by specific national institutions and norms. Thus, the result is a mix between the requirements of integration into global markets and specific institutional settings as well as specific sets of norms and values dominant in the respective societies.

Two hypotheses are brought forward in explaining divergence. First, institutional settings relevant for economic reforms are those elements of the domestic institutions that mediate between the state and society.

Corporatist structures foster veto-points to reforms, allow for deviation from a market-efficient adjustment to globalisation and increase the weight of special interest influence on economic policy. If corporatist institutions hinder reforms and can not be overruled, the state will only be able to undertake incomplete adjustments to globalisation.[3] Second, socio-economic norms and ideas are the result of decade-long socialisation processes and incorporate specific elements of a society's identity. Therefore, they cannot be rapidly changed and lead to path-dependent answers to new challenges such as globalisation. As norms and ideas cannot be changed rapidly according to new challenges, reforms only seem viable if they can be incorporated into existing norms, thus leading to a re-definition of norms.

The article is structured as follows. First, a brief appraisal is given on the causes and the impact of globalisation on national economic policies. Second, based on exemplification of the effects of globalisation, the two hypotheses will be conceptualised in order to analyse the development of economic policy in Germany. Empirical testing of the hypotheses is carried out in two cases: reforms and *Standortdebatte* of the 1990s and economic aspects of unification. A conclusion on the causes for divergence is given in the last section.

THE CASE FOR CONVERGENCE: GLOBALISATION AND NATIONAL ECONOMIES[4]

The term 'globalisation' has become problematic because of its varying definitions in the academic literature which increase the probability of misunderstandings. In addition, 'globalisation' is increasingly used as a tool for special interests in the public debate. In this article, 'globalisation' is used as a synonym for 'global markets', which seems more precise, because in this way the term is restricted to the economic dimension and provides the definitional distinction between 'the market' and 'the state' necessary for any theoretical conceptualisation of the interaction between the two. Global markets function in accordance with the logic of profit maximisation of private, transnational and potentially globally operating actors. Therefore, global markets are clearly distinguishable from the allocation of public goods as undertaken by governments, which are restricted by the confines of the nation-state and aim in principle at the common weal. To avoid the impression of simplification and reductionism, four caveats on the relationship between the state and global markets must be made.

First, the development of global markets is not a process occurring independently from the policies of national governments. States and global markets mutually influence each other. Without the liberalising policies of nation-states and multilateral governmental organisations (such as GATT/WTO, IMF), global markets would not have emerged in their present form.[5] That is not to say that states are powerless against global markets, or that regionalism will inevitably occur, as Ohmae suggests.[6] On the contrary, states continue to shape economic developments and seem to maintain freedom of manoeuvre for diverging national institutional settings and policies.[7]

Second, the development of global markets is – historically speaking – not a new phenomenon. The trans-border integration of production and capital flows was very strong at the end of the nineteenth century.[8] This era of openness ended with the two world wars and the world economic crisis after 1929. In the 1950s until the 1970s, 'embedded liberalism'[9] shaped the economic policy of the industrialised world, that is, a mix of restrictions on capital movement, fixed exchange rates, relatively open trade in goods and inward-oriented neo-Keynesianism. Therefore, the rapid increase of global markets since the 1970s is relevant to the analysis of the impact of globalisation today, and not its presence in the nineteenth century.

Third, the term 'global' does not imply that economic transactions are *predominantly* global. It only indicates that the share of cross-border activities is *increasing* in proportion to global output. 'Global' actors do not necessarily operate in every country or worldwide. Rather, their activities are in the process of global expansion and extension to a growing number of countries. Transnational activities in finance, trade and production focus 60–80 per cent on the OECD countries of Europe, North America and East Asia. Thus, global markets are characterised by their ability to *potentially* extend to any country, if the respective government offers attractive conditions. At present, states are integrated into global markets to very different degrees.

Fourth, only a small portion of GNP of the OECD countries is created by transnational activities. Investment, production and consumption are still predominantly 'domestic'. Decisive for the relevance of global markets today is their rapid increase since the 1970s, that is, the growing share of foreign trade, transnational division of labour and financial transactions in total GNP.

The core characteristics of the development of global markets are the transnational interconnectedness of national economies and the exogenous easing of cross-border transfers of resources for private actors.[10] As a consequence, economic policies that meet the expectations of global markets can be 'rewarded' more than before, while policies that do not follow the requirements of world market competition can be 'punished' more by a withdrawal or a withholding of mobile resources. If governments ignore the expectations of global markets, it can be assumed that the respective country will suffer effects such as a weakening of its currency (inflationary pressures) and a withholding or withdrawal of investment (less production and jobs) to a greater extent than in the 1960s. In addition, transnational economic activities make the financing of the government's budget difficult, as mobile actors can escape taxation more easily than immobile actors.[11]

As a consequence, the costs of redistributive, inward-oriented interventionist policies (such as neo-Keynesianism) rise as deficit spending becomes more expensive and tight regulations hinder competitive production.[12] At the same time, the incentives for world market-oriented reforms rise as they can stimulate the inflow of investment as well as production and trade. This pressure is accentuated by the potentially global allocation possibilities for transnational actors, which make states compete as locations for mobile resources. Transnational actors also attain greater political 'voice' vis-à-vis governments as they can threaten – with more credibility than inward-oriented actors – to relocate their activities abroad ('exit'), if the government does not provide more profitable conditions.

This does not imply that governmental policy-making is restricted *per se*. It is rather subject to a change in the cost of certain policy options and the benefits of other policy options. The direct cost of a policy that ignores the expectations and the competitive pressures of transnational actors rises in proportion to the integration of an economy into global markets (for example, through trade, investment, capital markets). Indirect costs arise independently from the degree of integration into global markets as opportunity costs (missing participation in mobile resources). An important element of the impact of global markets is that transnational actors are not (only) 'external', but incorporate those domestic-based companies and jobs that depend on the world market. Therefore, the line dividing different interests vis-à-vis globalisation is primarily not between employers and employees, but between world market-oriented companies and not globally competitive companies.

From this brief account of the characteristics of global markets there follow three hypotheses on the impact of global markets on states. All three suggest that global markets in principle stimulate a liberal, world market-oriented reform of national economic policy.

Crises.   Global markets react to the locational disadvantages of inward-looking interventionist policies with a withdrawal of resources and can thus influence the economic development of a country negatively.

Interests.   The growing integration of economic sectors into global markets and the increasing competition weaken the orientation of private business towards the domestic market and strengthen their orientation towards the competitive requirements on the world market. Thus, liberal, world market-oriented interests gain relevance.

Instruments. Because of the de-nationalisation of the economy, policies that foremost consider domestic market requirements will be weakened as transnational activities can easier escape the governmental grip than purely domestic actors can.

THE CASE FOR DIVERGENCE: INSTITUTIONS, NORMS AND ECONOMIC POLICY-MAKING

While the pressures of globalisation are similar to all states, national specificities may lead to variation in the answers to globalisation. Two variables were identified in the introduction that can make a difference between national responses to the impact of global markets: institutions and norms. Garrett's hypothesis[13] that a party-bias heavily influences the policy answers to globalisation is not included because his proposition only moderately fits the German case. In Germany, social democrats (SPD) and the Christian parties (CDU/CSU) show only minor differences regarding the maintenance of the welfare state and the answers to globalisation. This became evident with the Kohl and the Schröder administrations' similar unwillingness or inability to undertake far-reaching structural reforms.[14] Therefore, the analysis in the fifth section focuses on the hypotheses on institutions and norms.

Institutions

Institutions relevant to the formulation of economic policies are especially those which mediate between the government and society, that is, the organisation of economic interests and their participation in political decision-making matter in this regard.[15] How is the triangle between government, employers and employees organised? We can distinguish on the one hand corporatist countries, which give trade unions and employer associations a powerful and autonomous participation in guiding economic development. This applies, for example, to most continental European countries such as France, Germany and the Netherlands. Corporatist groups can be distinguished from other interest groups by their institutionalised influence on economic regulations and their institutionalised inclusion into the governmental decision-making process. On the other hand, competition and market-oriented countries such as the

United Kingdom after Margaret Thatcher's reforms of the 1980s and the United States see their economic policy decided by the government and only marginally submitted to the institutionalised influence of organised interests.[16]

Governments in corporatist countries such as in our case, Germany, have to embed their decision-making in close consultation with organised interests and see – where these interests possess autonomy – their influence on the economy restricted.[17] Therefore, reforms as an answer to globalisation have to be supported by corporatist groups or they will remain patchy as the government is dependent on organised interests to achieve acceptance and implementation for reforms. If the government wants to promote an economically efficient adjustment to globalisation and sees itself dependent on corporatist groups, it has to relocate political decision-making out of the reach of these groups or hope that they will change their course, as in the Netherlands or Denmark. In the latter, traditional corporatism changed towards a new 'supply-side corporativism'.[18]

Norms

Dominant norms are ideas about how a society should be organised and which principles it should follow that reach sufficient commonality (among the citizens) and specificity (with regard to their meaning) in order to form constraints for policy-making.[19] Norms develop in socialisation processes and reflect the collective experiences of societies, which in turn are part of what can be called a national 'identity'. Therefore, norms cannot usually change as quickly as material circumstances can and stimulate path-dependent policy courses. For an economic policy to be accepted among voters, it has to be embedded in the dominant norms of a given society. In the socio-economic field, relevant norms are, for example, consensus and solidarity. Governments in consensus-driven countries, such as Germany and the Netherlands, traditionally try to include all relevant societal interests in their decisions in order to reach acceptability. Competition-driven countries such as the United Kingdom accept the overruling of important groups to a greater degree. Therefore, consensus-driven societies reinforce the institutional power of corporatist interest groups by the norm of societal consensus (consensus as the cultural side of corporatism).

The solidarity norm refers to the idea that society – represented by the national government – should provide assistance to the socially or economically underprivileged. Thus, the state is made responsible for delivering a social 'safety net' in the form of unemployment assistance, health care and pension systems. The solidarity norm is especially relevant in the Scandinavian countries, Germany, the Netherlands and France. In the public debate about economic policies, these countries clearly reject the competition and market-driven models in the United States and the United Kingdom even if this implies a lesser ability to create jobs.

As the competitive pressures of globalisation stimulate liberalisation and deregulation, they will ultimately produce 'losers' in those countries that formerly followed an inward-oriented state-led policy. Those groups which were privileged by the former economic model will be especially negatively affected. Their legitimate resistance to liberalising reforms would not decisively affect governments of competition-driven countries, but would certainly hinder those in consensus-driven countries in undertaking reforms. The solidarity norm might also make liberalising reforms difficult for governments, since the state is held responsible for the well-being of all citizens and globalisation increases the cost of funds to assist 'losers' of reforms. The answers to globalisation in these countries will therefore be heavily influenced by countervailing norms. The only possibility for an economically efficient adjustment to global markets in countries guided by the norms of consensus and solidarity seems to be a redefinition of norms by finding a synthesis between the path dependency of norms and the new challenge of global competition.

'SOZIALE MARKTWIRTSCHAFT' AND ECONOMIC POLICY IN THE 1970s AND 1980s

The German post-war economic model of *Soziale Marktwirtschaft* (social market economy) aimed at the goals of attaining economic competitiveness and political stability simultaneously.[20] This was to be achieved by a combination of dense regulations by the state, market competition and strong participation of corporatist groups in economic policy decision-making: 'Capital tolerated intervention by the state and social institutions to create more equitable distribution of national income. In return, state and social actors provided the economic infrastructure and ever-rising skill levels among the labour force necessary for German firms to compete in high-quality, high value-added sectors of international markets.'[21] In practice, this organised liberalism was meant to reach political stability by socio-economic inclusiveness through a far-reaching social security system and by political inclusiveness through the intense participation of employers' associations and unions in the steering of the economy.

The latter rested first on co-ordination mechanisms such as the *Konzertierte Aktion* and today the *Bündnis für Arbeit*, which included the government, unions and employers in setting general principles for acceptable wage increases, for job creation and governmental subsidies as well as transfer payments. Secondly, it was based on the autonomy of corporatist groups in deciding working conditions (including wages) in the model of *Tarifautonomie* (free collective bargaining). Employees' power also rests on their influence on a company's policy as members of the company's supervisory board (*Aufsichtsrat*).[22] In addition, the works councils (*Betriebsräte*) have the right to co-decide issues involving working conditions (*Mitbestimmung*). Both of these mechanisms are based on federal law following the idea of compromise and consensual decision-making. Wage contracts between employers' associations and unions usually become binding throughout the respective economic sector also for those employers and employees which are not members of the respective associations. Another formative element of the German model is the tight regulation of the labour market, which aims at political stability and follows from the influence of unions and led to strong restrictions of the employer's ability to lay off employees. The institutionalised influence of employees on a company's fate politically also rests on the principle of the social responsibility of property stated in the German constitution.[23] This determination on the use of property for the 'common weal' represents a codification of the societal norm of material 'solidarity'. An instance for this norm were the difficulties the Anglo-American idea of 'shareholder-value' (in governing a company's priorities) had in becoming acceptable to the population after the modest financial market liberalisation in the 1980s.

This system and the neo-Keynesian policies dominant in the post-war decades came under pressure with the emergence of global markets from the end of the 1970s: Germany lagged behind its competitors due to high production costs while regulations and rising global interest rates increased opportunity costs for entrepreneurs as well as the costs of governmental deficit spending.[24] These pressures contributed to the end of the social-liberal coalition in 1982 and to the modest reforms of the Christian-liberal administration in 1982–98. The change of coalition partners by the liberal FDP was essentially due to a growing incompatibility of the interests of the SPD's and FDP's most important clientele groups. The effects of global markets had caused the preferences of these interest groups to diverge. As Scharpf explains,[25] the social democratic-liberal coalition was based on the two groups' mutual interest in the growth of production. Simplified, this means that the profits of the entrepreneurial group (represented by the FDP) were stimulated by the demand management policy (sale of goods), whereas labour (represented by the SPD) was able to realise a real increase in purchasing power through wage agreements above the inflation level and through growing state expenditures. This convergence of interests collapsed in 1979–82. The expanding unit labour costs lowered the profit margins of entrepreneurial activity, while at the same time alternative opportunities for profit (transnational capital investment) became more attractive due to the global wave of high interest rates.[26] The opportunities for making a profit on global financial markets were completely independent of national growth and employment rates. However, in order to seek these profit opportunities, it was more important to have a greater share of freely disposable capital (for example, by means of tax reductions) than higher aggregate demand, that is economic growth.[27]

In the last analysis, the Kohl government did not carry out a comprehensive deregulation and liberalisation of the economy after 1982 as Prime Minister Thatcher had done in the United Kingdom after 1979. Instead, Kohl continued the policy begun by Helmut Schmidt in 1981 of consolidating the budget (reducing the deficit and the public debt) by modestly cutting into the social security net and supplemented this policy with tax reductions for business, careful deregulation and measures to fight inflation. The patchwork character of the reforms was due primarily to the corporatist organisation of West German society and economy, coupled with the narrow majority the government had in the Bundestag, which made it unwise to annoy even the smallest group of voters, if they were well organised. Lobbying groups in areas that seriously needed reform, such as agriculture, the 'sunset' sectors (coal, shipbuilding, textiles, steel), trade unions and in part the entrepreneurial side often hindered the orientation toward competition which would have taken account of growing global competition in the goods and capital markets.[28] Major impulses for the implementation of further deregulation and for the political acceptability of liberal policies came from progress in European integration after 1986. Through the completion of the European Single Market and the criteria for monetary stability in the European Monetary Union the German government 'tied its hands' to a liberalising course and increased its acceptability by delegating responsibility to European institutions.[29]

When unification happened in 1990, Germany was on the one hand exposed more to global markets through transborder economic integration and embedded to a greater degree into the European economy, which had become more liberal in line with the Single Market Project. On the other hand, despite the modest economic reforms of the 1980s, Germany was still shaped by the basic characteristics of the 'Social Market Economy' as well as by corporatism and the high density of regulations that were formative in the 1960s and 1970s. This brief account of economic policy until 1990 leads to the core questions of this article: Why did German economic policy in the 1990s diverge from the convergence-pressures of globalisation and from the reformist stance of neighbouring countries such as the Netherlands? How far did institutions and norms shape the answers to globalisation in Germany?

GERMAN ANSWERS TO THE PRESSURES OF GLOBALISATION IN THE 1990s

The development of economic policy and the potential influence of institutions and norms will be analysed in two instances. First, the overall reform impetus with regard to the debate about locational problems in global competition, the *Standortdebatte*. Second, two core elements of unification policy, wage-setting and transfer-payments to the East.

Reforms and the 'Standortdebatte'

One of the major obstacles for a change in the German economic model is the opposing interpretations of the need for reforms among policy-makers and corporatist groups. These diverging interpretations led to a juxtaposition of the ideas of 'competitiveness' and 'welfare' as well as to opposing actions by corporatist groups with institutionalised power and autonomy.

On one side of the *Standortdebatte*, trade unions, some economists and a large part of the Social Democratic Party (SPD) argue that the conditions for production and investment are quite good and point at the export performance of German companies as evidence. The Deutscher Gewerkschaftsbund (DGB) published *Standort 2001: Deutschland in solider Position* and cited figures from the WTO and economic institutes indicating that Germany was the 'World's Export-Champion' in 1999 by exporting per capita US$6,598 compared with US$3,299 for Japan and US$2,546 for the USA.[30] Therefore, the unions, large parts of the SPD and the voters do not see an ultimate necessity to undertake fundamental reforms, reject changes in the welfare system and demand wage rises above inflation. Economists arguing in the same direction also point at opinion polls among entrepreneurs which show that the rising investment of German companies abroad is mainly motivated by market access and not by unattractive investment conditions at home.[31]

After the trade union-backed SPD gained power in 1998 some modest reforms of the Kohl government were taken back and labour influence in companies was strengthened (*Betriebsverfassungsgesetz*) by law. Both show the strong influence of corporatist groups on economic policy-making. While employers had their chance during the Kohl government in the 1980s (tax reductions), this time it was the unions' turn. Basically, Schröder continued the paradigm of 'divergence within convergence' vis-à-vis the pressures of globalisation. On the one hand, the new government did not undertake fundamental reforms and even decreased the attractiveness of the *Standort* with some measures such as strengthening unions' powers in firms and tightening labour market regulations (for example, for the self-employed). On the other hand, it tried to improve competitiveness by tax relief for companies, the reduction of labour costs (*Lohnnebenkosten*, see below) through the 'ecological tax' and austerity with regard to the federal budget.[32] In sum, the new regulations of the Schröder government and the corporatist influence partly ran counter to the pressures of global competitiveness and provided relative autonomy vis-à-vis global convergence. The change in government gave the unions more direct influence, as the employers had during the Kohl government. Both corporatist groups always had considerable influence because of the consensus norm as well as their institutionalised autonomy and the co-determination powers. An instance of this power was the ability of the unions to eliminate the impact of a federal law in the mid-1990s regulating wage-payments in times of sickness (*Lohnfortzahlung im Krankheitsfall*): Because of the *Tarifautonomie*, the unions were able to negotiate regulations with the employer associations which counteracted the effects of the federal law.[33]

On the other side of the *Standortdebatte*, employer associations such as the Bundesverband der Deutschen Industrie (BDI) and the Bundesvereinigung der Deutschen Arbeitgeberverbände (BDA), as well as liberal economists and politicians, argue that export performance alone is not a decisive indicator for the quality of the *Standort*, because a closer look at success in exports shows that it is paid for with lower profit margins, that the technological level of products declined and that Germany lost market share abroad to its competitors.[34] Therefore, production conditions in Germany should be improved by reducing costs in order to allow for greater R&D expenditure, better competitiveness and higher profits, which in turn would make investment and job creation in Germany more attractive. According to this line of thought, the reduction of production costs is to be achieved foremost by lower *Lohnnebenkosten*, this is mainly the social security (unemployment, pension and health) contributions which are by law co-financed by the employers as a percentage of the employees' wages and salaries. In addition, the – in international comparison – strict laws on the dismissal of employees are to be relaxed in order to give employers the possibility to reduce/augment their workforce according to the market. More flexibility with regard to work-time and a reduction in company taxes are also seen as vital for the improvement of the *Standort Deutschland*. In the end, the liberalisation demanded would change the German economic model as well as its welfare system.

This brief account clearly shows that Germany is divided with regard to a basic change of its socio-economic course. Together with the strong influence and autonomy of employer and employee organisations and the 'institutionalised norm' of political stability through welfare state provisions, this division blocks change. The only, and important, instance on which consensus exists is the need – but not the strategy – to create jobs, as unemployment oscillated around ten per cent in the 1990s. While the pro-welfare state position wants this to be achieved without changing the welfare system, the other position sees a reform of the welfare state and more individual responsibility as necessary for creating jobs. As a consequence, various round tables of the Kohl government and Schröder's *Bündnis für Arbeit* (alliance for jobs) failed completely because the participating corporatist groups (DGB, BDA and so on) diametrically opposed each other and because both governments were unable or unwilling to override the groups' opposing positions. At the same time, it is clear to most economists that global competitiveness and welfare systems do not *per se* contradict each other and that lower wages have in principle as little to do with the competitiveness of an industrialised country as liberalisation has with the end of the welfare state – it all depends on how the welfare state is defined.[35] While globalisation changes the costs and benefits of certain policy instruments, transfer payments by the government are not *per se* detrimental to competitiveness if they are not financed by deficit spending.[36]

In a comparison between Germany, the Netherlands and Denmark, Cox shows[37] that all three countries have similar institutional and normative settings, but while German politics did not change fundamentally in the 1990s, the two other countries undertook structural reforms. According to Cox, the two smaller countries achieved change through a redefinition of norms. The welfare norm was re-interpreted first by 'reciprocity' and 'fairness', that is, a duty of solidarity for the recipients of assistance. In addition to the solidarity of the society with recipients of help, these now have to show their solidarity by, for example, performing social work or by accepting lower living standards if they receive unemployment assistance. The second part of the redefinition points to individual responsibility in avoiding moral hazard problems of the welfare system and in contributing to economic competitiveness. Also, in Denmark and the Netherlands, the German dichotomy between 'welfare state' and 'global competitiveness' was overcome by integrating both: while the welfare system is now seen as strengthened by competitiveness (growth), competitiveness in turn is seen as dependent on a functioning welfare state which offers resources for re-training and assistance to those who bear the costs of adjustment to globalisation.

In sum, the German *Standortdebatte* shows the relevance of norms and corporatist institutions in preventing fundamental reforms by juxtaposing 'welfare' and 'competitiveness' instead of integrating both, as the Dutch and Danes did. The *Standortdebatte* also reveals the unwillingness of German policy-makers in creating an integrating and redefining discourse, which would allow change. It is interesting to note that German policy-makers and public opinion continue to support the idea of political inclusiveness and corporatist influence also in instances where the perception of failure is dominant. While the round table for the creation of jobs composed of the government, unions and employer associations (*Bündnis für Arbeit*) failed to reach any kind of compromise, it is seen by 72 per cent of the population as a 'good institution'.[38] The influence of norms ('consensus') seems to trigger path-dependent support even when the policy at stake does not accomplish its goals.

German Unification and Economic Policy

Unification in 1990 could have been an opportunity to adjust the West German economic model to the changing global economy. Instead, the old model was transferred in every detail to the East. Core elements of economic unification can thus provide an example for the influence of institutions and norms on economic policy-making. Before going into the specifics of the economic unification process, two caveats must be made. First, the economic aspects of unification, as all other components, were shaped by the time pressures of the historical 'window of opportunity' which the agreement of the Soviet Union to unification was seen as. Second, electoral considerations of all parties gained priority over the economic rationale, thus leading to economic mistakes widely discussed in the literature.[39] Hartwich even comes to the conclusion that the German political establishment completely lacked economic rationale in the unification process.[40] The relevance of corporatist institutions and societal norms in the unification process are analysed with regard to the micro-level (wage-policy) and the macro-level (transfer payments).

Wages

East German labour productivity in 1990 reached between 30 and 50 per cent of West German productivity. In the following years, Eastern productivity only rose slowly, while wages quickly (nearly) matched Western levels.[41] Even though the wage level in the 'Social Market Economy' in the West was traditionally attached to the respective productivity, this link was not transferred to the East, as East German wages from 1990 on followed a different logic. Western unions and employers' associations expanded to the East and both had an interest in the East's wages rising quickly to match those of the West.[42] While the unions wanted to prevent low-wage pressure on Western wages and to deliver East German workers a reason to join them, the employers' associations intended to prevent low-wage competition from East German companies. The result was a de-coupling of wage levels and productivity, which made investment in the East unattractive unless the state provided subsidies. Instead of introducing market forces in the new Eastern Länder, corporatist power and autonomy shaped an economic situation which can be labelled 'social corporatist economy'. Gerlinde Sinn concludes: 'In the end, the claim of West German corporatism to impose West German wages, regulations and norms on the New Länder [East Germany] had little in common with a fair and free market.'[43]

High wages in comparison to Eastern productivity often made production in the East prohibitively expensive without governmental incentives and contributed to the high level of unemployment in the East as well as to the breakdown of the formerly important East European markets for the East German economy.[44] As a consequence, natural comparative advantages of the East such as lower wages and living costs were eliminated and production was only viable with subsidies, tax reductions and other incentives by the state. This of course inceased the cost of unification for West German taxpayers considerably and contributed to rising budget deficits for the federal government. Decisive for the modelling of wage policy in the East was the institutionalised autonomy of collective bargaining by the corporatist groups (*Tarifautonomie*). Therefore, a disregard of the growing pressures from global markets only became possible through the institutional characteristics of the West (now also East) German economic model. Without the autonomy and the power of unions and employers' associations wage rises might have taken place in accordance with productivity. An instance for this alternative scenario are the still very low East German membership rates in the two corporatist groupings and the refusal of many companies there to pay the standard wage agreed upon by the organisations. This has led to conflicts between, on one side, 'independent' and, on the other, 'organised' employees and employers.[45]

Transfer Payments

Financial assistance to economic recovery in the new Länder and to the living standards of East Germans reached 4–6 per cent of West German GNP per year in the 1990s.[46] This enormous amount was transferred from the West to the East for example in the form of subsidies, investment in infrastructure, unemployment payments and assistance to the budgets of communities and Länder whose tax revenues were too small for the functioning of public entities and services. West–East transfers were financed by deficit spending (funded through increasing debts of the federal government) and by a special 'solidarity surcharge' on income tax for all Germans (*Solidaritätszuschlag*).[47] As East German income taxes were marginal, the 'solidarity-surcharge' was – and still is – a West German phenomenon. The *Solidaritätszuschlag* underlines the relevance of the societal norm of 'solidarity' with the underprivileged.

It is interesting to note that this 'solidarity' was – as in the case of welfare state provisions in general (see above) – not conceived reciprocally: East Germans did not have to return the solidarity, for example by performing social work, and did not have to wait a longer time to reach Western income and public service levels in exchange for Western 'solidarity' payments. As in the case of the *Standortdebatte*, the solidarity-norm was not re-defined in order to reach more individual responsibility, reciprocity in solidarity and a normative synergy between competitiveness and welfare, as the Dutch and Danes did. In the end, 'solidarity' even seems to prevail above 'equality' as living costs in the East are lower than in West Germany and as East German Länder and communities are at times better financially equipped than some of their Western counterparts.

Rather than using the challenge of unification to adapt to convergence pressures from globalisation, the power of corporatist institutions led to a truly uncompetitive modelling of East German production costs. Corporatism and the power of norms led to income levels and expectations not in accordance with market principles as well as to higher taxes, thus reducing private purchasing power and material incentives for economic activity also in West Germany. In addition, governmental deficit spending induced a rise in interest rates which discouraged private investment throughout the country and contributed to the demise of the European Monetary System in 1992.[48]

CONCLUSION

Evidence clearly indicates that German economic policy was heavily influenced by the institutional setting of its economic model and by societal norms constraining and directing policy-making. Thus, divergence from the pressures of globalisation towards convergence around a liberal, competitiveness-enhancing course can be explained at core instances of German economic policy-making by the two variables of institutions (corporatist groups) and norms (consensus and solidarity). This does not mean that other variables did not have an influence on economic policy. The concept of 'comparative institutional advantage' developed by Hall and Soskice[49] on the advantages the institutional support of co-ordinated market economies provides for production can also contribute to the explanation of the reaction of these economies to competitive pressures from globalisation. However, the German case clearly shows the relevance of the institutionalisation of corporatist power and of societal norms in explaining the deviation of economic policy and parameters from the liberalising pressures of globalisation.

The institutional setting gave corporatist groups power and autonomy to influence economic policy-making according to the interests of their respective clientele. This led to a stalemate with regard to reforms because the government was not able or willing to override opposing positions in the *Standortdebatte*. In addition, the government had to tolerate corporatist wage-setting in East Germany which obstructed a closer link to productivity, hindered East German competitiveness and contributed to the high costs of unification, which in turn ran counter to West German competitiveness through tax surcharges and rising public indebtedness.

In addition, the norms of 'consensus' and 'solidarity' led to divergent policy answers, because the first made reforms conditional on being accepted by all relevant groups (increasing the weight of corporatist power) and because the second hindered an increase of individual responsibility, a transformation of the welfare state and a market-driven approach to East German recovery. Unlike the Netherlands and Denmark, no redefinition of these norms occurred in Germany, thus perpetuating the dichotomy between 'competitiveness' and 'welfare' instead of integrating the two.

Institutions and norms modified the pressures globalisation exerts on the three pathways 'crises', 'interests' and 'instruments' introduced in the second section. The perception of a crisis in competitiveness and of the reasons for high unemployment as well as the adequacy of potential answers was contested among corporatist groups and led to opposed interpretations as to whether a structural crisis actually exists which would have made corresponding reforms necessary. Even where consensus existed on diagnosing a crisis (such as with regard to unemployment), the need for reforms and the acceptability of costs (changes in the welfare state and in labour market regulations) remained highly controversial. While globalisation has strengthened the interest of some domestic groups in better conditions for competing on the world market,[50] it did not diminish the institutional power of those groups who see the interests of their members threatened by economic liberalisation. Given the institutional (corporatist autonomy) and normative (consensus) setting in Germany, the latter were able to protect their interests and prevent far-reaching reforms. The weakening of the efficiency of (and the increasing costs for) interventionist governmental instruments by globalisation did lead to some converging answers but apparently also allowed for divergence. While corporate taxation and state-controlled production costs (such as *Lohnnebenkosten*) were modestly reduced by the Kohl and the Schröder governments, labour market regulations were partly tightened and unification was financed by tax surcharges and by deficit spending which led to high interest rates detrimental to investment. Unification did not influence policy responses to globalisation, but was shaped by the same corporatist power and norms that influenced overall economic policy-making.

The case study on German answers to the convergence pressures from globalisation shows that countries do posses autonomy for diverging economic policy. These diverging answers carry costs such as high unemployment and problems in competitiveness also seen in the German case. The core result of this study is that the domestic level matters for the policy responses to globalisation. The institutional setting for those groups mediating between society and the government as well as societal norms on how economic policy should be conducted clearly influence economic policy-making in the age of globalisation.

NOTES

1. See Vincent Cable, 'The Diminished Nation-State: A Study in the Loss of Economic Power', *Daedalus*, 124/2 (1995), pp.23–53; Daniel W. Drezner, 'Globalisation and Policy Convergence', *International Studies Review*, 3/1 (2001), pp.53–78; Stefan A. Schirm, *Globale Märkte, nationale Politik und regionale Kooperation in Europa und den Amerikas* (Baden-Baden: Nomos, 1999); Stefan A. Schirm, 'Krisen, Interessen und Instrumente. Zur Konzeption der Wirkungen globaler Märkte auf Staaten', *Zeitschrift für Politikwissenschaft*, 9/2 (1999), pp.479–98.
2. Peter A. Hall and David Soskice, 'An Introduction to Varieties of Capitalism', in Peter A. Hall and David Soskice (eds.), *Varieties of Capitalism. The Institutional Foundations of Comparative Advantage* (New York: OUP, 2001), pp.1–68; David Soskice, 'Globalisierung und institutionelle Divergenz: Die USA und Deutschland im Vergleich', *Geschichte und Gesellschaft*, 25 (1999), pp.201–25.
3. Two strategies that can increase governmental autonomy (in adjusting to globalisation) vis-à-vis domestic interest groups have been concepualised and tested in a previous paper: The transfer of economic policy decision making out of the reach of corporatist groups (1) to independent regulatory bodies and (2) to the multilateral-regional policy-making level. See Stefan A. Schirm, 'Wie Globalisierung nationale Regierungen stärkt. Zur politischen Ökonomie staatlicher Antworten auf Globalisierung', in Christine Landfried (ed.), *Politik in einer entgrenzten Welt. 21. Wissenschaftlicher Kongress der DVPW* (Köln, 2002 forthcoming).
4. This section is based on Stefan A. Schirm, *Globalisation and the New Regionalism. Global Markets, Domestic Politics and Regional Cooperation* (Cambridge: Polity Press, 2002), chapter 2.
5. Robert Wade, 'Globalization and its Limits: Reports of the Death of National Economy are Greatly Exaggerated', in Suzanne Berger and Ronald Dore (eds.), *National Diversity and Global Capitalism* (Ithaca, NY: Cornell University Press, 1996), pp.60–88.
6. Kenichi Ohmae, *The End of the Nation State: The Rise of Regional Economies* (New York: Free Press, 1995).
7. Berger and Dore (eds.), *National Diversity and Global Capitalism*; Soskice, 'Globalisierung und institutionelle Divergenz'; Layna Mosley, 'Room to Move: International Financial Markets and National Welfare States', *International Organisation*, 54/4 (2000), pp.737–73.
8. Paul Hirst and Grahame Thompson, *Globalisation in Question. The International Economy and the Possibilities of Governance* (Cambridge: Polity Press, 1996), p.2.
9. John G. Ruggie, 'Territoriality and Beyond: Problematizing Modernity in International Realtions', *International Organisation*, 47/1 (1982), pp.139–74.
10. Jeffrey A. Frieden and Ronald Rogowski, 'The Impact of the International Economy on National Policy: An Analytical Overview', in Robert O. Keohane and Helen V. Milner (eds.), *Internationalization and Domestic Politics* (Cambridge: CUP, 1996), pp.25–47.
11. *The Economist*, 31 May 1997, pp.17–19.
12. Geoffrey Garrett, 'The Causes of Globalisation', *Comparative Political Studies*, 33/6–7 (2000), pp.941–91; Erich Gundlach, 'Globalisation: Economic Challenges and the Political Response', *Intereconomics*, 35/3 (2000), pp.114–18; Elmar Altvater, 'Operationsfeld Weltmarkt oder: Vom souveränen Nationalstaat zum nationalen Wettbewerbsstaat', *Prokla*,

24/4 (1994), p.523.

13. Geoffrey Garrett, *Partisan Politics in the Global Economy* (Cambridge: CUP, 1998).

14. Garrett's approach also has a drawback with regard to Germany in assuming a left–centre–right cleavage in economic policy making when he states: 'Left-wing and centrist Christian democratic parties have long been more willing to expand the welfare state than their counterparts on the right' (ibid., p.7). The only relevant 'counterpart on the right' for CDU is its Bavarian 'sister-party' CSU, which traditionally practises stronger state-intervention than the CDU.

15. In focusing on the relevance of societal and political institutions for economic policy, this paper also draws on arguments of the New Institutional Economics, see e.g. Ingo Pies, 'Normative Institutionenökonomik: Programm, Methode und Anwendungen auf den europäischen Einigungsprozeß', in Martin Leschke (ed.), *Probleme der deutschen und der europäischen Integration: Institutionenökonomische Analysen* (Münster/Hamburg: LIT, 1994), pp.1–33.

16. Hall and Soskice (eds.), *Varieties of Capitalism*, pp.8, 19, call the two groups 'liberal market economies' and 'coordinated market economies'.

17. Reinhard Heinisch, 'Coping with Economic Integration: Corporatist Strategies in Germany and Austria in the 1990s', *West European Politics*, 23/3 (2000), pp.67–96.

18. Bernhard Weßels, 'Die Entwicklung des deutschen Korporativismus', *Aus Politik und Zeitgeschichte*, B 26–27 (2000), p.21; see also below.

19. On the commonality and specificity of social norms, see Henning Boekle, Volker Rittberger and Wolfgang Wagner, 'Constructivist Foreign Policy Theory', in Volker Rittberger (ed.), *German Foreign Policy since Unification. Theories and Case Studies* (Manchester: MUP, 2001), pp.109–10.

20. Hans-Hermann Hartwich, *Die Europäisierung des deutschen Wirtschaftssystems. Alte Fundamente, neue Realitäten, Zukunftsperspektiven* (Opladen: Leske + Budrich, 1998), pp.33–126; Heinisch, 'Coping with Economic Integration'; Manfred G. Schmidt, 'Still on the Middle Way? Germany's Political Economy at the Beginning of the Twenty-First Century', *German Politics*, 10/3 (2001), pp.1–12; Jonathan Story, 'Globalisation, the European Union and German Financial Reform: The Political Economy of "Finanzplatz Deutschland"', in Geoffrey R.D. Underhill (ed.), *The New World Order in International Finance* (Houndmills: Macmillan, 1997), pp.245–73.

21. John Leslie, 'The Politics of *Standort*: Germany's Debate About Competitiveness', in Gale A. Mattox, Geoffrey D. Oliver and Jonathan B. Tucker (ed.), *Germany in Transition. A Unified Nation's Search For Identity* (Boulder, CO: Westview, 1999), p.63.

22. 50% of the members of the supervisory board are representatives of the employees, two-thirds of them are elected by the employees and one-third is appointed by the union. The president of the supervisory board is always a representative of the employers and has the decisive vote in case of parity of votes.

23. Article 14, Paragraph 2 of the German constitution (Grundgesetz) states: 'Eigentum verpflichtet. Sein Gebrauch soll zugleich dem Wohle der Allgemeinheit dienen.'

24. Schirm, *Globalisation and the New Regionalism*, chapter 3.3.

25. Fritz W. Scharpf, *Sozialdemokratische krisenpolitik in Europa* (Frankfurt/M: Campus, 1987), pp.194–8.

26. Whereas in the case of low (1975: 2.3%) or negative real interest rates in the mid-1970s almost every profitable business had been worth investing in, real interest rates of up to 5.9% (1981) meant that production now had to compete for funds with portfolio investment on capital markets.

27. Scharpf, *Sozialdemokratische krisenpolitik in Europa*, p.195, concludes: 'Whereas before capital interests and labour interests could only succeed together, despite constant conflicts over distribution, now the growth policy had become less important to the FDP clientele than the distribution and tax policies – which determined the amount of the earned capital income one could keep.'

28. Herbert Giersch, Karl-Heinz Paque and Holger Schmieding, *The Fading Miracle. Four Decades of Market Economy in Germany* (Cambridge: CUP, 1992), p.235.

29. Schirm, *Globalisation and the New Regionalism*, chapter 3.3.

30. Deutscher Gewerkschaftsbund (DGB), *Standort 2001: Deutschland in solider Position* (Berlin, 2001), p.2.
31. Arne Heise, 'Der Standort Deutschland im globalen Wettbewerb', *WSI-Mitteilungen*, 48/11 (1995), pp.691–711.
32. The latter was also induced by the stability-citeria of the EMU, which limit the budget deficit to 3% of GDP.
33. Fritz W. Scharpf, 'Globalisierung als Beschränkung der Handlungsmöglichkeiten nationalstaatlicher Politik', MPIFG Discussion Paper 97/1 (Cologne, 1997), p.23.
34. Rolf Kroker, 'Deutschland – Angeschlagene Standortqualität', *WSI-Mitteilungen*, 48/11 (1995), p.706.
35. Arne Heise, 'Sind Effizienz und Gleichheit ökonomisch unverträglich?', *Berliner Debatte INITIAL*, 10/3 (1999), pp.115–25; Stefan Müller and Martin Kornmeier, 'Globalisierung als Herausforderung für den Standort Deutschland', *Aus Politik und Zeitgeschichte* B9 (2001), pp.6–14; Harald Trabold, 'Zum Verhältnis von Globalisierung und Sozialstaat', *Aus Politik und Zeitgeschichte*, B48 (2000), pp.23–30.
36. See section above and Geoffrey Garrett, 'Global Markets and National Politics: Collision Course or Virtuous Circle?', *International Organisation*, 52/4 (1998), pp.787–824.
37. Robert H. Cox, 'The Social Construction of an Imperative: Why Welfare Reform Happened in Denmark and the Netherlands but not in Germany', *World Politics*, 53/3 (2001), pp.463–98.
38. *Der Spiegel*, 5 (2001), p.20.
39. Gerlinde Sinn, 'Politikversagen bei der wirtschaftlichen Vereinigung Deutschland', in Martin Leschke (ed.), *Probleme der deutschen und der europäischen Integration: Institutionenökonomische Analysen* (Münster/Hamburg: LIT, 1994), pp.139–57; Hans-Werner Sinn, *Volkswirtschaftliche Probleme der Deutschen Wiedervereinigung* (Opladen: Westdeutscher Verlag, 1996); Horst Siebert, Holger Schmieding and Peter Nunnenkamp, 'The Transformation of a Socialist Economy. Lessons of German Unification', *Kiel Working Paper* No. 469 (Kiel, 1994); Paul J.J. Welfens, 'German Economic Unification and European Integration: Prosperity without Stability?', in Paul J.J. Welfens (ed.), *Economic Aspects of German Unification. Expectations, Transition Dynamics and International Perspectives* (Berlin: Springer, 2nd edn., 1996), pp.359–408.
40. Hartwich, *Die Europäisierung des deutschen Wirtschaftssystems*, p.135.
41. Sinn, 'Politikversagen bei der wirtschaftlichen Vereinigung Deutschland', pp.151–2; Sinn, *Volkswirtschaftliche Probleme der Deutschen Wiedervereinigung*, pp.36–7.
42. Average productivity in the East rose after unification primarily because those jobs with the lowest productivity were those to disappear first. Thus, rapidly growing unemployment contributed to rising average productivity.
43. Sinn, 'Politikversagen bei der wirtschaftlichen Vereinigung Deutschland', p.140.
44. Another reason for the elimination of export opportunities was the politically determined exchange rate of 1:1 to which the East Mark was converted to DM. The effective exchange rate was 1 DM:4 East Mark (Welfens, 'German Economic Unification and European Integration', p.363).
45. While the public sector pays wages in accordance with sector-wide agreements, only half of the private enterprises pay wages in accord with the respective industries' agreement (Schmidt, 'Still on the Middle Way?', p.9). Private business employment does not – by far – reach the West German share in total employment.
46. Reimut Zohlnhöfer, 'Deutschland im finanzpolitischen Konflikt zwischen Wiedervereinigung und europäischer Integration', *Zeitschrift für Politikwissenschaft*, 11/4 (2001), p.1549.
47. The share of public spending in GDP raised from 45.8 % (1989) to 50.6 % (1993) (Schmidt, 'Still on the Middle Way?', p.8).
48. Welfens, 'German Economic Unification and European Integration', p.367.
49. Hall and Soskice, 'An Introduction to Varieties of Capitalism', p.37.
50. Schirm, *Globalisation and the New Regionalism*, chapter 3.3.

Abstracts

Analysing German Unification: State, Nation and the Quest for Political Community, *by Mi-Kyung Kim and John D. Robertson*

After unification, the nature of German politics can be characterised by the continuous incongruence between German state and German nation from Rokkan's theoretical perspective. We suggest that this incongruent nature of the united German politics might have been resulted from the path-dependency of the mode and timing in the process of German unification itself. That is, in the process of the unification, the lack of 'constitutional agreement' between the West and the East Germany has influenced the persistent problem of 'political community' in the context of the united Germany.

Historical Consciousness and the Changing of German Political Culture, *by Felix Philipp Lutz*

Historical consciousness in unified Germany 13 years after the fall of the German Democratic Republic is undergoing a profound change whose direction is not yet clearly visible. The article describes the status and contents of historical consciousness of the period from autumn 1989 until the end of the twentieth century. Historical consciousness is at the heart of German political culture and derives from existential experiences during the Third Reich and World War II and the period of reconstruction after 1945. However, German unification in 1990 was the starting point for a new foreign policy and an ongoing change in historical consciousness, partly also due to generational change.

Trust in Democratic Institutions in Germany: Theory and Evidence Ten Years After Unification, *by Robert Rohrschneider and Rüdiger Schmitt-Beck*

Central to the stability of a regime is that citizens trust a nation's institutional framework. Based on this premise, this article looks at how much Eastern and Western Germans trust several institutions of Germany's political system. More generally, it examines the empirical validity of three potential individual-level sources of institutional trust: (1) citizens' ideological values (a value model); (2) publics' appraisals of the economic performance of institutions (a performance model); (3) citizens' ties to other individuals (a social capital model). We find that institutional trust is quite low, especially in the East. We also show that institutional trust is significantly driven by all three factors.

The 'Double' Public: Germany After Reunification, *by Winand Gellner and Gerd Strohmeier*

This article explores (1) how and why mass media have promoted the inner-German process of reunification, (2) why the media might even have slowed down or blocked the process, and (3) why it is important to think of Germany as consisting of two different publics. The analysis emphasizes the impact of political culture on political communication processes. In the West, a predominantly liberal/competitive political culture, with populist/ dogmatic tendencies, developed. However, during the process of reunification there was an erratic revolutionary change in East Germany, moving from a controlled/collective political culture to a more populist/ dogmatic pattern, with only minimum expression of liberal/competitive cultural traits. Thus we conclude that strong differences in the three dimensions account for the existence of two publics in Germany, which makes integration a challenge.

The Consequences of German Unification on the Federal Chancellor's Decision-Making, *by Karl-Rudolf Korte*

The political system of Germany is characterised by a combination of parliamentary structures and negotiating systems. The web of connections characterising the decision-making processes of the so-called 'negotiating state' leads to a loss of 'inner sovereignty' while the media enforces the concentration on the Federal Chancellor as the main actor on the political stage. By comparing Gerhard Schröder's and Helmut Kohl's styles of governance, the author identifies seven possibilities for Federal Chancellors to place themselves in a better position to increase their formal and informal power resources.

The German Party System: Continuity and Change, *by* *Thomas Saalfeld*

This article investigates continuity and change in the German party system since unification against the backdrop of longer-term developments in the party system of Germany and other advanced industrial societies. It tests four influential interpretations of the development of the German party system since 1990: (1) the danger of a re-fractionalisation of the German party system; (2) a nearly complete transfer of the West German party system to the East of Germany; (3) the interaction between institutional transfer from West to East and East German political and cultural traditions and constraints; and (4) the main parties in Eastern Germany provide a model for the West German parties and may eventually lead to institutional transfer from East to West. The empirical evidence assembled in this chapter suggests that the first two interpretations capture some elements of the developments but cannot be corroborated entirely. The most plausible interpretation is the third. The fourth interpretation can be corroborated in terms of the organisational structure of CDU and SPD in East Germany, whereas the effects of these developments for the rest of Germany remain a matter for speculation.

The Impact of Unification on German Federalism, *by* *Arthur B. Gunlicks*

While it is clear that the Berlin Republic represents far more than a change in name from the Bonn Republic, it is not so clear whether it is qualitatively different from its predecessor. Evidence exists for both sides of the question. This article deals with some of the most significant changes in German federalism since unification. It looks at territorial changes; constitutional changes at the federal and Land levels; the strengthened role of the Land governments in European policy-making; the perennial topic of fiscal federalism and the other perennial topic of Land boundary changes; the party system at the Land level; and the strong interest in direct democracy that has emerged since 1990. Whether these changes qualify as sufficient to justify the thesis that German federalism has become a different kind of federalism since 1990 is doubtful, but certainly important changes have taken place. Some of these are more a result of unification than others, but unification has had some impact on all of them.

Local Government and Politics in East Germany, *by Hellmut Wollmann*

This study begins with an examination of the secular institutional transformation of East Germany's local government since the early 1990s following the collapse of the communist regime and during the process of German unification. In its spectacular mix of institutional demolition and reconstruction this transformation bore many traces of what Joseph Schumpeter has called 'creative destruction'. The article addresses the 'performance' of the newly created political and administrative structures of local government a decade after transformation. It argues that the performance of East Germany's institutions and actors has attained the 'normalcy' of West German administrative practice remarkably rapidly. Finally, East Germany's institutional development is considered within a comparative perspective, focusing on other Central and East European countries, particularly Poland and Hungary.

Economic Consequences of German Unification, *by Michael Münter and Roland Sturm*

The process of economic unification has been more complex than most observers had predicted in 1989/90. This article develops the thesis that three main themes are central to the success or failure of economic unification: (1) fiscal policies; (2) employment policies; and (3) perceptions of a divergence of living standards in East and West Germany. We conclude that (1) financial transfers were less efficient than expected; (2) the unemployment problem has not been solved; and (3) though standards of living have converged in some respects, the prevailing perception in the East is still one of discrimination.

A Change of Course? German Foreign and Security Policy After Unification, *by Franz-Josef Meiers*

In spite of a decisive shift in the structural constraints facing the Federal Republic of Germany (FRG), Germany's foreign and security policy since unification has been marked by a high degree of continuity. Germany remains committed to NATO and the EU. European integration, the transatlantic link, and the commitment to multilateral co-operation continue to be the guiding principles of united Germany. This study offers an explanation for the complex pattern of continuity and change of Germany's foreign and security policy that has emerged since unification. This is illustrated by five issue areas which were and are of strategic importance to Germany: (1) Germany and the deepening of the European integration process; (2) Germany and the European Security and Defense Identity (ESDI); (3) Germany and the 'new NATO'; (4) Germany and the participation in out-of-area missions; and (5) Germany and the reform of the armed forces.

The Power of Institutions and Norms in Shaping National Answers to Globalisation: German Economic Policy After Unification, *by Stefan A. Schirm*

Globalisation changes the costs and benefits of economic policy options, stimulating convergence around a liberal paradigm. Although a trend towards liberalisation can be observed in OECD countries, divergence from this trend remains astonishingly strong. Germany provides an example of divergence in not changing its traditional economic model. Two hypotheses are proposed in explaining divergence from globalisation's pressure for convergence: First, domestic institutions that mediate between state and society (corporatism) influence national answers to globalisation. Second, socioeconomic norms (consensus and solidarity) make change dependent on a re-definition of norms. These hypotheses are tested with regard to Germany's economic policy since unification.

Notes on Contributors

Winand Gellner is Professor of Political Science at the University of Passau. He has published widely on a variety of comparative politics issues. His primary research interests are mass media and the political process in developed democracies, especially Germany, the UK, and the USA; institutional think-tanks in comparative perspective; health policy, European integration; parties and interest groups. He is Chief Editor of www.politik-im-netz.com.

Arthur B. Gunlicks is a Professor of Political Science and Chair of the Department at the University of Richmond, Virginia. Publications include *The Länder and German Federalism* (forthcoming), *German Public Policy and Federalism* (ed., forthcoming), *Local Government in the German Federal System* (1986), and numerous journal articles and book chapters on German federalism, local government, political parties, and campaign and party finance.

Mi-Kyung Kim is a Ph.D. candidate in Political Science at the Texas A&M University. Her dissertation is on 'Explaining Variation in Regional Institutionalization in Europe and Asia: The Legacy of Karl Polanyi's Political Economy'. Research interests include comparative regionalism in Europe and Asia, political economy of coalition governments, and the political economy of state authority.

Karl-Rudolf Korte teaches political science at Gerhard-Mercator University at Duisburg in Germany. Since 2000 he has been the head of the research group 'governance' at the Centrum für Angewandte Politikforschung (CAP), Munich. He has published widely on the German chancellorship and German political affairs.

Felix Philipp Lutz is Head of the Department 'Future Trends/Markets and Politics' in the Berlin office of Prognos AG, and Professor of International Relations and Business Administration at Schiller International University, Heidelberg. He has published in the fields of international relations, political culture, and contemporary German history.

Franz-Josef Meiers is a Senior Fellow at the Center for European Integration Studies at the University of Bonn. His articles on German foreign and security policy have appeared in various scholarly journals including *Survival, Politique Étrangère, European Security* and *Internationale Politik*. His most recent publication is *La Réforme de la Bundeswehr: adaptation ou rénovation intégrale?* (2001).

Michael Münter is Lecturer at the Institute of Political Science at the University of Erlangen-Nuremberg. He is currently working on his Ph.D. thesis on devolution in the United Kingdom. His most recent publication is *Grüne Alternativen für Europa?, Die Europapolitik der Grünen bis 1990* (2001).

John D. Robertson is Professor of Political Science at Texas A&M University. He has published widely in major political science journals, including *American Political Science Review, American Journal of Political Science, Journal of Politics, International Studies Quarterly*, and *International Political Science Review*. He is co-author of *Comparative Analysis of Nations: Quantitative Approaches* (2002).

Robert Rohrschneider is Professor of Political Science at Indiana University, Bloomington. His articles on comparative political behaviour have appeared in various scholarly journals, such as the *American Political Science Review, American Journal of Political Science, Journal of Politics*, and *Comparative Political Studies*. His *Learning Democracy: Democratic and Economic Values in Unified Germany* (1999) was awarded the 1998 Stein Rokkan prize.

Rüdiger Schmitt-Beck is Scientific Director at the Center for Survey Research and Methodology (ZUMA) at Mannheim. He has published widely in the field of comparative politics, especially on topics of political communication, electoral behaviour, political culture, social movements and political participation. His most recent book is *Politische Kommunikation und Wählerverhalten* (2002).

Thomas Saalfeld is a Senior Lecturer in Politics at the University of Kent at Canterbury. Publications include *Bundestagswahl '98: End of an Era?* (1999, co-ed. Stephen Padgett), and *Members of Parliament in Western Europe: Roles and Behaviour* (1997, co-ed. Wolfgang C. Müller). He has published articles in publications such as the *European Journal of Political Research, International Studies Quarterly, Journal of Legislative Studies, Parliamentary Affairs, Politics, Rivista Italiana di Scienza Politica*, and *West European Politics*.

Stefan A. Schirm is Professor of Political Science at the University of Stuttgart. His research interests focus on the impact of globalisation, regional co-operation in Europe and the Americas, and global economic governance. Recent publications include *Globalization and the New Regionalism. Global Markets, Domestic Politics and Regional Cooperation* (2002).

Roland Sturm is Chair of Political Science and Head of Department at the University of Erlangen-Nuremberg. His research focuses on regions and regional policies; the politics of European integration; German politics; comparative politics and comparative public policy; and economic policies.

Gerd Strohmeier is a Lecturer in Political Science working on his habilitation at the University of Passau (D.Phil. 2001). He has published widely on elections, mass media, political parties, European integration, and campaigns and political communication. He is deputy editor of www.politik-im-netz.com (the leading online portal in German political science).

Hellmut Wollmann is Professor Emeritus of Public Administration at the Institute of Social Science at Humboldt University Berlin. He has published widely in the areas of comparative (local) government, institutional transformation in formerly socialist countries, and the evaluation of public sector reforms.

Index

Books of Related Interest

Continuity and Change in German Politics: Beyond the Politics of Centrality Festschrift for Gordon Smith

Professor Stephen Padgett, *University of Strathclyde* and
Professor Thomas Poguntke, *Keele University*

Over three decades, Gordon Smith has written authoritatively on
almost every aspect of German politics. In this volume, leading UK
and German scholars use themes from his work in an examination
of the evolution of the German polity in the face of socio-economic
change, globalisation, European integration and the domestic
upheaval of unification. Chapters include Germany's place in the
wider context of European politics, government and political
leadership, part system change, political economy and political
culture. Spanning the years from the era of Brandt and Schmidt to
Schroder, the book presents a multi-faceted portrait of Germany at
the turn of the Millennium.

160 pages 2002
0 7146 5238 5 cloth
0 7146 8220 9 paper

FRANK CASS PUBLISHERS
Crown House, 47 Chase Side, Southgate, London N14 5BP
Tel: +44 (0)20 8920 2100 Fax: +44 (0)20 8447 8548 E-mail: info@frankcass.com
NORTH AMERICA
5824 NE Hassalo Street, Portland, OR 97213 3644, USA
Tel: 800 944 6190 Fax: 503 280 8832 E-mail: cass@isbs.com
Website: www.frankcass.com

Bundestagswahl '98

End of an Era

Stephen Padgett, *Professor of Politics, University of Liverpool* and **Thomas Saalfeld**, *University of Kent* (Eds)

'*a penetrating analysis of the German election*'
Contemporary Review

The German election of 1998 brought to an end sixteen years of Christian – Liberal government under Helmut Kohl, ushering in the first Red–Green coalition in a major west European country. Reflecting far-reaching changes in economic and social life, this upheaval in the electoral landscape signals a political reorientation, which will have major consequences for Germany in the new millennium. This book provides an analysis of electoral change against the background of the changing anatomy of German Society.

224 pages 1999
0 7146 5019 6 cloth
0 7146 8076 1 paper
A special issue of the journal German Politics

FRANK CASS PUBLISHERS
Crown House, 47 Chase Side, Southgate, London N14 5BP
Tel: +44 (0)20 8920 2100 Fax: +44 (0)20 8447 8548 E-mail: info@frankcass.com
NORTH AMERICA
5824 NE Hassalo Street, Portland, OR 97213 3644, USA
Tel: 800 944 6190 Fax: 503 280 8832 E-mail: cass@isbs.com
Website: www.frankcass.com